Russian Cosmism

Russian Cosmism

edited by Boris Groys

e-flux
New York, New York

The MIT Press
Cambridge, Massachusetts
London, England

This book was set in ITC Stone Serif Std and Helvetica LT Std by Toppan Best-set Premedia Limited.

Library of Congress Cataloging-in-Publication Data

Names: Groĭs, Boris, editor.
Title: Russian cosmism / edited by Boris Groys.
Description: Cambridge, MA : EFlux-MIT Press, 2018. | Includes
bibliographical references and index.
Identifiers: LCCN 2017023585 | ISBN 9780262037433 (hardcover : alk. paper)
ISBN 9780262552882 (paperback)
Subjects: LCSH: Philosophy, Russian. | Cosmology.
Classification: LCC B4231 .R78 2018 | DDC 197—dc23 LC record available at
https://lccn.loc.gov/2017023585

Contents

Foreword

Walter Benjamin has a beautiful passage on Paul Klee's *Angelus Novus*, the angel of history. For Benjamin, what the angel sees when looking backward is a pile of rubble: death, destruction, failure. Everyone dies; all projects fail; cities and civilizations fall into ruin. History is this graveyard: a genocide of people and their ideas. It is hard to argue with such a sublime spectacle of time's destruction, and it often appears that only religion can explain human helplessness in the face of such power. In nineteenth-century Russia, however, a little-known philosopher named Nikolai Fedorov began to develop a very different view of history and the past. Fedorov believed that death is not natural, but more like a flaw in the design of the human—something to be overcome by technological and scientific means, similar to the ways in which medicine seeks to cure disease. But while medicine seeks to cure afflictions in the living, a more sweeping approach is necessary to cure those afflicted with death itself.

First, death must be understood in a new way. Similar to understanding the soul as continuing to exist in spite of having left the body, we can understand death as a change in a human's material state. For Fedorov, our ethical obligation to use reason and knowledge to care for the sick extends to the curing of death: the dead must be brought back to life—not as souls in heaven, but in material form, in this world, with all their memories and knowledge. From this point of view, history, the past, and the graveyard become a field full of amazing potential: nothing is finished and everyone and everything must continue. Fedorov's philosophy of the "common task" thus calls for a total reorientation of social relations, productive forces, economy, and politics toward the singular goal of achieving physical immortality and material resurrection. We cannot consider any person to be really dead and gone until we have exhausted every possibility for reviving him or her.

Fedorov was an Orthodox Christian writing just prior to the October Revolution, yet it appears he was deeply influenced by Western Enlightenment ideas. Following the revolution, the materialist, scientific, and futuristic emphasis of his philosophy became extremely appealing to a younger generation of revolutionary anarchist and Marxist thinkers who incorporated his ideas under their own brand of Biocosmism. The Biocosmists continued Fedorov's vision without its religious implications, while still advancing its technoscientific vision of immortality, resurrection for all, and freedom of travel in universal space.

Space travel was extremely significant for the Cosmist imaginary, and Fedorov's understanding of outer space is fascinating for being as religious as it is materialist: it is both the space of heaven and of the afterlife. The conquest of death would thus be achieved by living through the colonization of space and heaven as a singular unity. For Biocosmists, outer space would remain the territory of immortal life and infinite resources, especially considering that all resurrected generations of humans, animals, and all other previously living substance on Earth would quickly exceed the capacities of our planet. This created an immediate need to explore space travel, and it can be argued that these fantastic ideas of immortal life in cosmic space gave rise to the origins of the Soviet space program. Konstantin Tsiolkovsky, an early pioneer of Soviet rocket science, studied with Fedorov and similarly worked toward colonizing universal space to access a cosmic panpsychism.

Today, the imperial or expansionist undertones of space colonization make the utopian or metaphysical aims of the early Russian Cosmists stand in stark contrast to the brute resource-plunder of European territorial expansion. It can be said that even the US space program, while being technologically more advanced, remained a spiritually impoverished exercise trapped within the same colonial drive for territorial control in the absence of any significant cultural project. A question arises concerning how non-Western avant-gardes summoned technology to serve cultural practices or spiritual cosmologies beyond the steamroller of Western industrial modernity. The eccentricity of early Russian utopianism points to a universal materialism decidedly more humane and spiritually far more encompassing than the mechanistic functionalism or free expressionism of its Western artistic or architectural contemporaries.

In the Russian cultural field of the time, Cosmist ideas inspired a vast majority of the Soviet avant-garde, including visual artists, poets, filmmakers, theater directors, fiction authors, architects, composers—nearly everyone who was engaged in the production of advanced culture. Biocosmists participated in the Proletkult (the largest cultural association formed in the Soviet Union after the revolution), published essays and manifestos in leading newspapers, and started their own journals and organizations in Moscow and Saint Petersburg. Many were publicly supportive of Leon Trotsky in his confrontation with Stalin, but this ended tragically with Stalin's victory: the vast majority were jailed or sent to labor camps while others were repressed or executed. Starting in the early 1930s, expressing Cosmist ideas in any form became extremely dangerous. The space program, however, continued, largely for military purposes.

The writings in this volume represent different strains of Russian Cosmism and Biocosmism. Many have only recently been published in Russian for the first time since their suppression in the 1930s, and almost none have been translated or published in English. It is a great pleasure and an honor to make these works available to an international public.

Anton Vidokle and Brian Kuan Wood

Introduction: Russian Cosmism and the Technology of Immortality

Boris Groys

We have grown accustomed to understanding human beings as determined by the social milieu in which they live. Modernity taught us that we are organisms dependent on our environment, mere knots in networks of information. Globalization has only made us more self-conscious of our dependence on events taking place around the world—politically, economically, ecologically. But our planet is not an island in the galaxy. It depends on processes taking place in interstellar space—dark matter, waves and particles, stars exploding, and galaxies collapsing. The fate of humanity also depends on these cosmic processes because all of these cosmic waves and particles pass through human bodies. The survival of living organisms on the surface of the Earth depends on conditions determined by the position of the Earth within the cosmic whole.

A specifically modern anxiety arises from our dependence on uncontrollable and even unknown cosmic events. Cosmic anxiety is the anxiety that results from being part of a cosmos that we cannot control. Periodically, contemporary mass culture becomes obsessed with explicit visions of this anxiety: we see depictions of asteroids coming from deep cosmic space to destroy the Earth, or an invasion by a rapacious alien species. But this anxiety also takes subtler forms. Georges Bataille, for instance, built his theory of the "accursed share" on the fact that the Sun sends more energy to the Earth than the organisms living on its surface can immediately absorb:

> Solar radiation results in a superabundance of energy on the surface of the globe. ... Living matter receives this energy and accumulates it within the limits given by the space that is available to it. ... Vegetation quickly occupies the available space. Animals make it a field of slaughter and extend its possibilities this way. ... In this respect, the wild beast is at the summit: its continual depredation of depredators represents an immense squandering of energy.[1]

This excess of solar energy makes a necessity of waste—if the surplus is not consumed through ecstatic festivals and sexual orgies, it will be spent on violence and war. Cosmic energies are the reason human culture and politics are eternally shifting between order and disorder.

Bataille's solar myth is strongly reminiscent of the interpretation of world history as defined by the activity of the Sun—an interpretation that was formulated by Russian historian and biologist Alexander Chizhevsky in the 1920s and '30s. During this time, Chizhevsky's ideas also spread to the West, especially to France and the United States, and some of his texts were published in English and French—meaning his ideas could easily reach Bataille.[2] However, Chizhevsky's central text, in which his theory is extensively formulated and supported by empirical data, was published only relatively recently in Russian.[3] Chizhevsky collected a huge amount of empirical data—ranging from ancient Roman and early Chinese sources up to information from the 1930s—to show a close correlation between periods of higher activity of the Sun and mass revolutionary movements. It is, of course, the Russian Revolution in 1917 that gave the decisive impulse to his research. Chizhevsky asks: Why, under similar social, economic, and political constellations, do masses in some cases become mobilized and revolutionized, but in other cases remain passive and indifferent? The answer he offers is this: to be able to start a revolutionary movement, human beings must be mobilized not only on the level of the spirit but also on the level of the body. The human spirit can be mobilized through an ideology but, according to Chizhevsky, the degree of mobilization of the human body, like of all organisms living on Earth, is dependent on the cycles of solar activity. Through astronomical and historical data, Chizhevksy shows that the greatest revolutions coincided with the greatest activity of the Sun. His findings also suggest that the historical process is characterized by a succession of active and passive periods corresponding to eleven-year cycles of solar activity (the highest degree of activity follows a twenty-two-year cycle). But it seems the most interesting part of his results, for our time, concerns the relationship between the activity of the Sun and British parliamentary elections. These results show that the influence of the Sun dictates not only the choice between revolution and the status quo, but also between left-wing and right-wing politics in the framework of regular parliamentary processes. Moments of change in solar activity are correlated precisely with changes in the English government. Chizhevsky shows that for the period between 1830 and 1924, the summary activity of the Sun during the rule of liberal governments was 155.6 percent higher than during the rule of conservative governments. Conservative governments never held power when the number of sunspots was over ninety-three.

Chizhevsky suggests that knowing the correlation between the activity of the Sun and the political activity of the masses can prepare the political classes for seemingly unexpected changes in public mood. During the financial crisis in 2008, some specialists remembered the so-called Kondratiev waves—Nikolai Kondratiev, a student of Chizhevsky, applied his theory to economic cycles to predict further cycles, including the 2008 crisis. On a political level, one is reminded of the years 1968, 1989, and 2010–11. However, the political effects of larger numbers of sunspots are often ambiguous. Chizhevsky specifically warns that growth in solar activity can lead not only to the adoption of a progressive agenda by the masses, but also to the rise of irrational and reactionary populist movements. Here, shifts from periods of political calm to those of collective ecstasy and violence and vice versa are explained by the dependence of political processes on the interplay of cosmic forces.

Friedrich Nietzsche described human culture as being dependent on the eternal battle between Apollonian and Dionysian forces, or in other words, between cosmos and chaos, order and anarchy, stability and revolution. Only two ways of reacting to the battle between cosmos and chaos are possible: the ecstatic embrace of chaos or an attempt to control the cosmos and secure its victory over chaos. The first option inspired many avant-garde writers and artists during the first decades of the twentieth century, especially the artists of the Russian avant-garde. In 1913, some of the most prominent members of that movement at the time, including Kazimir Malevich, Velimir Khlebnikov, Alexei Kruchenykh, and Mikhail Matyushin, participated in the creation and premiere of the futurist mystery-opera *Victory Over the Sun*.[4] The work celebrated the extinction of the Sun and the descent of cosmos into chaos—symbolized by the black square that Malevich painted for the first time as part of the opera's scenography. By the beginning of the twentieth century the embrace of chaos seemed imminent, as no one could be expected to believe any longer in the stability of divine or natural order. The very idea of a stable order, be it religious or rationalist, appeared to lose its ontological guarantee. New technology seemed to permanently replace, make obsolete, and ultimately destroy old things, old traditions, and familiar ways of life, thus undermining lingering faith in the "traditional world order." Technological development, subjected to the logic of progress, presented itself as a force of chaos that would not tolerate any stable order. The future came to be seen as the enemy of both past and present. Precisely because of that view, the futurists celebrated the future, as it held the promise that everything that had been—and still was—would disappear.

One can say that Russian Cosmism proposed a counterproject to the futuristic project of the Russian avant-garde—even if both projects started from the same basic presupposition, namely the decisive role of technology. Russian futurists saw in technology the force that would destroy the "old world" and open the way for building the new world from point zero. In contrast, Russian Cosmists hoped that technology would become a truly strong messianic force that could fulfill the expectations already transmitted from one past generation to the next.

Russian Cosmism found its initial philosophical conceptualization in the "Philosophy of the Common Task" that Nikolai Fedorov developed in the late nineteenth century.[5] Fedorov's writings may have been met with little public attention during his lifetime, but they nevertheless reached illustrious readers like Leo Tolstoy, Fyodor Dostoevsky, and Vladimir Solovyov, who were fascinated and influenced by Fedorov's project. After the philosopher's death in 1903, his work gained ever-increasing currency, although in essence it remained limited to a Russian readership. In brief, the project of the common task consists in the creation of the technological, social, and political conditions under which it would be possible to resurrect by technological and artificial means all people who have ever lived.

In a sense, Fedorov developed his project of the resurrection of past generations as an attempt to "materialize" Hegelian philosophy. Hegel understood the historical process as a work of negation: we should negate the past and present to let the historical new emerge. According to Hegel's *Phenomenology of Spirit*, the goal of history consists, however, in the spiritual reconstruction of all its past epochs.[6] Thus, Hegel believed that through his *Phenomenology* he had achieved the ultimate reconciliation and even synthesis between past and future. However, for Fedorov this synthesis was insufficient because it took place merely inside the limited realm of the "spiritual"—in other words, through memory and imagination.

Instead, Fedorov wanted a true synthesis of past and future that could only mean the material resurrection of all the dead. The Christian promise to overcome death is reinterpreted here as a promise of the victory of cosmos over chaos, achieved by means of secular politics and technology. One could say that Fedorov, like later Russian Cosmists, inherited and radicalized the Marxist shift from divine grace to secular technology. The reaction of the Russian Cosmists to Nietzschean radical atheism was in many ways similar to Marx's reaction to the atheism of the French Enlightenment, or that of Feuerbach.[7] Traditional atheism rejected Christianity as a false promise to secure the survival and even immortality of humankind. The enlightened individual was understood as one who accepts his finiteness, mortality, and dependence on the materiality of the world, especially on cosmic forces, economic needs, and sexual drives. Of course, Marx was also a child of the Enlightenment, but he did not want to reject the Christian promise of happiness and harmony at the end of times. Rather, he wanted to realize this promise by means of a communist society that could take the fate of the Earth in its hands instead of relying on divine grace. Fedorov goes even further than Marx in his project of achieving immortality and resurrection of the dead through technology and rational social organization.

Indeed, Fedorov no longer believed in the immortality of the soul existing independently of the body. In his view, physical, material existence was the only possible form of existence. And Fedorov believed just as firmly in technology: because everything is material, physical, everything is technically manipulable. Above all, however, Fedorov believed in the power of social organization; in that sense he was a socialist through and through.

However, there is one essential difference between the Marxist project and the Cosmist project. The communist "paradise on Earth" that is supposed to be achieved through the combination of revolutionary struggle and creative work is understood as a realization of harmony between humanity and nature, to which also belongs the inevitability of so-called natural death. Fedorov interpreted this acceptance of natural death as an internal contradiction in the socialist theories of the nineteenth century. Future generations were supposed to enjoy socialist justice only at the price of the cynical acceptance of an outrageous historical injustice: the exclusion of all previous generations from the realm of socialist utopia. Socialism thus functioned as an exploitation of the dead in favor of the living—and as an exploitation of those alive today in favor of those who will live later. But is it possible to think of technology in terms different from those of historical progress?

Fedorov believed that such technology directed toward the past is possible—and, in fact, already exists. For him it takes shape in art technology and, particularly, in technology used by art museums.[8] The museum does not punish the obsoleteness of individual items by removing and destroying them. Thus the museum is fundamentally at odds with progress. Progress consists in replacing old things with new things. The museum, by contrast, is a machine for making things last, making them immortal. Because each human being is a body among other bodies, a thing among other things, humans can also be blessed with the immortality of the museum. The Christian immortality of the soul is replaced here by the immortality of things or bodies in the museum. And divine grace is replaced by curatorial decisions and the technology of museum preservation.

According to Fedorov, art uses technology with the goal of preserving old things and lifestyles. There is no progress in art. Art does not wait for a better society of the future to come—it immortalizes here and now. Human beings can also be interpreted as readymades—as potential artworks. Not only all of the living but all people who have ever lived must rise from the dead as artworks and be preserved in museums. Technology as a whole must become the technology of art. And the state must become the museum of its population. Just as the museum's administration is responsible not only for the general holdings of the museum's collection but also for the intact state of every given work of art, ensuring that the individual artworks are conserved and restored when they show signs of decay, the state should bear responsibility for the resurrection and continued life of every individual person.

In the famous phrase by Michel Foucault, the modern state can be defined by the fact that it has the right "to make live and to let die," in contrast to the sovereign states of the older variety that "take life or let live."[9] The modern state is concerned with birth rates, health, and providing its population with the necessities of life—all understood as statistical values. Thus, according to Foucault, the modern state functions primarily as a "biopower" whose justification is that it secures the survival of the human masses, of the human species. The survival of the individual is, of course, not guaranteed by this. If the survival of the population is one of the state's goals, then the "natural" death of any given individual is passively accepted by the state as an unavoidable event and thus treated as a private matter of that individual. The death of an individual is thus the insurmountable limit of biopower organized into a state. And this limit is accepted by the modern state that respects the private sphere of natural death. This limit, by the way, is not even questioned by Foucault himself. However, for Fedorov the state can no longer permit itself to allow individuals to die privately or the dead to rest peacefully in their graves. Death's limits must be overcome by the state. Biopower must become total.

This totality is achieved by equating art and politics, life and technology, state and museum. Overcoming the boundaries between life and art is here not a matter of introducing art into life but, rather, is a radical museumification of life—the idea that life can and should attain the privilege of immortality in a museum. By means of the unification of living space and museum space, biopower extends itself into infinity: it becomes the organized technology of eternal life. Such a total biopower is, of course, no longer "democratic": no one expects the artworks that are preserved in a museum collection to democratically elect the museum curator who will care for them. As soon as human beings become radically modern—that is, as soon as they are understood as bodies among other bodies, things among other things—they have to accept that state-organized technology will treat them accordingly. This acceptance has a crucial precondition, however: the explicit goal for new power must be eternal life here on Earth for everyone. Only then does the state cease to be a partial, limited biopower of the sort described by Foucault; only then does it become a total biopower.

Thus the museum can be seen as a place where technology becomes self-reflective—and begins to protect, exhibit, and contemplate its own past and present. Technology is mostly understood as an extension of the capabilities of humans in their attempt to put the external world under their control. However, technology will dominate not only space but also time—and thus practice not only negation but also protection and sustainability. In his famous essay on the question of technology, Heidegger rightly says that the primary goal of technology is to secure the storage and availability of resources and commodities. He shows that, historically, the development of technology was directed toward our decreasing dependence on the accidents to which the natural supply of resources is inevitably related. A person becomes increasingly independent from the Sun by storing its energy in different forms, and in general over time we have become increasingly independent of annual seasons and the instability of the weather.[10] Heidegger does not say so explicitly, but technology is for him primarily the interruption of the flow of time, the production of reservoirs of time in which time ceases to flow toward the future—so that a return to previous moments of time becomes possible. Thus, one can leave a museum and then return and find again the same artwork one contemplated on a previous visit. According to Heidegger, the goal of technology is precisely to immunize us against change, to liberate us from dependency on physics, on fate, on circumstance. Heidegger sees this development as extremely dangerous. But why?

Heidegger explains this danger in the following way: if everything becomes a resource that is stored and made available, then the human being also begins to be considered a resource—as human capital, we would say now, as a collection of possibilities, capabilities, and skills.[11] In this way humanity becomes degraded—through a search for stability and security the individual turns him- or herself into a thing. The reason for Heidegger's dislike of technology becomes clear. Technology is able to change its direction and turn the individual from its subject into its object. Becoming objectified means for Heidegger becoming usable and used. But is this equation between thing and tool valid? Certainly it is not valid in the case of art. Artworks are not used, but rather are exhibited or looked at. And, if a museum is doing its job well, they are kept in good condition, restored, and so forth. The use of the artworks is their contemplation—and contemplation leaves the artworks undamaged. Thus, turning a human being into a thing does not necessarily diminish his or her dignity. Technological self-reflection does not annul human rights but, in fact, radicalizes them by treating the human being as an artwork.

However, art serves not only to conserve objects but also to improve them. As previously noted, Fedorov spoke of the resurrection of the dead in a way that could suggest that they should be awakened as, so to speak, readymades—as they truly were before dying. But resurrection also means, of course, a transformation. To become immortal is not to remain as one was before, while still mortal. The world of the mortal is not the same as the world of the immortal. In the Christian tradition, immortality was associated with a profound transformation of body and soul.[12] So it is not surprising that the generation of Fedorov's followers who entered the scene after the October Revolution combined the project of the technological resurrection of the dead with the project of improving human nature.

In their first manifesto (1922), representatives of the Biocosmists-Immortalists, a political party that had its roots in Russian anarchism, wrote: "We take the essential and real rights of man to be the right to exist (immortality, resurrection, rejuvenation) and the freedom to move in cosmic space (and not the supposed rights announced when the bourgeois revolution was declared in 1789)."[13] Hence Alexander Svyatogor, one of the leading Biocosmist theoreticians, subjected the classical doctrine of anarchism to a fundamental criticism by pointing out that there must be a central power to ensure these new basic rights. Svyatogor took immortality to be at once the goal and the prerequisite for a future communist society, since true social solidarity could only reign among immortals: death separates people; private property cannot truly be eliminated if every human being owns a private piece of time. Total biopower, by contrast, signifies the collectivization not only of space but also of time. In eternity, conflicts between the individual and society are eliminated; those same conflicts could not be eliminated in any finite span of time. The achievement of immortality is the highest goal for every individual. For that reason, the individual will always remain faithful to society if society makes immortality its goal. At the same time, not only does this total sort of society make it possible for people to experience life without temporal or spatial limits; the communist society of immortals will also be "interplanetary," that is, it will occupy the entire space of the cosmos. Svyatogor tries to distinguish himself from Fedorov by characterizing the latter thinker as old-fashioned, even archaic, because of Fedorov's emphasis on the fact that all human beings are related and fraternal. Even so, the family resemblance between Fedorov and the Biocosmists is all too obvious.

To put it in sociopolitical terms, both writers tried to combine capitalist and socialist utopias. The capitalist utopia is, obviously, a utopia of self-preservation that allows for the accumulation of capital.[14] The bourgeois subject was traditionally criticized for not being able to sacrifice or self-sacrifice. And, indeed, in bourgeois society, life is regarded as the highest value. Even if natural death is accepted as inevitable, the conscious sacrifice of human life is seen as morally reprehensible. In fact, natural death often becomes politicized and interpreted as an effect of criminal action or neglect. For example, if people die from natural catastrophes, governmental administrations are criticized for not organizing efforts at early prevention. And if people die from illness or old age, one blames the medical system, and so forth. That is why the revolutionary movements of romanticism and anarchism embraced and celebrated destructive cosmic energies as undermining the bourgeois order by demonstrating to the bourgeois individual the futility of its strategy of self-preservation. Such was the Nietzschean strategy shared, as I already mentioned, by members of the Russian avant-garde and later by Bataille and Deleuze. Here the bourgeois individual was required to—voluntarily or involuntarily—sacrifice his or her will to self-preservation to be able to enter the totality of cosmic life, and to dissolve her- or himself in this totality.

According to the teachings of Russian Cosmism, the modern, bourgeois subject also had to sacrifice her or his will to self-preservation by subjecting it to the general plan governing society, which was organized on the principles of collectivist socialism. But this relinquishment of self-preservation had to be compensated by society because it had to make immortality, that is, the eternal preservation of every individual, its highest goal. Here the capitalist subject enters the cosmic whole without losing her or his main values—individual life and the will to self-preservation.

The path from radical anarchism to the acceptance of Soviet power as one (possible) authority of a total biopower is characteristic not only of the Biocosmists, but also of many other fellow travelers of the October Revolution. For example, Valerian Muravyev converted from being a fierce opponent of the Bolshevik Revolution to being its advocate. This transformation occurred the moment he discovered in Soviet power a promise of "mastery over time," that is, the artificial production of eternity. He too saw art as a model for politics—as the only technology that could overcome time. He too called for a departure from a purely "symbolic" art in favor of using art to make society as a whole, and indeed the entire cosmos, into an object of human design. Far more radically than most authors of his time, Muravyev was prepared to view the human being as an artwork. Muravyev understood resurrection as following logically from the process of copying; and even earlier than Walter Benjamin, Muravyev observed that there could be no difference between the "original human being" and his or her copy under conditions of technological reproducibility.[15] Muravyev thus sought to purify the concept of the human being of the metaphysical and religious remnants to which Fedorov and the Biocosmists still clung. For Muravyev the human being was simply a specific combination of particular chemical elements, just like every other thing in the world. For that reason, Muravyev hoped to eliminate gender difference in the future and to create a nongendered, purely artificial method for producing human beings. The human beings of the future would thus have no guilt with respect to their dead ancestors: they would owe their existence to the same technologically organized state that guaranteed the duration of their existence, their immortality.

The technologically and politically guaranteed resurrection of dead ancestors is thus the last step in the secularization of Christianity, for secularization remains partial if it merely negates, censors, and prohibits the hopes, desires, and demands for eternal life that religion articulates. It is not enough to say that there is no immortality and to prohibit people from seeking it. For if people are told that they cannot hope for immortality because they lack souls and are simply things, they can rightly ask why these things cannot be preserved. Indeed, after the death of the soul it is the corpse that remains. Is not this purely material corpse an object that can be treated technologically, like any other material object? If the transition from the "animate" body to the "inanimate" corpse is a purely material process, then this process can also be technologically reverted. What makes such a reversal impossible? The answer usually given to this question is that a human being is indeed somehow different from a mere thing and thus cannot be preserved, produced, and reproduced like a mere thing. But what is this "something else" if not a soul? That is why the thinkers of Russian Cosmism wanted to thoroughly purify society of "idealism," replacing the immortality of the soul guaranteed by God with an immortality of the body guaranteed by the state—thereby bringing to a close the transition to a new era and a new, total biopower.

These biopolitical projects may have been utopian to the extent that they were not based on already-existing scientific knowledge or technology. But at the same time, as is so often true of such cases, they stimulated the development of purely scientific and technological programs. In the 1920s, such programs inspired by radical biopolitical projects were both numerous and varied. One of the most spectacular and influential of them was doubtless the rocket research that Konstantin Tsiolkovsky conducted with the goal of transporting the resurrected ancestors discussed by Fedorov to other planets; this became the starting point of later Soviet space travel. Tsiolkovsky himself was a follower of cosmic biopolitics who wanted to fulfill in practice what Fedorov called the "patrification of the heavens" (the transformation of the planets into habitable places for our resurrected ancestors). Tsiolkovsky's many writings were, apart from delving into strictly technical problems, devoted to the social organization of the universe. Tsiolkovsky still believed strongly in human creativity, even though in the best biopolitical tradition he saw the human being as a mere body, a thing, which, by definition, could not be creative. Most of his texts are devoted to solving this philosophical problem. Tsiolkovsky's solution consisted in seeing the human brain as merely a specific and purely material part of the universe. Thus all of the processes that take place in the human brain are ultimately processes that have their origin in the whole universe: according to this logic, the will of an individual human being is at the same time the will of the universe. Human creativity is an expression of the creativity of the universe. If the human brain is a part of the cosmos and transmits cosmic energies, then the human being becomes cosmic. Of course, natural selection must, argued Tsiolkovsky, decide whose brain best expresses the will of the universe. Tsiolkovsky was relatively skeptical about the human race's chances of winning this competition. Tsiolkovsky believed that "higher beings" have the right and even the duty to destroy "lower beings," just as gardeners do when they tend their gardens; and he did not preclude the possibility that, among all the other beings populating cosmic space, humans are on the lower end.[16] However, he hoped that the human race could reach perfection and happiness and, thus, allow all the individual atoms and molecules that constitute the human body to be happy, too. Tsiolkovsky believed that the smallest material elements can experience happiness and pain, and thus the creation of a society of happy, satisfied people would also be a cosmic event. The individual atoms would be either without any feeling (being elements of stones, water, etc.) or happy (being elements of happy human bodies). This vision of the future left out plants and animals—and, indeed, Tsiolkovsky believed that they should be exterminated because they would never be able to reach true happiness, which could only be the work of reason.

Another fascinating biopolitical experiment, although not as influential, was the Institute for Blood Transfusion that Alexander Bogdanov founded and directed in the 1920s. Bogdanov had been a close ally of Lenin's when they were young and was a cofounder of the intellectual and political movement within the Russian Social Democratic Party that led to Bolshevism. Later, however, he increasingly distanced himself from contemporary politics and was sharply criticized by Lenin for his favorable view of Ernst Mach and his positivist philosophy.[17] After the revolution, Bogdanov directed the famous Proletkult movement, in which he promoted "nonprofessional" writing and art produced by ordinary workers. Later, Bogdanov became enthusiastic about experiments with blood transfusion, which he hoped would slow the aging process, if not stop it completely. Blood transfusions from younger generations to older ones were supposed to rejuvenate the elderly and establish a solidarity and balance among the generations that Bogdanov considered essential to establishing a just socialist society.[18] As it happened, Bogdanov died from such a blood transfusion: he intentionally exchanged his blood with the blood of a young female student who was so ill that the doctors had given up hope for her recovery. After receiving the other end of the blood transfusion that killed Bogdanov, the student recovered. Retrospectively, it is difficult to say if this was a mistake on Bogdanov's part or an "irrational" act of self-sacrifice. In his theoretical treatises, Bogdanov preaches rationality and scientific knowledge. However, in his fiction he thematizes irrationality and self-destruction. Thus, in one of his novels, *Red Star*, Bogdanov describes a fantastic, ideal "communist" society on Mars based on pure rationality. The human hero of his novel identifies with the values of this society. However, he suddenly becomes carried away by a wave of irrational, blind hatred against a Martian scientist and tries to kill him because this scientist, in the style of Tsiolkovsky, has proposed to destroy the human race, since it is incapable of achieving true rational order.[19] And in the short story "Immortality Day," included in this volume, Bogdanov describes a happy and satisfied scientist who sacrifices his immortality in order to experience suffering and death.[20]

For the present-day reader, Bogdanov's reports on the Institute for Blood Transfusion evoke above all Bram Stoker's *Dracula*. This analogy is by no means coincidental. The society of vampires—that is, of immortal bodies—over which Dracula reigns is a society of total biopower par excellence. The novel—which was written in 1897, around the same time as Fedorov's project of the common task was formulated—describes the reign of total biopower not as a utopia, however, but rather as a dystopia. The "human" heroes of the novel bitterly defend their right to a natural death. The idea of a struggle against a society of vampires that produces and guarantees the immortality of the body has continued ever since in the mass culture of the West—even if a certain seduction by vampiric forces is not denied. Aversion to corporeal immortality is certainly not new, as the stories of Faust, Frankenstein, and the Golem all demonstrate. Those stories, however, were written at a time in which faith in the immortality of the soul had not yet been completely abandoned. And, thus, it seemed better to die and preserve one's immortal soul than to become a soulless body. However, in our time we have lost faith in the possibility of the soul to exist separately from the body. And so corporeal immortality remains the only chance of life after death. The promise of technology substitutes for the promise of divine grace. Russian Cosmism was one of the earliest and most radical manifestations of this substitution.

Acknowledgments

There are many people to whom I am deeply grateful for inspiration and practical help in the process of preparing this book.

Here I will mention only a few of them.

I am grateful to Anton Vidokle not only for supporting this project but also—and maybe even more importantly—for his enthusiasm for Russian Cosmism.

I am also grateful to Arseny Zhilyaev for reading the translations and also for his own inspiring artistic work on Russian Cosmism.

And I thank Kaye Cain-Nielsen for her (very difficult) editorial work, and Anastasia Garrel and Anne Luther for helping me with references and endnotes.

Notes

1. Georges Bataille, *Accursed Share: An Essay on General Economy*, vol. 1, trans. Robert Hurley (New York: Zone Books, 1988), 29, 34.

2. For example: A. L. Chizhevsky, *Les Épidémies et les perturbations electromagnettiques* (Paris: Hippocrate, 1938).

3. A. L. Chizhevsky, "Zemlya v ob'yat'yakh solntsa" [The Earth in the Sun's embrace], 1931, in Chizhevsky, *Kosmicheskiy pul's zhizni* [Cosmic pulse of life] (Moscow: Mysl, 1995). See also Vincent Barnett, *Kondratiev and the Dynamics of Economic Development* (London: Macmillan, 1998).

4. *Victory Over the Sun*, ed. Patricia Railing, trans. Evgeny Steiner (London: Artists Bookworks, 2009), 2 vols.

5. Nikolai Fedorovich Fedorov, *What Is Man Created For? The Philosophy of the Common Task*, trans. and ed. Elisabeth Koutaissof and Marilyn Minto (Lausanne: Honeyglen Publishing/L'Age d'Homme, 1990). See also George M. Young, *The Russian Cosmists: The Esoteric Futurism of Nikolai Fedorov and His Followers* (New York: Oxford University Press, 2012).

6. G. W. F. Hegel, *Hegel's Phenomenology of Spirit*, trans. A. V. Miller (New York: Oxford University Press, 1977), 490–493.

7. See George M. Young, *The Russian Cosmists: The Esoteric Futurism of Nikolai Fedorov and His Followers* (New York: Oxford University Press, 2012).

8. Nikolai Fedorov, "The Museum, Its Meaning and Mission," trans. Stephen P. Van Trees, in *Avant-Garde Museology*, ed. Arseny Zhilyaev (New York: e-flux classics, distributed by the University of Minnesota Press, 2015).

9. Michel Foucault, *Society Must Be Defended: Lectures at the College de France, 1975–1976*, trans. David Macey (New York: Picador, 2003), 241–247.

10. Martin Heidegger, "The Question Concerning Technology," in *Basic Writings* (New York: Harper Perennial, 2008), 320–342.

11. Ibid., 323.

12. Giorgio Agamben, *The Open: Man and Animal*, trans. Kevin Attell (Stanford: Stanford University Press, 2003), 17–39.

13. Kreatorii Rossiiskikh i Moskovskikh Anarchistov-Biokosmistov, "Deklarativnaia rezolyutsiia," *Biokosmist*, no. 1 (1922): 1–3.

14. Max Horkheimer and Theodor W. Adorno, *Dialectic of Enlightenment*, ed. Gunzelin Schmid Noerr, trans. Edmund Jephcott (Stanford: Stanford University Press, 2002), 35ff.

15. Valerian Muravyev, "A Universal Productive Mathematics" [in Russian], *Vselenskoe Delo* [The deed of the universe], no. 22 (1934): 116–140. Translated by Thomas Campbell and published in this volume.

16. Konstantin Tsiolkovsky, "Volia Vselennoi," in *Genii sredi liudei* (Moscow: Mysl, 2002), 224–231, at 227.

17. Vladimir I. Lenin, *Materialism and Empirio-Criticism*, in *Lenin: Collected Works*, vol. 14 (Moscow: Progress Publishers, 1972), 17–362. Originally published as *Materialism and Empirio-Criticism* [in Russian] (Moscow: Zveno Publishers, 1909). Available in English at Marxists Internet Archive: marxists.org.

18. Alexander Bogdanov, *God raboty instituta perelivaniya krovi, 1926–1927* (Moscow, 1927), 33.

19. Alexander Bogdanov, *Red Star*, trans. Charles Rougle (Bloomington: Indiana University Press, 1984).

20. Alexander Bogdanov, "Immortality Day," originally published under the title "Immortal Fride: A. Bogdanov's Fantastic Narrative" [in Russian], *Probujdenue-SPb.*, no. 16 (1912): 497–505. Translated by Anastasiya Osipova and published in this volume.

1 "The World-Historical Cycles," from *The Earth in the Sun's Embrace*

Alexander Chizhevsky

Starting with the assumption that the historical distribution of popular mass movements is determined by solar force via its impact on the human neuropsychological apparatus—by increasing excitability and sharpening the people's reflexes—I have found it necessary to make a detailed analysis from this perspective of all the historical materials my research has accumulated.

To this end, I have engaged in a specific psychiatro-psychological analysis of each historical event under consideration. I have studied in detail the various changes and fluctuations in the course of the masses' psychological processes, insofar as these processes may be detectable through specialized forms of historical inquiry. By "psychological processes," I mean mass sentiments of a certain kind, which find objective expression in the corresponding conduct of the masses and those who lead them. I have conducted this work from perspectives both psychological and psychiatric, making detailed investigations into deviations in the behavior of the masses from particular norms. Thus it has become possible to study simultaneously both the inner psychological processes of the masses and the relationship of these processes with one or another state of solar activity, all from a single, unified point of view. For me, this work serves as the foundation of a science of mass movements.

Research into the relationship between the behavior of the masses during various historical events and the development of sunspots has allowed me to reach the following general conclusion: prolonged mass movements

"The World-Historical Cycles" was translated from Alexander Chizhevsky, *Kosmicheskiy pul's zhizni: Zemlya v obyatiyakh Solntsa. Geliotapaksia* [Cosmic pulse of life: Earth in the Sun's embrace], (Moscow: Mysl, 1995), 478–491.

flow according to the cycle of solar activity and demonstrate fluctuations synchronous with this cycle. The behavior of the masses, expressed in varying degrees of neuropsychological excitability, undergoes fluctuations that run precisely parallel to fluctuations in the intensity of the sunspots.

Analyzing the discrete course of each individual event and then comparing its known stages with the stages of other historical events that took place during comparable periods of solar activity, I easily concluded that, despite the absence of any real connection between them, they all run an identical course, making at certain moments comparable rises, pivots, and falls.

Based on this conclusion, I decided to divide every world-historical cycle into four epochs corresponding to the psychological processes taking place during this cycle. I gave the following titles to these four epochs:

1. The epoch of minimal excitability
2. The epoch of mounting excitability
3. The epoch of maximal excitability
4. The epoch of diminishing excitability

In relation to the objective impact of various degrees of excitability on human activity, I have also divided each cycle into four epochs describing human social activity:

1. The epoch of minimal activity
2. The epoch of increasing activity
3. The epoch of maximal activity
4. The epoch of decreasing activity

The time occupied by each age within an 11.1-year cycle runs as follows:

1. Epoch 1: three years
2. Epoch 2: two years
3. Epoch 3: three years
4. Epoch 4: three years

with periodic fluctuations to meet the complete duration of the cycle.

Of course, these generalizations correspond to historical synthesis—as a preliminary scheme of sufficient certainty.

The characteristics of the epochs of this cycle are closely connected to the formation of various international and domestic conjunctures from which sociohistorical phenomena arise.

Further, I will formulate the general socio-psychiatro-psychological characteristics for every epoch of our cycle. They represent the ideal forms lying at the basis of every cycle, freed from random phenomena dictated by temporal and geographic specificities.

There is no doubt that all of these phenomena are in actuality incomparably more complex than my schematization of their characteristics suggests. All of them deviate from this schematization in multiple directions. And yet they all vindicate these schematizations in any given historical moment. We should see them as shared tendencies whose reasons lie in the human physiological apparatus, but which may, thanks to one or another man-made institution, skew in any direction, justifying themselves only on the basis of general—yet fundamental—features.

The first epoch of the world-historical cycle: The period of minimal activity The characteristic features of this period are: the fragmentation of the masses;

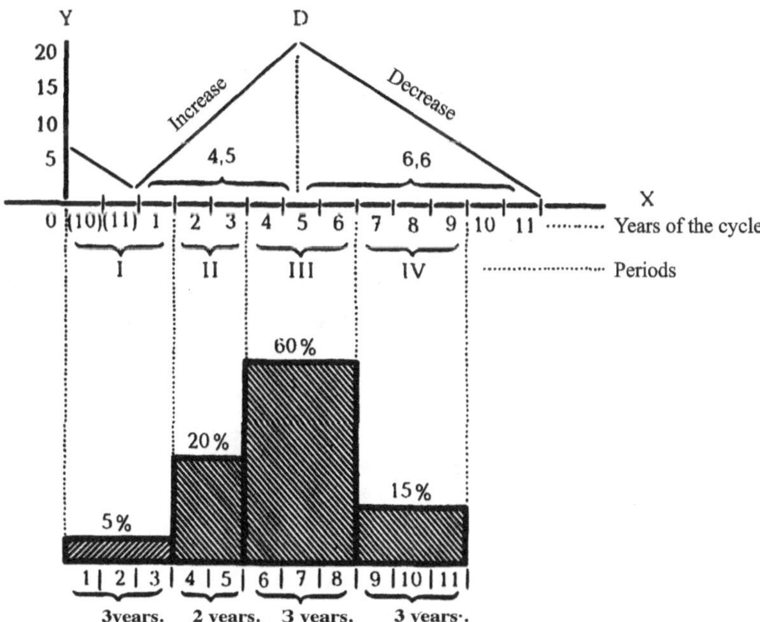

Figure 1.1
Ratio of the quantity of emergent historical events to years and periods of the cycle, as a percentage. Average output over 500 years (fifteenth–nineteenth centuries).

their indifference to political and military questions; their peaceful mood, docility, patience, and the like.

The emergence of these features among the masses in the first period of the cycle generally accompanies the absence of desire to struggle over an idea or right, and is marked by easy surrender, capitulation to capture, giving over of arms, flight from the battlefield, and so forth.

Such behavior on the part of private citizens or entire groups forces the authorities to take corresponding measures: the establishment of diplomatic relations, the conclusion of truces with the enemy, and finally a peace treaty, a surrender to the enemy under unfavorable conditions, the declaration of neutrality, the recalling of troops, and so forth. In the memoirs of those who endured it, and in the historical record, this time will forever mark itself by its embrace of peace, the disinclination to join conflict of any type, an end to military aggressions, and the triumph of principles of nonintervention in many areas of international and domestic military-political life. These facts are generally explained by the depletion of moral and physical powers, the neuropsychological fatigue that follows periods of agitation, the unraveling of national unity, the discontinuation of once-unifying causes, an inability to fight, the downfall and departure of those leaders who have lost the trust of the masses and thus power over them, and so on. Political life goes deaf, suffers suppression. The government becomes a heavy boot. The individual loses its presence in political life, burgeoning instead in the sphere of the intellect. The individual becomes oppressed by the mechanism of the state. A single person's protest is meaningless. The individual accepts violence, endures it, takes it as given. The dynamic unrest gives over to quiet.

The aspirations of humanity in other spheres of activity mutate as well: the current of social life, joining the stream of peace and quiet, is able to direct its course toward other ends—the resolution of other problems. Here begin man's spiritual activities; here are created his cultural values, art and science standing at the pinnacle of social life, exchanged for the churning froth of recent days, quickly and casually devaluing by their very achievements all that they have wrought. During periods of minimal activity, mankind tends toward calm, relaxes from the anxiety of years gone by, and gathers physical strength for the new era of unrest that is ineluctably approaching.

Research into the historical events taking place in the first epoch has permitted me to establish that periods of minimal excitability contribute to the conclusion of peace treaties; voyages of conquest, modest in scale; surrenders; occupations; the most radical abridgment of parliamentarianism; the strengthening of autocracy and oligarchy.

The second epoch of the world-historical cycle: The period of increasing activity The psychological and historic complexity of this period demanded the broadest inquiries, with the result that we were able to gather a significant amount of data about it. Here it will be necessary to confine ourselves to certain diagrammatic observations.

Even the very start of this period is characterized historically by a significant rise in the activity of the masses over the preceding period. There is no unity among the masses; parties and groups are only beginning to assemble themselves for the period of minimal excitability. The power of suggestion returns to the masses: statesmen, warriors, orators, the press—all recuperate their influence. Questions, both political and military, start to appear just over the horizon of calm public life and define themselves crisply. A focus on uniform military or political subjects, along with other animating forces, grows gradually sharper; certain ideas circulating among the masses begin to predominate.

Before crucial questions of state are answered, preparations for war have already begun, and the international situation starts to grow more complicated. Of course, one still hesitates in the decision to enter into direct conflict or fully declare war: one lingers, feeling the general excitability of the masses slowly rise. Soon—after a year or two, and sometimes even sooner—the unanimous demand of the masses for the resolution of these and other questions becomes urgent. Now even those far removed from military and political matters are forced to affiliate themselves with one or another political or military group. It is as though a "societal solution" has been saturated, which in time yields crystals that begin to grow. By this I mean that when one's environment is saturated, one need only to introduce into it an organizing principle, and all around, ideologically identical stratifications will form.

At the end of the second epoch, which can become volatile and which finds the mood of the masses impatient and nervous, we observe one of the more important phenomena in the politico-military life of society. I am speaking of the aspiration of unifying the various nationalities that make up a given society, in order to defend or assail the various political groups for their opposition to other political groups.

The significance of this epoch consists in its offering a basis for the further development of historical events in the expansion of a given cycle in a given human society, and to some degree even to foretell their passage into the period of maximal excitability.

The duration of the epoch I am addressing is by no means identical across human societies: its duration will be determined by, on the one hand, the state of solar activity, and, on the other, a diversity of politico-economic forces. Furthermore, the epoch in question takes on, depending on these same causations, various forms of expression.

We can divide the second epoch into three key phases. In order of their gradual development, these are: the emergence of ideas among the masses, the grouping of ideas, and the triumph of a single principal idea among the masses of a particular human society—and finally the start of the third epoch.

1. The emergence of basic ideas during the period's first phase depends directly on both intragovernmental, politico-economic forces and international, military-political forces, which in this case are equivalent in value: the economic condition of the state; the degree to which the authorities and apparatus of state are organized and stable; the international situation, with its threats of war, blockades, occupations, and the like; as well as various ideas current among the great masses. When at a given moment in a society there is no discontentment in the existing order of things, these phenomena can remain absent—so that the whole cycle remains relatively peaceful. There is, however, no guarantee that an abrupt disruption will not bring sharp complications later on in that cycle; indeed, nearly always, even the slightest instigation will be succeeded by a period marked by particular events in which the masses participate locally.
2. The bearer of ideas that have emerged in this form may serve as a psychic center for the formation of certain groups, each united around a single shared idea. This process is linked with class consciousness, the degree of people's material security, and the personal characteristics of each individual. Having taken shape in this way, groups may nominate leaders from within their own ranks in order to place

psychological imbalance under the control of a specific psychic center, where the attendant ideas are tallied together and transformed into unified directives and some specific formulas for activity by the organized group.

3. The third phase emerges from the second and consists of trying to find a single supreme idea, absorbing the many ideas of the group in a unity organized around a supreme center that subordinates the masses into mass concentration on the single idea.

All three phases of the second epoch can sometimes develop quite mechanically, without any organizing participation by active individuals, which prepares them for the perfectly unexpected effects of mass unity on the approaching beginning of the cycle's third epoch, the period of maximal activity. Thus, a necessity arises to address *primarily* the *primary* issues troubling the masses of the human society in question.

The third epoch of the world-historical cycle: The period of maximal activity This is the main stage in the development of each cycle, solving at established world-historical moments the most important historical problems and founding new historical eras. It spurs mankind toward the greatest achievements and madnesses. It brings ideas into full life with the spilling of blood and the clanging of iron. If we wanted to make a comparative historical analysis of this epoch's character, we would need to revisit the most crucial events of world history: all of them, as has been shown through earlier comparisons of the activities of the Sun with those of man, having taken place in the era of the charge of solar activity. It is in this epoch that the greatest revolutions and clashes of peoples take place, initiating new epochs in the life of mankind. This is the era that leaders of those peoples have often mistaken for singular historic events.

Here we must not dwell on the consideration of the significant quantity of materials gathered in research into the period of maximal excitability. Let us indicate just those decisive forces whose existence among the masses makes the emergence and development of these decisive events conditional upon itself:

1. The excitatory effect on the masses of the leaders of peoples, military figures, orators, the press, and so forth
2. The excitatory effect of the moods and ideas circulating among the masses

3. The rapidity of excitation from the unified psychic center
4. The measure of territorial reach by a mass movement
5. The integration and individualization of the masses

Never does the influence of leaders, military figures, orators, the press, and so forth reach such great heights as during the period of maximal charge from the activity of sunspots. In this period, a single timely word or gesture can suffice to move whole armies and masses of people. A single indication by a leader proves captivating under the multinational banners that constitute governments, opposition parties, and the elements of a society. In this epoch, the word of a leader—a word with wings—does something extraordinary: it is heeded, obeyed, while entire floods of admonishments, distributed at every step in the period of minimal activity, yielded no result. Now even the very name of the leader, spoken aloud, calls forth a mighty swell of inspiration. The masses walk behind their leader blindly, unthinking, imbued with powerful excitation and ecstasy.

Thus, gifted personalities are elevated by the masses in contradiction to traditional norms and settled laws. And at the peaks of mass movements we see the greatest military and political geniuses mankind has known: spiritual leaders, the champions of freedom, the founders of various social associations. All of them, having forced their way through a crowd of people like the vivid embodiment of the masses' aspiration at a given moment, establish their leadership and with its help declare new modes of human organizations, new forms of social life, new aspects of spiritual pursuit. Advances such as these, as close investigation shows, can be perfected only when the masses are unified, and this is observed most clearly during the epoch of intensifying activity by the Sun.

Powerful ideas circulate among the masses in the time leading up to the period of maximal excitability. Agitation by word of mouth and in print can decide the fate of a military or political movement.

The period of maximal activity can also be called the period in which the face of the masses and the sound of the people's voice are revealed. Historians reach an impasse on realizing that ideas about which people dared not speak just a year or two ago are now discussed openly and boldly; the masses grow more impatient, more restless, more excited; they begin to lift up their voices, to make demands, to take up arms. Demonstrations grow more malicious and unpleasant, people's assemblies are convened with little attention to peace: the masses make their demands aggressively, wielding the sword of full confidence in their own decisions; their impulses will no longer be constrained, and, immediately taken up by the people, will lead to the overthrow of all that has been cause for concern and disturbance. Individual caprices and excesses suddenly take on the force of law, and any man who tries to oppose them earns punishment; the population is controlled by a deep hatred for its enemies, whom it consigns to obliteration. In such an era, when the people begin to speak, the only two options are to obey or to renounce them.

In the period of maximal activity, the very slightest indication sometimes proves sufficient to enflame the masses into an uprising or war. Even a single whisper, loosed on the masses, can lead to general unrest and revolt. What in the period of minimal activity could have been expected to engender peaceful discussion can, in the maximal epoch we are considering, excite the masses, leading to uprisings, wars, and other bloody episodes. The masses thirst for a movement, troops are restrained only with difficulty, soldiers tend toward revolt, and the people toward anarchy. In short, excitation increases extraordinarily, and the human organism requires some sort of release. A sharp change can be observed in the neuropsychic tone of the masses, as can a spike in neuropsychic reaction to external stimuli. Individuals show that they are in no position to suppress their increased reflexive excitability, reacting exaggeratedly even to unimpressive, minor irritations.

The written records of periods of maximal activity testify to a staggering rapidity in the spread of popular uprisings, and mass movements in general. Consider, for example, how the spread of uprisings may unfold: an uprising takes hold of the country with unusual speed; a few days later huge areas have risen to their feet; as though some magic wand had been waved, the whole population seems to have joined with the rebels; rebellion breaks out in the government with the speed of a hurricane; rebellion breaks out at almost the same instant in various parts of the country, gathering huge groups of people under its banners; the din of the uprising sweeps across the entire nation with the speed of a thunderbolt; the flames of international warfare engulf a huge area, and all of the populace, from small to great, takes on some role in the uprising. Considering this, we can see why Titus Livius called social conflicts an "infectious plague."

Besides the speed at which mass movements spread, we should note the significance of their territorial reach. Indeed, an uprising begun in one nation may, under the right circumstances, spread across borders to neighboring countries. History offers many examples of wars, uprisings, and other mass movements traversing vast distances in short times—across many lands, and even whole continents.

The shared spirit of the masses, which is outlined especially clearly in this period prior to the resolution of any military or political issues, forms the basis of the preceding. Now, with a single call their leader can assemble beneath his banner tens, hundreds of thousands of people inspired by a single shared ideal, a single desire. Unanimity reigns in place of enmity, and common conviction ignites minds. This unanimity in the period of maximal activity is capable of miracles; even those who were recently enemies can be made into friends, allies against the gravest and most terrible dangers, or to resolve shared questions of importance to all. In such moments, ethnicity, partisanship, and social status are effaced, private quibbles grow calm, and everyone gathers where they are needed. In short, in the name of whatever military undertakings, campaigns, uprisings, and the like are taking place, general goodwill and peace emerge among opposing and formerly conflicting elements of the state. In such moments, the entire nation is ready to pursue any declared goal, together as one man. This understanding of unity and full solidarity among the masses obliterates all argument and conflict. Psychic contamination or interinfusion reaches its highest point, and the masses turn toward a collective identity, while the collective is individualized.

The sudden unity of the masses in the period of maximal activity is a means of revealing the will of the people and the limits of autocracy and oligarchy. While during the period of minimal activity the masses break into small and indifferent units, during the maximal period, assuming the presence of certain social forces, there will be something to oppose in any government, and a collective bound by the people's unanimity that is able to act as a powerful individual. As a consequence of this kind of conjunction of various popular masses during the epoch of the maximum, in certain instances we see a change in internal policy, concessions made to the masses, and reforms, while in others we see revolutions and civil wars. It is nearly always the case that, in a detailed analysis of those points in history at which the role of the masses could be manifested unclearly, one can see this role confirmed numerous times. For example, during periods of maximum intensity we often see combined a deepening of reactions, the restoration of a monarchy, the apogee of autocratic power, and so forth. The investigation of this point in history without doubt will show that it is again the masses who espouse this reactionary movement, although in the majority of cases during the period of maximal activity the masses are anarchic, revolutionary, and opposed to the government. And so, on the basis of social factors, a conflict erupts.

The intensity of this struggle reveals the entire broad spectrum of human madness, immoderation, and passion. Spontaneous violence, bitterness, berserking, epileptic delirium, thirst for power, epidemics of murder, panic, pogroms, desperate invasions, wild battles, mass exterminations, and bloody struggles, not to mention uprisings, rebellion, and the spectacles of fanaticism and heroism, all reach their apogees. The masses and mobs become capable of celebrating even the most awful violence, atrocities, and murders. They devise torturous executions. Insanity dominates. What had been considered savage and impossible during the period of minimal activity may well become the moral and sublime ideal pursued in the period of maximum activity. One gets the impression that during this time the centers of higher consciousness are suppressed, and primordial, instinctive reactions take over.

And so the ground is prepared for the resolution of world-historical problems—the same ground on which the systems of human societies become established. Events take place here that have few parallels in earlier periods of the cycle. Through my own research, I have established that the greatest revolutions, wars, and mass movements leading to changes of government, constituting the turning points of history, and rocking the course of human life on every earthly continent have tended to coincide with epochs of heightened solar activity and to reach their peak in moments of the most intense solar activity. In fact, in every age and among all peoples, the epochs of maximal activity have always attracted the fascination of thinkers and historians who, with attention and surprise, have managed to observe sharp changes in the psychological composition of the masses during these periods. The descriptions of these particular periods have been preserved in the annals of history from the time of Herodotus. Beginning with ancient accounts, we can delineate the precise borders separating the epochs of maximal excitation very clearly from the epochs of rise and decline. Already in the majestic writings of Herodotus, in which we can glimpse the struggles on the plains of Marathon or at the Battle of Thermopylae, and in the works of Tacitus, which relate the horrors seen at the fall of Carthage, these epochs are defined by certain special characteristics. And onward throughout the rest of history, we see ideas born during these epochs igniting huge masses of people, giving rise to military leadership, animating hundreds of thousands of human lives, uniting societies, leading to the fulfillment of actions, achievements, and madness—all the bricks from which the temples of human society are built. Immediately, a question arises: if the emergence of great historical events is determined by a mass excitation of minds that is somehow connected with solar activity, can we assume that the rate of mankind's historical evolution would have been considerably slowed by the absence of this force that periodically contributes to an excitation of the overall activity of the human masses? In any event, this question does not contradict the energetic understanding of the world's development, of which one part is the world-historical or social process.

The study of historical events during the third epoch has allowed us to establish a series of facts according to which the period of maximal activity contributes to the unification of the masses; the emergence of leaders, military figures, state actors; the triumph of ideas held by the masses; the maximal development of parliamentarianism; democratic and social reforms; democracy and limitations on the power of autocracy; uprisings, riots, unrest, insurrections, revolutions; wars, campaigns, invasions, persecutions; and other flashes of mass human activity.

The fourth epoch of the world-historical cycle: The period of decreasing activity The period of decreasing activity is, in historico-psychological terms, no less interesting than the periods that come before it. It may also abound in formative events, although usually during this period only those that appeared earlier are completed.

The period of decreasing activity is like an echo of the earlier, tempestuous period of struggle and disquiet whose highest degrees of intensity have already passed, and is marked by a shared desire for calm and peace. If a war is underway, its fire will gradually fade, a laxness will overtake the discipline of the forces, and the pace of military activity will slow.

Now for the first time there is a sense that there has been enough of war, plunder, and bloodshed. The honoring of military commitments and treaties is no longer thought necessary; allied countries cease providing one another military support; separatism becomes all the more common a political position; military alliances fall apart.

Those troop movements still ongoing recall the convulsions of the dying, and gangs of warriors thirst for peace with the very impatience that not long ago characterized their thirst for war. At the same time, the movement of enemy forces, if sufficiently disciplined, meets no serious resistance. Meanwhile, the whole country has just come to know the enemy by fire and sword. Gradually, the army has been transformed into a heedless mob, its ranks rapidly thinning; soldiers coalesce into groups set on returning home, and the martial mood that had prevailed among the masses is supplanted by a peaceful one.

Leaders, military brass, and orators lose the power by which, during the previous period, they had enthralled the masses and forced them into submission. The masses take to suggestion only with great difficulty; parliamentary debate no longer captivates the country.

Rather than flaring up, newly arisen wars quickly die down, resulting in a world built on conditions of leniency. If a year or two earlier it had been easy to spur on rebellion, it now no longer is, and attempts at doing so will come to nothing. Historians may be surprised that the elements of opposition do not manage to unify, as they had in the same nation not long ago; they do not sow unrest or crop up simultaneously in different places, but rather grow less common and remain unresolved, their laxness exerting a corrosive effect on all military and political alliances.

This lack of unanimity in the fourth epoch of the cycle is a submerged stone on which any new uprising, any mass action, risks being broken, since concerted activity has in this period been made unlikely by the diminishment and weakening of the forces binding it together. Campaigns already underway and military expeditions are carried out without inspiration, sometimes in a spirit of obvious disinterest. The masses' enthusiastic support for reforms, people's government, wars, uprisings, and so on begins to wane, supplanted by total indifference. Indeed, they all express a tendency toward propitiation, and talk of peace begins to be heard. It is rumored even in the most belligerent countries.

The decline in unified communication by the masses sows discord and leads to arguments within collectives, alliances, and governments. This last development renders all human groupings indecisive and unfit for combat.

Declared in all its complex totality, this development moves toward a rejection of recent assertions, and demands that had previously been proclaimed by foaming mouths are turned down to a minimum.

Finally, the general decline in excitability alternates with a depressive psychophysical condition. It is a time of political stagnation and inaction. People's assemblies and representative bodies are dissolved without protest, uprisings are easily put down, no wars break out, and peace talks can be mechanistically carried out under the indifference of the masses, the way often paved by physical exhaustion.

With these characteristics, we have unveiled a series of phenomena developing in various epochs of the cycle, and have attempted to move toward the establishment of laws that govern how these phenomena unfold.

Here I shall say again that the characteristics of the epochs enumerated above are in essence idealizations, synthetically derived from the large number of world-historical cycles we have investigated. The actually occurring social process tends to approach these ideal characteristics, prevented from completely coinciding with them by various deviations of geographic and temporal forces. Thus the development of each historical cycle in fact bears only a partial resemblance to the sinusoidal course of the phenomenon, with its gradual rise in the curve and its consequent fall. We can say, however, that mankind, taken as a whole under the sign of the integral as the limit of accumulation, undergoes living, feeling, and thinking in accordance with these characteristics in the flow of corresponding epochs of the solar cycle.

Further, we can say that mankind's mass activity is based on a type of regular alternation between tensions and relaxations, exaltations and depressions, work and rest, and that this alternation is functionally dependent on the degree of intensity in the activity of the Sun.

From all of the above we can derive the morphological law of the world-historic process, which I have formulated as follows.

The current of the world-historical process consists of an unceasing series of cycles that proceed in synchronicity with the cycles of periodic sunspot activity, with each cycle occupying a mathematical average of eleven years.

Every cycle possesses the following sociopsychological characteristics:

1. In an epoch of maximum sunspots, the most intense economic, political, and military forces drive the mass behavior of humanity across the Earth, exploding into revolutions, uprisings, wars, struggles, and migrations, creating new formations in the development of particular states and new historical eras in the development of humanity and the concurrent integration of the masses through their activity and majority rule.
2. In the epoch of minimum sunspots, the intensity of the military and political activity of all humanity gives way to creative activity and an all-around decline in political and military enthusiasm, peace and calm creative work in the sphere of organizing the foundations of government, international relations, science, and art in the face of the disintegration and demoralization of the masses and the strengthening of the authorities' tendencies toward absolutism.
3. The intermediary stages between the epochs of the cycle's maximum and minimum are characterized by respective intermediate sociopsychological characteristics.

Deviations from this morphological law of the world-historical process are produced by causes independent of the cosmic force, and are but the sociohistorical consequence of key events falling within the era of maximal activity that have not managed by one force or another to wind up within the bounds of the epoch that has summoned them.

The preceding allows us to take a single world-historical cycle consisting of four epochs as the template of a basic unit for measuring time in the world-historical process, a kind of sociopsychological "metric" of history, since the sociopsychological structure of one cycle corresponds to the sociopsychological structure of all others.

We may call the new field of knowledge that has arisen on the basis of these considerations "historiometry," understanding it to be a science for measuring historical time by way of concrete physical units. The first and most fundamental unit for tracking historical time in this way is the single sunspot cycle, which is equivalent on average to eleven years. In relation to the world-historical process, the time occupied by a single solar unit can be called one historiometric cycle.

In science, there are not many apodictic positions to be discovered. Science's fundamental achievements can be boiled down to assertions that rest on certain degrees, greater or lesser, of plausibility. Most often, we are satisfied with approximate values, and, based on them, we carry out the creative work that leads to the establishment of fairly strict statistical norms. We reach these statistical norms by studying the distribution of mass events across time and their classification in the flow of particular epochs of the cycle.

Thus, I have laid out in concise and diagrammatic terms the morphological identity of all historical cycles, the "universal" tendencies driving the conduct of the human masses across the four epochs of the cycle. There can be no doubt that all these phenomena, developed in human societies, are incomparably more complex and confusing in reality than their representations in my scheme. However, by using this scheme, which I concede is far from perfect and necessarily approximate in many respects, we can nonetheless proceed forward in an objective investigation of the issue.

In the process of gathering, studying, and synthesizing synchronistic materials, I made broad use of comparative methods, calling out a complete series of the most important sociopsychological issues.

As it happened, changes in the behavior of the masses could be seen in especially stark relief during the development of prolonged historical phenomena. The inspiration and increase of the energies of the masses were clearly delineated, as was the gradual decline of these energies during their transition to a state of fatigue and apathy. Then, after some time, it again became possible to observe a general revival, disquiet, mood of excitation, and, finally, the rise in political and military enthusiasm that is intrinsic to the period of maximal activity. Thus, prolonged historical phenomena make excellent examples of the characteristic changes in the conduct of the masses that occur throughout the cycle. All of the most impactful historical phenomena extending across the country and rolling on for several decades were in their development subject to fluctuations in accordance with the epochs through which they unfolded, which can easily be observed in the changes of any historical event in connection with the changes of the process of sunspot development.

Naturally, the cycle cannot always be delineated into epochs with such clarity. There are times when we can proceed through their determination only by groping forward in the darkness, guessing, as it were, where the borders fall between different epochs in the mood of the masses, in their

Table 1.1
Diagrammatic summary of the data for a complete cycle.

	Sunspot Activity		Behavior of the Masses				
Name of Period/Epoch	No. of Epoch	Relative No. of Sunspots	Emergent Historiometric Events	No. of Historical Events by Period (%)	No. of Historical Events in Each Year of Each Period (%)	Sociological Characteristics of Mass Behavior	Historical Phenomena
Period of Minimal Excitability (Era of Depressions)	I	Minimum	Emergence of mass sociopolitical movements	5	1.7	Differentiation of the masses, indifference to social issues, a peaceful mood, pliability, tolerance, depressive stance, mass statics, etc.	Signing of peace treaties; aggressive campaigns undertaken without participation by the masses; surrenders, occupations, maximal constraints on parliamentarianism, strengthening of autocracy
Period of Increasing Excitability	II	Gradual increase in sunspots and groups of sunspots	Gradual increase in movements	20	10.0	1. Emergence of social ideas and building of collectives; 2. Grouping of ideas and the masses; 3. Emergence of fundamental ideas and general unity among the masses	Hesitations in the resolution of military and political issues; preparations for war; growing worsening of international relations; the start of conspiracies; the specification of politico-military tendencies

Table 1.1 (continued)

Name of Period/Epoch	Sunspot Activity: No. of Epoch	Sunspot Activity: Relative No. of Sunspots	Behavior of the Masses: Emergent Historiometric Events	No. of Historical Events by Period (%)	No. of Historical Events in Each Year of Each Period (%)	Sociological Characteristics of Mass Behavior	Historical Phenomena
Period of Maximal Excitability (Era of Concentrations)	III	Maximum	Maximum	60	20.0	I. (a) Effect on the masses of popular leaders, military figures, the press, orators, etc.; (b) influence of ideas on the masses II. (a) speed of development of mass movements; (b) breadth of territory of movements; (c) integration of the masses; individualization of collectives; (d) dynamics of the masses	Advancement of leaders, military brass, state actors; triumph of ideas held among the masses; maximal development of parliamentarism; democratic and social reforms; power wielded by the people; limitations on autocracy. Revolutions, uprisings, revolts, riots, wars, marches, expeditions, emigrations, resettlements, persecutions, and other flare-ups of mass activity
Period of Decreasing Excitability	IV	Gradual decrease in sunspots and groups of sunspots	Gradual decrease in movements	15	5.0	Progressing belatedness of public relations to public stimuli; degradation of concentrated activity, enthusiasm, inspirations, etc.	Breakdown of military or political organizations, separatism; repudiations of claims of international or sovereign order; dispersal or disintegration of people's councils; easy suppression of uprisings; completion of events originating in previous period

Notes: Average duration of sunspot cycle: 11.1 years. Average duration of period within the cycle: 5.16 years. Average duration of historiometric cycle: 11 years. Average duration of periods within historiometric cycle: 3 years (I, III, IV); 2 years (II). Given phenomena develop under conditions inclinations, their military or political reasoning, in the historical spirit of a given moment.

In history, of course, we encounter a huge variety of phenomena that do not at first glance seem capable of inclusion under a single shared rubric. At one point, we may find the masses fully passive while the rulers rattle their sabers for war. Only a short time later we may see those same masses rising as one to heed the call of war. At another time, we may observe quite a different phenomenon: the masses active, and the government remaining quiet, ignoring the voice of those masses, until one day revolution breaks out. We have no cause to think that during the period of maximal sunspot activity humanity becomes significantly more bellicose. Even if this were true, it could only be partly so. Humanity has simply in these moments reached a greater level of excitation, and here lies the basis of its conduct. We must in fact understand that, during the epoch of maximal activity and in times of war, calls for peace can arise with equal force, if prior events have contributed to this. Then, the masses will demand peace just as forcefully as they had earlier clamored for war.

To the same degree that social and economic forces play a critical role in the development of mass phenomena, the course of these phenomena must in certain circumstances deviate significantly from the course of developments on the Sun. So for example, if the politico-economic ground has caused a significant rise in emotion among the masses, and the government has been unable to suppress this rise through various measures (for instance, arresting its leaders), a mass movement may erupt at the first quick jump in sunspot activity and reach its apex in the period of the maximum. And if that mass movement were to be hindered, or if it simply adopted a slow pace on its own, this could be reflected in a year of maximal charge from sunspots, but also in the two years following it.

It is this understanding that largely accounts for the fact that a rapid increase in sunspots after the minimum sometimes calls forth an entire series of historical events, quickly dying down (in parallel with a simultaneous decrease in solar activity), only to emerge again in anticipation of the period of the maximum, all the more sharply and dramatically.

In fact, one phenomenon stubbornly calls attention to itself repeatedly across many cycles: the abrupt transition from a minimum of sunspot activity to a maximum elicits urgent crises in the behavior of the masses. At once, in certain separate places, movements arise that, having quieted down earlier, now explode once more in the period of maximal solar activity. This phenomenon somewhat recalls chemical reactions whose beginnings are marked by volatile transformations of matter.

In the comparative measure of separate epochs in the history of various peoples, we are repeatedly confronted by facts that clearly demonstrate how huge is the role played in the life of a people by the difference in character between two epochs of sunspot activity, the maximum and the minimum, both opposite in their effects on the collective behavior of the masses.

Throughout history, we are repeatedly confronted by phenomena with deeply enigmatic properties. Accordingly, there are times when utterly identical sets of phenomena nonetheless produce different results. In one case, a war of A against B may end in the total victory of A's forces and the defeat of B's, despite all of B's advantages and cunning military leadership. B's forces will flee and disintegrate, while A's will move deep into enemy territory and claim it with seemingly great ease. In another case, the picture may change: now B's forces can handle their enemy. They hunger to meet him in battle, with the outcome that A's campaign against B is decided by steel and blood. This striking difference between military enterprises that nonetheless bear so substantial a formal resemblance to one another can be seen in especially stark relief if the campaigns are carried out in rapid succession, such as the campaigns of Ancient Greek civil feuds, or the medieval wars of the Germanic states against Italy.

Generally speaking, there is no shortage of examples of the varying impact that periods of sunspot activity have on similar events. The complexity of these events can be so great at times that it is not always possible to clearly identify that impact; but something deadly exceeds all of this complexity, independently of the will of interacting collectives, controlling the course of events with the greatest compulsion toward conformity with the energetic influence of the Sun.

In studying the history of campaigns by Alexander the Great, Julius Caesar, Charlemagne, Frederick the Great, Napoleon, and other famous military leaders, it may seem that these ingenious leaders understood how to raise their own and their enemies' regiments up out of any and all dependence on the activity of the Sun. I am unable to concur with such an opinion, however. It is difficult to say what they based the timing of their campaigns on, but there is no doubt that they have often conformed to the mood of the masses of the nations they opposed. Further considering this question,

I have come to the conclusion that the greatest, most ambitious, and most aggressive campaigns of antiquity, the Middle Ages, and the modern day all took place within epochs of minimal intensity of sunspot activity. It remains for us to address the question of whether any of these conquests might have been achieved had it begun a few years later, in the epoch of maximum activity. Would the great leaders of the resistance in that case not have met them from the other side, ruling out surrender, and rather significantly reducing the extent of the conquest and limiting the number of trophies? One can only wonder how leaders in the epoch of the minimum could succeed in uniting and rallying their forces and compelling obedience to their wishes.

In those cases where we encounter a slowdown in the development of military enterprises, expeditions, and campaigns thanks to the resistance of the enemy, we see, comparing the dates of the campaigns, that they are completed in the epoch of the maximum. In those cases where the incursion of troops into hostile terrain is met with resignation, with an absence of general enthusiasm among the enemy, with relative indifference; when the country does not rise to its feet, fails to throw all its strength on the altar of self-defense; when the citizenry greets the invading forces with little more than a spiteful grimace rather than rising up to the last man; then, comparing the historical date with sunspot activity, we can see that it has fallen during a period of minimal activity by the Sun. In such periods, the leaders who carry out aggressive invasions find good reason to echo Julius Caesar: *Veni, vidi, vici*; I came, I saw, I conquered.

A detailed investigation of this issue has led me to conclude that expeditions of conquest undertaken during periods of minimal solar activity usually conclude with comparatively easy and simple victories. If it has elite forces, united under the charisma of a leader or the thirst for plunder, a state can send expeditions of conquest into other countries during a period of minimal activity. The forces move forward, seize land, impose taxes, grandly insult the dignity and national pride of the citizens of the land they have conquered, all without encountering any serious obstacles to their triumphal march. In a period of minimal activity only those nations that can identify gifted military leaders will know triumph. Instances of bloodless conquest generally coincide with the epoch of the least activity by the Sun. The history of European colonialism confirms this rule neatly.

In such moments, the historian will be particularly surprised to observe that a people proud of its past and strong at present will nonetheless meekly and timorously endure the greatest offense its enemy can make—the occupation of land, the seizure of fortresses and cities, the rape of women—all without eliciting any unified rebellion or general uprising, while even a minor charge, with the unanimity of the masses, could stir the occupied garrisons and return their lost honor to them. But if the enemy tarries too long in leaving the conquered country, with the maturation into the epoch of the maximum, among the masses a murmur will begin to build, quietly at first, but gaining in strength, until, finally, the day arrives when the whole of the people stands as one against its enemy and drives him from the fatherland.

In the sphere of intragovernmental policy, periods of minimal activity by the Sun are characterized by a general calming of political passions, the relative indifference of the broad masses toward politics, and so on. In connection with this phenomenon one characteristic psychological feature of the epoch of the minimum emerges, repeated invariably across many historical periods. This, to be precise, is that the independence and separation of governmental powers from the masses reaches its apogee, autocratic power rises to the highest point in its development, and parliamentarianism is driven down to zero.

In this period, when the masses of people are occupied with peaceful labor and when the political passions that had agitated the masses in the epoch of the maximum are waning, governmental power can sometimes be left quite mechanistically to helm the ship of state. Without the influence of the pacified masses, authorities become unable to address the needs and demands of the country. Autocratic power in these moments reaches the limit of its development and, without encountering a counterweight to its actions, gains the ability to set forth laws that may run directly contrary to the needs of the people.

At the same time, one frequently occurring phenomenon draws attention to itself in connection with the problem of leadership and the masses. The spontaneous indifference of the masses to sociopolitical issues and the accompanying increase in the despotism of the ruling party bring on a number of complications that can often prove totally insoluble for historians. One of the striking examples that characterizes the psychological composition of the masses in the epoch of minimal excitation is the downfall of social actors from the shimmering pedestals of grandeur and glory on which they had been placed during the epoch of the maximum. If these social actors or popular military leaders were promoted in the epoch of the maximum while managing to accumulate power over the masses at a time when they were united, when their collective behavior was comparable to that of a single powerful individual, their subsequent downfall in the epoch of the minimum appears wholly logical and natural: the masses have become inert, splitting into opposing parties, and new gods and heroes are suddenly heaped with reproach and apostasy. History is full of examples of such overthrows of societal and popular leaders during years of minimal solar activity.

Translated by Ian Dreiblatt

2 From "Mass Movements and Short Periods of Solar Activity," in *The Earth in the Sun's Embrace*

Alexander Chizhevsky

In the book's previous chapters, I have repeatedly pointed out that the life of the popular masses in different countries is subject to fluctuations that, depending on solar activity, find their expression and shape in the periodic upsurges and depressions of parliamentary life, in changes of the liberal and conservative parties standing at the helm of government. The constant alternation of popular social exaltation and popular social depression has compelled me to study the degree to which the alternation in question has been reflected in parliamentary history and the degree to which parliamentarianism has been dependent on the influence exerted by the Sun's periodic activity.

No one, of course, would deny the obvious fact that parliamentary elections and the life of parliament in general are hardly spontaneous, and that there is a significant amount of artificiality in their operations. This is evidenced by the entire history of parliamentarianism, from ancient times to the present. At the same time, however, it cannot be denied that the principal stages of the life of parliament—elections—occur under the sign of public attention and popular pressure, which in the given instance is especially interesting. We also know that elections are accompanied by a struggle. Passions flare during this struggle, and there is no doubt the outcomes of elections often depend on the extent to which the neuropsychological mechanisms of voters are inhibited or disinhibited. Since the particular state of the nervous system is dependent on the

"Mass Movements and Short Periods of Solar Activity" was translated from part 3, chapter 4 of Alexander Chizhevsky, *Kosmicheskiy pul's zhizni: Zemlya v obyatiyakh Solntsa. Geliotapaksia* [Cosmic pulse of life: Earth in the Sun's embrace] (Moscow: Mysl, 1995), 300–320.

state of the environment, elections might also be of considerable interest to us.

Indeed, approval or disapproval, voting or silence, involvement or non-involvement in debates, and other techniques for voicing one's opinions at elections are to a certain extent guided not only by conscious deliberation but by the body's overall neuropsychological fitness, as are all other actions and human deeds in which not only the higher mental functions but also the emotional sphere are involved. At the same time, neuropsychological fitness could also depend to a certain degree on the environment. This dependency leaves a mark on the behavior of the masses that might go unnoticed in individuals. We thus see the masses reacting in the same way to particular stimuli. The uniform action of the masses depends to a certain degree on the uniform impact exercised on all these individuals by the world around them.

I have focused on the history of the English Parliament, the oldest such body and, obviously, the body that over its centuries-long history has adapted to a large variety of popular moods in the country.

Until the Reform Act of 1832, the long history of the English Parliament and ministries is of no substantial interest to us because the popular masses did not take part in elections. Thus, in the late eighteenth century, only 160,000 men had the franchise among a population, in England and Wales, of eight million people, and even that franchise was far from uniform. Large cities such as Birmingham and Manchester were not represented at all. At the same time, many sparsely populated villages—the so-called rotten boroughs—enjoyed the right to send members to the House of Commons. Such villages were completely controlled by local lords, who influenced the outcome of elections. Sometimes, a seat in Parliament was simply purchased.

The need to reform parliamentary elections had been quite apparent since the eighteenth century. Chosen on the basis of an outmoded electoral system, the House of Commons could no longer be regarded as representing the entire country. The urban population was growing, but the towns and cities were not represented in Parliament. In 1769, a year marked by peak solar activity, the first league for electoral reform emerged. Beginning with William Pitt Sr., who tabled a bill in 1770, more or less radical reform bills were tabled in the House of Commons.

Power passed back and forth between the Whigs and Tories until finally, in 1807, the Tories gained power for twenty-three years. This fact is sufficiently explained by the strengthening economic position of agriculture, a sector dominated by the Tories.

The nature of English political parties changed dramatically in the early nineteenth century. During the eighteenth century, both Whigs and Tories mainly recruited from the same class and differed little from one another in terms of their ideas. So too the struggle between them resembled less a struggle between two distinct parties, and more a squabble between different factions of the same party. But when, in the early nineteenth century, the Tories became the party of agriculture, while the Whigs became the party of commerce and industry, and both parties were put on a sound organizational footing, the rivalry between them became the main arena of political struggle in England.

With the growth of political institutions and political rivalry, the obsolete electoral system was becoming useless. In the first quarter of the last century, the House of Commons represented the people only to a minimal extent. There were 400,000 to 500,000 voters among a population of 24 million people, and even so they were extremely unevenly apportioned by district. England's bourgeoisie demanded electoral reform. The Whigs inscribed this demand on their banner, but the Tories resisted in every way they could. The tense circumstances dragged on until 1830, a year of intense solar activity, when elections gave the Whigs the majority in the Commons. Lord Grey formed the new cabinet, which included electoral reform champion Lord John Russell. The next year, Russell tabled a reform bill in the Commons that applied only to England and Wales. After long debate, the bill was rejected by an alliance between one faction of Whigs and the Conservatives. Grey responded by dissolving the Commons. In the newly elected Commons, the supporters of reform had a considerable majority owing to a huge pro-reform social movement. The reform was passed by the Commons, but the Lords rejected the bill. To push the reform bill through, Grey asked the king to knight supporters of the reform. The king refused to do this and asked Tory leaders to form a Conservative government. In light, however, of the immense upsurge in public support for the reform and the popular mood, the Tories turned down the king's offer. The reform bill was then tabled in the Commons for the third time and passed during its second reading. The Lords did not debate the bill, because on the day the vote had been scheduled, its opponents deliberately failed to attend the session. Thus, in 1832, the reform bill was passed into law.

The number of voters doubled after the reform, extending to 3 percent of the entire populace. The number of MPs remained the same, but their distribution changed. By renewing the Commons, the reform made it the voice of the English middle classes, and thanks to their numbers the MPs themselves were less subject to governmental pressure.

The 1832 elections, held under the aegis of the new law, returned an unprecedented majority of three hundred seats for the Liberals. Since then, the history of the English Parliament has seen a systematic alternation between Conservative and Liberal cabinets, as directly defined by the makeup of the Commons, that is, by the outcomes of the elections themselves.

Since England's popular masses are involved in the elections to some extent, the change of governments also has a certain relation to the problem we are studying as a barometer of moods among large groups of people, moods that emerge for particular reasons.

I found it quite interesting to trace whether there was correspondence in time between switches from Liberal to Conservative governments in England, on the one hand, and periods of maximum and minimum solar activity, on the other. A priori, based on all of the above, it was necessary to assume a coincidence between periods when the Liberals were in government and periods of maximum solar activity, between Conservative governments and solar minima. This assumption followed from all my previous research. Indeed, during the course of my basic research, I had occasion to note cases of abrupt upsurges in parliamentarianism during periods of maximum solar activity.

Indeed, in 1834, when there was a solar minimum, Grey and Melbourne's Liberal ministry was replaced during 1834–1835 by Peel's Conservative ministry, which in 1835 was forced to resign as new elections in 1835 had returned a Liberal majority to the Commons. This coincided with an abrupt upsurge in solar activity that reached its peak in 1838. The Liberal Melbourne once again undertook to form a new cabinet, a cabinet that stayed in office for the entire cycle of the solar maximum until the Sun's activity diminished in 1841. The year saw new elections to the Commons that returned a majority of sorts for the Conservatives, and Peel again formed a cabinet.

Peel's Conservative ministry held on for the entire solar minimum until 1846 when, simultaneously with an acute upsurge in solar activity, Peel had to yield to Russell's Liberal cabinet. The latter lasted throughout the entire solar maximum until 1852 when, along with a downturn in solar activity, it was replaced by the Conservatives, led by Derby. However, fresh elections in 1852 were not entirely favorable to him, and his ministry had to resign. Aberdeen formed the new cabinet. Although it was dominated by Liberals, it also included several Conservatives. The first exception to the pattern we have thus far been tracing emerged: Aberdeen's Liberal ministry held office during a solar minimum. In 1855, Aberdeen was succeeded by Palmerston, who retained the previous cabinet, sans Aberdeen and the Liberal Gladstone. The presence of Peel's supporters in the ministry imparted more of a Conservative flavor to it than a Liberal one. This ministry vigorously reformed the military administration and firmly prosecuted the Crimean War (1853–1856). In 1858, Palmerston's ministry suffered a defeat in the Commons thanks to an act of his that outraged English society. In the wake of Orsini's attempt on the life of Napoleon III, Palmerston tabled his Murder Bill, aimed at combating such conspiracies on English soil. English society was so firm in its conviction that England should grant asylum to political exiles that Palmerston's bill incensed public opinion. He had to go, and a new cabinet was formed by the Conservative Derby (1858). In 1859, however, along with an ascending solar maximum, general elections gave a majority to the Liberals, and Derby's ministry had to yield to Palmerston's Liberal ministry, which included Gladstone and Russell. Once again, there commenced a period of remarkable coherence in the alternation between Liberal and Conservative ministries, and the alternation between solar maxima and solar minima.

Palmerston and Russell's Liberal ministry remained at its post for the entire maximum cycle, from 1859 to 1866. Power was again returned to Derby's Conservatives in 1866: Derby and Disraeli formed their third cabinet, which lasted throughout the solar minimum from 1866 to 1868. In 1868, however, the ministry of Disraeli (who had succeeded Derby in 1868) suffered a defeat on the Irish question and dissolved the Commons. The voters opted for the Liberals. Disraeli resigned. Gladstone formed the so-called great Liberal ministry. It stayed in power for an entire solar maximum, from 1868 to 1874.

By the end of his administration, however, Gladstone had made enemies of influential groups in society who in 1874 constituted a strong coalition supporting the Conservatives. Gladstone resigned, and Disraeli was charged with forming a new cabinet. The reign of the Conservatives thus once more coincided with the following solar minimum, 1874–1880. A bad harvest and social unrest in Ireland brought triumph to the Liberal Party in the 1880 elections, and once again the Liberal Party's administration, from 1880 to 1885, coincided with a solar maximum, from 1882 to 1884.

In 1885, Gladstone was forced to resign after suffering defeat in the Commons on budget and military matters. The Conservative Salisbury formed a cabinet that stayed in power from 1885 to 1892, not counting a six-month break in 1886 when power belonged to the Liberals. Salisbury's administration once again fit nicely with the solar minimum that lasted from 1888 to 1890. In 1892, during an increase in solar activity, the Conservative ministry had to resign, yielding to the Liberals. Gladstone formed his fourth cabinet, which remained in power from 1892 to 1894, an entire solar maximum. In 1894, Gladstone resigned, and he was replaced by a member of his own party, Rosebery, who continued Gladstone's policies until fresh elections in 1895 returned the Conservatives.

From 1895 to 1905, England had a Conservative ministry, led by Salisbury (1895–1902) and Balfour (1902–1905). We had a solar minimum in the period 1900–1902. In a year marked by a maximum, 1905, however, Balfour's ministry was replaced by the Liberal ministry of Campbell-Bannerman (1905–1908), which stayed in power throughout the maximum (1905–1907).

He was succeeded in 1908 by another Liberal ministry, that of Asquith, which remained in power until 1916, that is, during a minimum cycle that lasted from 1912 to 1913, which is the second exception to the rule. In 1916, Asquith was succeeded by the Liberal ministry of Lloyd George, which neatly coincided with the maximum of 1916–1918 and resigned in 1922.

The year 1922 marked the beginning of a minimum (1922–1924) that saw the Conservative ministries of Bonar Law and Baldwin (1922–1924) replaced simultaneously in 1924 with the first spikes in solar activity after the minimum by MacDonald's Labour ministry. Owing to political reasons, this ministry did not enjoy the public's trust, and it resigned. It was replaced by Baldwin's Conservative ministry, whose administration coincided with a solar maximum. This is the third exception to the rule.

To arrive at a fuller explication of the accuracy and closeness of the given dependency, I have resorted to the following method. I added the relative annual numbers of sunspots, according to Wolfer's latest data, separately for periods of Liberal and Conservative ministries, as per the history of the English Parliament. Moreover, in years in which reelections took place, I divided the sunspots in half, attributing half to the previous period, and the other half to the subsequent ministry. I then divided the sums of Wolf-Wolfer numbers I had obtained for the periods of the various ministries by the number of these ministries to arrive at the arithmetic average. These arithmetic averages, in fact, served as my first criterion. I adduce all these operations due to the outstanding interest represented by the conclusions based on them.

We can summarize the results in a single table. When we look at the table, we can see sharp fluctuations in the average Wolf-Wolfer number over periods of Liberal and Conservative ministries. This difference can be visualized as follows:

Liberal ministries	53.5	79.8	72.5	20.1	51.9	76.2	47.2	57.9	etc.
Conservative ministries	17.5	23.3	27.1	37.2	11.4	12.6	19.6	23.1	7.0

If we add all the figures for the Liberal and Conservative ministries separately and divide them again by the number of ministries, we get the arithmetic average for the Liberal and Conservative periods. The arithmetic average of Wolf-Wolfer numbers during Liberal periods is 54.7, while it is 21.4 during Conservative periods. This means that solar activity is 155.6 percent more intense during Liberal ministries than Conservative ministries.

Comparing the data on English cabinets with the table of Wolf-Wolfer numbers, we can say the following. The English Conservatives have never once been in power when the relative number of sunspots was higher than 93. Only in 1859, when the Wolf-Wolfer number was 93, were the Conservatives in power for part of the year, after which they were ousted by the Liberals. Only twice have the Conservatives been in power when the Wolf-Wolfer number was between 60 and 70, and only once when it fluctuated between 70 and 80. The relative number of sunspots has fluctuated

Table 2.1

Period of Ministry	Year	Relative Number of Sunspots	Arithmetic Average
1830–1832	1830	71.0	43.9
	1831	47.8	
	1832	27.5 ÷ 2 = 13.7	
		131.9	
1832–1834	1832	27.5 ÷ 2 = 13.7	9.6
	1833	8.5	Σ 53.5
	1834	13.2 ÷ 2 = 6.6	
		28.8	
1834–1835	1834	13.2 ÷ 2 = 6.6	17.5
	1835	56.9 ÷ 2 = 28.4	
		35.0	
1835–1841	1835	56.9 ÷ 2 = 28.4	79.8
	1836	121.5	
	1837	138.3	
	1838	103.2	
	1839	85.8	
	1840	63.2	
	1841	36.8 ÷ 2 = 18.4	
		558.8	
1841–1846	1841	36.8 ÷ 2= 18.4	23.3
	1842	24.2	
	1843	10.7	
	1844	15.0	
	1845	40.1	
	1846	61.5 ÷ 2 = 30.7	
		139.5	
1846–1852	1846	61.5 ÷ 2 = 30.7	72.5
	1847	98.5	
	1848	124.3	
	1849	95.9	
	1850	66.5	
	1851	64.5	
	1852	54.2 ÷ 2 = 27.1	
		507.5	
1852–1858	1852	54.2 ÷ 2= 27.1	27.1
	1853	39.0	20.1
	1854	20.6	
	1855	6.7	
	1856	4.3	
	1857	22.8	
	1858	54.8 ÷ 2 = 27.4	
		120.8	
1858–1859	1858	54.8 ÷ 2 = 27.4	37.2
	1859	93.8 ÷ 2 = 46.9	
		74.3	

Table 2.1 (continued)

Period of Ministry	Year	Relative Number of Sunspots	Arithmetic Average
1859–1866	1859	93.8 ÷ 2 = 46.9	51.9
	1860	95.7	
	1861	77.2	
	1862	59.1	
	1863	44.0	
	1864	47.0	
	1865	30.5	
	1866	16.2 ÷ 2 = 8.1	
		408.5	
1866–1868	1866	16.3 ÷ 2 = 8.1	11.0
	1867	7.3	
	1868	37.3 ÷ 2 = 18.6	
		34.0	
1868–1874	1868	37.3 ÷ 2 = 18.6	76.2
	1869	73.9	
	1870	139.1	
	1871	111.2	
	1872	101.7	
	1873	66.3	
	1874	44.7 ÷ 2 = 22.3	
		533.1	
1874–1880	1874	44.7 ÷ 2 = 22.3	12.6
	1875	17.1	
	1876	11.3	
	1877	12.3	
	1878	3.4	
	1879	6.0	
	1880	32.3 ÷ 2 = 16.1	
		88.5	
1880–1885	1880	32.3 ÷ 2 = 16.1	47.2
	1881	54.3	
	1882	59.7	
	1883	63.7	
	1884	63.5	
	1885	52.2 ÷ 2 = 26.1	
		283.4	
1885–1892	1885	52.2 ÷ 2 = 26.1	19.6
	1886	25.4	
	1887	13.1	
	1888	6.8	
	1889	6.3	
	1890	7.1	
	1891	35.6	
	1892	73.0 ÷ 2 = 36.5	
		156.9	

Table 2.1 (continued)

Period of Ministry	Year	Relative Number of Sunspots	Arithmetic Average
1892–1895	1892	73.0 ÷ 2 = 36.5	57.9
	1893	84.9	
	1894	78.0	
	1895	64.0 ÷ 2 = 32.0	
		231.4	
1895–1905	1895	64.0 ÷ 2 = 32.0	23.1
	1896	41.8	
	1897	26.2	
	1898	26.7	
	1899	12.1	
	1900	9.5	
	1901	2.7	
	1902	5.0	
	1903	24.4	
	1904	42.0	
	1905	63.5 ÷ 2 = 31.7	
		254.1	
1905–1908	1905	63.5 ÷ 2 = 31.7	42.9
	1906	53.8	
	1907	62.0	
	1908	48.5 ÷ 2 = 24.2	
		171.2	
1908–1916	1908	48.5 ÷ 2 = 24.2	20.3
	1909	43.9	
	1910	18.6	
	1911	5.7	
	1912	3.6	
	1913	1.4	
	1914	9.6	
	1915	47.4	
	1916	57.1 ÷ 2 = 28.5	
		182.9	
1916–1922	1916	57.1 ÷ 2 = 28.5	49.6
	1917	103.9	
	1918	80.6	
	1919	63.6	
	1920	37.6	
	1921	26.1	
	1922	14.2 ÷ 2 = 7.1	
		347.4	
1922–1924	1922	14.2 ÷ 2 = 7.1	7.0
	1923	5.8	
	1924	16.7 ÷ 2 = 8.3	
		21.2	
1924	1924	16.7	

Table 2.2

Solar Activity	Period of Ministry	Average Wolf-Wolfer No. for Period	Ministries	Notes
Maximum, 1830	1830–1834	53.5	Liberal: Grey, Russell; from 1832: Grey, Melbourne	
Minimum, 1833	1834–1835	17.5	Conservative: Peel	
Maximum, 1837	1835–1841	79.8	Liberal: Melbourne	
Minimum, 1843	1841–1846	23.3	Conservative: Peel	
Maximum, 1848	1846–1852 1852	72.5 27.1	Liberal: Russell Conservative: Derby	
Minimum, 1856	1852–1858 1858–1859	20.1 37.2	Liberal: Aberdeen, Palmerston Conservative: Derby	1st exception
Maximum, 1860	1859–1860	51.9	Liberal: Palmerston, Russell	
Minimum, 1867	1866–1868	11.4	Conservative: Derby, Disraeli	
Maximum, 1870	1868–1874	76.2	Liberal: Gladstone	
Minimum, 1878	1874–1880	12.6	Conservative: Disraeli	
Maximum, 1883	1880–1885	47.2	Liberal: Gladstone	
Minimum, 1889	1885–1892	19.6	Conservative: Salisbury	
Maximum, 1893	1892–1895	57.9	Liberal: Gladstone, Rosebery	
Minimum, 1901	1895–1905	23.1	Conservative: Salisbury, Balfour	
Maximum, 1905	1905–1908	42.9	Liberal: Campbell-Bannerman	
Minimum, 1913	1908–1916	20.3	Liberal: Asquith	2nd exception
Maximum, 1917	1917–1922	49.6	Liberal: Lloyd George	
Minimum, 1923	1922–1924	7.0	Conservative: Bonar Law, Baldwin	
Maximum, 1927	1924 since 1925	16.7	Labour: MacDonald Conservative: Baldwin	3rd exception

between 1 and 30 to 40 at all other times when the Conservative Party was in power.

The relative numbers of sunspots paint a completely different picture during periods when the Liberal Party has been in power. Here we see the highest increases in solar activity over the entire hundred-year period: 138, 124, 139, 103, and so on.

Comparing our results with the dates of solar maxima and minima, we arrive at the following conclusions.

1. During solar maxima, elections to the English House of Commons return overwhelming majorities for the Liberal Party.
2. During solar minima, the Conservative Party wins the majority of votes.

During the period from 1830 to 1928, there have been three exceptions to the rule out of a total of thirty-three elections, namely, the Liberal ministry of 1852–1858, which ruled during a solar minimum; the Liberal ministry of 1908–1916, which ruled during a solar minimum; and the Conservative ministry elected in 1925 as a solar maximum was brewing. However, it follows from the history of these ministries that the exceptions merely proved the rule. Thus, for example, MacDonald's Labour ministry, elected during the first upsurge in solar activity after a minimum in 1924, had to resign because of the lack of confidence it incited in voters.

If we take these three exceptions into account, the figure we mentioned above, 155.6 percent, drops to 129 percent.

I have tried to present the relationship between the Sun's periodic activity and the vicissitudes of the English Parliament in two tables, which illustrate with complete clarity the dependency I have discovered. The following curious consequences ensue from the first table.

Liberal ministries prevailed during periods when solar activity was in the ascendant (from 1846 to 1874). They were in government twenty-three years of the twenty-eight years in this period. Conservative ministries dominated during periods of relatively low maxima (from 1874 to 1913). They were also in government twenty-three years of the thirty-nine years in this period. We should note, however, that the greater the upsurge in solar activity, the longer the Liberals were at the helm, for example, 1835–1841, 1846–1852, 1859–1866, and 1868–1874. On the contrary, the longer minima lasted, the longer the Conservatives stayed in power: for example, 1874–1880, 1885–1892, and 1895–1905.

[...]

If we take the dynamics of any physical phenomenon on Earth that depends on the Sun's periodic activity, for example, some aspect of the weather, we would not obtain a better coincidence of patterns than in this case. Consequently, we can say that the English Parliament in its alternations is subject to the Sun just as nicely as many physical phenomena that are directly dependent on the influence of sunspot formation.

From this fact, however, it does not follow that parliamentarianism in other countries should reveal such an exact correspondence on the dynamics of solar activity. It may very well be that, in other countries, parliament is not such a subtle sounding board of the neuropsychic vibrations emitted by the masses, vibrations that arise under the combined energetic influence of the social and physicochemical environments in which human organisms dwell.

But nor should we think the parliaments of other countries do not reveal the same conformities to the dynamics of the solar process as the English Parliament has revealed. This conclusion would be erroneous. Since mankind's popular behavior generally depends on the Sun's radiation, in other countries where popular political life takes the shape of parliamentarianism it must follow the Sun's directives to some extent, in accordance with local social factors. I have not investigated the issue more closely, but I have found in the history of other countries complete confirmation of this logical conclusion, which follows from the theory's fundamental tenets.

Translated by Thomas Campbell

3 Astronomy and Architecture

Nikolai Fedorov

Having unified all sciences within astronomy, and all the arts within architecture—for, indeed, such a union is of the simplest, most accessible order, requiring no scholarly expertise—we cannot but puzzle over, or, better still, intone the very question of why, if the former (i.e., astronomy) is a world knowledge, the latter (i.e., architecture) should not be called a world order, or world governance: why architecture cannot be called the application of a knowledge that is produced by astronomy. However, this should be the connection, the quite natural connection, between knowledge, that is, science, and action, that is, art.

Remember, if you will, the Riddle of the Sphinx. But replace one of its legs with a lightning rod lifted upward into the sky on an aerostat, and then this creature, for which three cubits of earth would have sufficed, will touch its newly created paw to the clouds and, drawing furious strength from the atmosphere, will subdue tempests, silence hurricanes, turn winds to the course of its will, scatter rains across fields as it deems fit. It was in the person of Benjamin Franklin that America bore witness to the launch of Europe's first aerostat, but it does not seem to have occurred to the lightning rod's inventor how his instrument might be employed in the extraction of rain—though he was known to answer those who questioned to what use a new invention might be put by asking in turn, "Of what use is a newborn baby?" Yet a century has passed, and the toy remains but a toy; the child has not yet escaped his bedsheets, though at his very birth the opportunity presented itself to make of this toy a great implement. But the urban citizenry has not understood famine, and the aerostat has remained until the present a mere toy. The idea has now occurred to one of our staunchest Slavophiles of equipping this craft with a lightning rod that will make it an instrument of salvation from hunger, but Germany, in the person of Professor Fuss, has declared the Slavic invention useless.

Imagine now that the energy sent to the Earth by the Sun, which presently scatters off into space, could instead be conducted onto the Earth, thanks to a massive configuration of lightning rod–aerostats, implements that will drive solar light to our planet. Imagine that this solar energy, once directed earthward, might alter the density of its new home, weaken the bonds of its gravity, giving rise in turn to the possibility of manipulating its celestial course through the heavens, rendering the planet Earth, in effect, a great electric boat. No sooner will this creation have gazed up to the heavens than it will begin sailing the celestial seas, with the sum total of the human race rendered as captain, crew, and maintenance staff of this Earth Ship. This will surely leave no doubt that it is not the Sun that moves through space but the Earth, just as one riding in a skiff feels no doubt it is the skiff that moves and not the shore. Military duty will no longer amount to a summons to war, to the dutiful defense of the fatherland by its sons, because all fatherlands will be joined as one; rather, military service will become a call for sons to join in the shared paternal business that can be attended to solely by directing the course of the Earth and all the matters taking place upon it. Science will come to be defined as knowledge of the Earth as a heavenly body, coupled with the knowledge of other planets that resemble it, if the Copernican hypothesis describing the substance of other planets as resembling Earth's is to be trusted; and if so, then it is by that other discipline, the application of science, that the course not only of the Earth, but of whatever planets may prove moveable by the same methods, is to be directed. The building up of Earth, too, will be accomplished by that same application: its transformation into a temple, and the other planets into new dwellings.

The transition to these dwellings depends not upon a single World Order, but rather upon the ordering of organic life itself, that is, upon Body Order, knowledge of the configuration and production of our bodies, as well as the art of managing them. This same question, the question of the relationship between World Order and World Governance (architecture) and World Knowledge (astronomy), can be addressed to the structure of living bodies in their relationship to the science of life—that is, biology. Why then, we may well ask, does biology, which seeks knowledge of the structure of bodies subject to destruction and of the life of living beings doomed to death, not find its own application in the recreation of bodies destroyed? For the arts (sculpture, painting) offer but to replace those bodies destroyed, with stone, with metal, with figurations not easily effaced (or, indeed, sometimes made in clay and so quite easily effaced). Why do these images occur—by no means images of all men, but rather only a select few—and why are arts like sculpture and painting but the weak applications of anatomy, manifestations of the complete purposelessness of physiology, the merely illusionary applications of biology—mere phantoms, that is to say, of life? And thus biology, discovering no serviceable application, turns from the science of life to the science of how a living being dies bit by bit, approaching its death by gradations. Death, if it is to be properly defined, must be understood as the transference of one being, or of two beings merged into one, into a third, via the medium of birth—that is, the emergence of any new life is always associated with a destruction of previous life. Herein we find manifested the law of that blind force that can create only while it destroys. Art, if it is the work of a rational being, must consist precisely in the resurrection of everything destroyed by blind force, in redressing the work blind force has wrought through the inaction of the intelligent force.

Only once we adopt the view that biology is a part of astronomy, that we act properly in uniting all sciences—biology accordingly among them—within astronomy, only then should we expect to understand why biology is the science of life as much as of death, for, viewing life solely in terms of its connection with the World Order, we will be able to reveal why life, as it seems, began as merely one-day life, then became one-year life, then became many-year life, and under which conditions, accordingly, it can be infinitely prolonged—the essential question for any rational being. At the same time, it will be clear to us that at the present moment, when the Earth is isolated from other worlds by vast spaces, life, eternal in its foundations, may be manifest only in the changing of generations.

But can biology be called an astronomical, a heavenly, a universal science, if life is known and probably exists solely on the Earth, this one heavenly body? If, however, biology—being a form of knowledge—is negligible in volume, in the space occupied by its object, then biology—as an art of resurrection—knows bounds of neither time nor space. Being a cemetery, the Earth holds within it as many generations as there are worlds in the universe not ruled by reason (in point of fact, we know of no other worlds ruled by reason), and a great many of these worlds are utterly ill-suited to support life; so that through the resurrection of the deceased generations biology may have some hope of settling—that is, of bringing under enlightened governance—all worlds. In this way, by ensuring that life is installed on all worlds, this universe will be made a biological one.

Those men, animated and transformed, cease to be born and to become workers—that is, they learn to re-create themselves out of elementary material components (which celestial chemistry, the chemistry of spectral analysis, finds across the universe); those sons of humanity learn to travel to other planets, and now on each they will duplicate exactly what has been done on Earth—that is, by the instrument of the lightning rod–aerostat, all of the energy of the Sun will be directed onto each planet, thereby freed of gravity's bonds and turned into a great, electric boat.

Translated by Ian Dreiblatt

4 Our Affirmations

Alexander Svyatogor

Even when I was publishing articles and lecturing on the radical ideas of *immortalism* and space travel during the early days of the Revolution, I was distilling them to a few affirmations that, although far from complete, constituted a fairly satisfactory definition of our credo. It seemed particularly important to create an awareness of our ideas in their most basic form, as close as possible in format to slogans, to express our scientific or philosophical ideas in a nutshell, because there was a real necessity to do so.

The most important thing for us is the immortality of the individual and its life in the cosmos. We made this value our goal, thus formulating our teleological point of view. Our philosophy is first and foremost a great teleology, and all philosophical problems are shaped by our great objectives.

We looked to our undying instinct for immortality and our unquenchable thirst for great creativity, trusting in our Biocosmic consciousness of the objective world's reality. Objective reality is an infinite arena for the great struggle in which everything that possesses individuality and integrity asserts its supreme existence.

Our ethical stance is an ethics of action understood in terms of the realization of the great objectives of Biocosmism. Our ethical norms are defined by our ultimate goal (in this respect, we take an opposite view to Kant's, for whom values and objectives stem from ethical norms). Our ethics are supported by our cosmology—and, indeed, were our world to be harmoniously complete and finished, there would be no room for our individual actions or those of others.

I have based the most important statements of our ideas concerning Biocosmism on the philosophical premises presented here as concisely and clearly as possible, condensing them into the following clauses:

1. Death diminishes man and debases the human character: fear for one's life gives rise to cowardice, baseness, falsity, and ugliness. Death is also responsible for the deepening root of social injustice, monstrous private ownership, and the antagonism between individuals, nationalities, and classes. This restriction in time—that is, death—represents the age-old foundation for the spiritual and material decomposition of both the individual and society.

2. But, man has within him an instinct for immortality, at once powerful and unquenchable, and can never, therefore, be reconciled with the order of death. Death is so logically senseless, ethically inadmissible, and aesthetically ugly that the question of immortality inevitably emerges in a person's consciousness. In his inability to face death, man has looked for salvation in religion and mysticism in the hope of immortality, if only for the soul.

3. At a time when religion has finally become obsolete, when a religious and mystical solution to the question of immortality can no longer be offered as real bread, and death's stronghold has been shaken biologically, mankind has, at last, come close to solving the realization of individual immortality as the immortality of the individual in the fullness of its physical and spiritual powers.

4. In Biocosmism, every individual—and indeed mankind as a whole—will find complete freedom only in the struggle for individual immortality. Biocosmism maintains that this struggle represents the true basis for the spiritual and material union of the people, that the individual and society will grow to unprecedented heights in terms of strength and creativity, and that, through its involvement in this struggle, human character will enjoy unparalleled advances.

5. Note that Biocosmism also regards the question of personal immortality, or *immortalism,* as a question of resurrection. Resurrection is, above all, a logical conclusion to personal immortality and a guarantee against the chance death—avoidable in principle—of a person already assured of personal immortality. The question of resurrection is also a question of renewal of life of those who have lived before.

6. Biocosmism raises the question of *interplanetarianism* at the same time as immortalism. If death (a restriction in time) is the primary root of evil in the life of the individual and society, then its secondary root is caused by a restriction in space, which is to say, the primary position accorded by

one's home, hometown, native land or state, and race. At the end of the day, even internationalism relates merely to a certain locality within the universe.

7. Mankind has already approached the question of interplanetarianism, since an era of space travel will immediately follow an era of air travel. Interplanetarianism involves the problem of how to master cosmic space, how to become a citizen of the cosmos and an active participant in life in space, regulating and transforming the cosmic bodies at will through our wisdom, and reshaping the old and creating new worlds.

8. The questions of immortalism and interplanetarianism must not be viewed independently or linked mechanically. They are both intimately interconnected, constituting a single organic whole united under a single term: Biocosmism.

9. Even if there is an element of fantasy to Biocosmism, this fantasy of ours should not be relegated entirely to the realms of utopia. Since it depends on the latest advances in science and technology, the fantasy of Biocosmism has matured sufficiently for the questions of immortalism and interplanetarianism to become the "order of the day." We contend that Biocosmism is the new supreme life-plan for the single individual as well as humankind as a whole, and that it is now time to set about realizing this plan.

10. We believe that the time has now come for us to present the questions associated with Biocosmism as life's urgent objectives. Our belief is based on our opinion that a worldwide struggle between the oppressed and their oppressors and between labor and capital is now unfolding before us. This struggle seeks to destroy class divisions; in our view, this is a prerequisite to the organizing of universal questions associated with Biocosmism. The Revolution will undoubtedly embrace Biocosmism, so that defining, collecting, and organizing the tendencies embodied within it will become the most important task of the revolutionaries. With the Revolution under way, an outline of the questions pertinent to Biocosmism, the highest possible plan, is essential in order to bring victory to those in revolt. This understanding of Revolution allows us not to postpone the realization of the ideas of Biocosmism to the postrevolutionary future, but rather to begin with the implementation of the ideas of Biocosmism right now.

11. In the struggle for Biocosmism, it would be unthinkable either to imitate or concur with religious or mystical tendencies. Instead of immortality

beyond the grave and immortality in spirit, our goal is to promote here on Earth, in the real cosmos, the immortality of the individual—with all its spiritual and physical powers. Our relationship with religion and mysticism is, therefore, irredeemably negative. In the same way, instead of a dreamy, poetic, imaginative penetration of the universe, we favor a realistic interpretation of space travel as the immediate task of technology.

12. In the struggle for Biocosmism, we are reliant on the latest scientific and technological achievements, striving to transform them at the same time as philosophy, sociology, economics, art, and so on, in keeping with our teleology; that is to say, their form and content must be developed to accord with the great objectives of Biocosmism. This is why Biocosmism represents the beginning of a completely new culture, a new order of things, and a new objective reality.

These twelve clauses make up the "First Commandments of Biocosmism." They comprise the ideological core from which our burgeoning creativity, propaganda, and struggle spring and continue to spread. We bring to the world the greatest gospel of them all; until now, it was difficult to comprehend the unprecedented immensity of a movement that we, the Biocosmists, are initiating in Russia, at the center of the Great Revolution.

Up until this point, mankind has resembled the people described by one of the philosophers of antiquity, who lived in a cave where they saw only the shadows of things. But today, thanks to the Biocosmic avant-garde, mankind more strongly resembles those people at the moment when they emerged from the cave, looking at real things lit up by the light of the Sun, even choosing to look at the Sun itself. We are sure that, in the very near future, if not immediately, men will perceive themselves and the world through our lens and happily walk beneath our Biocosmic banner.

Of course, in our movement, mistakes are possible, and death probably awaits us as its first messengers and warriors. But even the prospect of serious mistakes and failures does not trouble us, in the same way that the danger of protracted defeat does not trouble the determined conqueror. He who has great goals before him, who is completely sure of himself, strong and absolutely firm in his resolve, ultimately emerges victorious.

Translated by Caroline Rees

5 The Doctrine of the Fathers and Anarchism-Biocosmism

Alexander Svyatogor

1

We, who have raised the flag of a new ideology, are interested in the role of anarchism in the Revolution—primarily in the aspects concerning its thought. We will examine the main direction taken by this thought, which is divided into two chronological periods.

During its first period, this thought remains 100 percent faithful to the "doctrine of the fathers." It is, in fact, unequivocally and slavishly subordinate to it. Bound by tradition and uncritical, it stands united. "Unified anarchism" is therefore the right term for this first, uncritical period.

The second, critical period begins as a consequence of the unsuccessful leap into anarchy. Severe revolutionary reality (it could not be otherwise) has led to a revision of the principles of its founding fathers.

Both periods have revealed the inadequacy of the doctrine of the fathers, calling into question the validity of anarchist thought per se and consequently driving it into a state of impasse. We believe that deliverance is possible only through Biocosmism.

2

We will deal with anarchist thought as follows. We are not concerned here with the chiefly national and historical reasons for its main characteristics. Neither will we attempt a causal explanation of its character, or try to justify it from an impartial, historical point of view. It is clear that it proved unworkable during the Revolution and is, therefore, indefensible.

We believe that weakness and immaturity are its main characteristics. It has all the signs of immaturity and its critical side is too weak and underdeveloped. It is absolutely unable to make any independent judgment as to reality and its content. It is unable to analyze the succession of experiences and events that have occurred, and has no idea of the workings of a whole complex of reasons and great ideas behind them. Its powers of analysis are purely formalistic, as well as superficial and unrealistic. The same is true of its capacity for synthesis.

Immature and weak thinking easily becomes subordinate to authority. The weaker it is, the more subordinate it becomes, with a correspondingly diminished field of vision and sense of independence. Anarchist thought is too dependent on authority. It has raised the fathers' doctrine to the status of *vox Dei* and become a slave to tradition. It is true that it is outwardly active, but its energy is one in which individuality is subservient to doctrine and blindly follows authority to the letter.

It is naturally subordinate, unoriginal, and one-sided because it is weak and repressed, and this has had a drastic effect on its outward form. It wears an eloquent mantle of rhetorical utterances and expressions, but how monotone, hackneyed, stereotypical, and deadpan all these are! Not one word is truly alive, authoritative, and original, able to provoke serious attention or, at the very least, attest to a sense of independent inquiry.

These are the principal characteristics of anarchist thought in the first period. Then, because of the pressure of disappointments, a critical element begins to be voiced, but still cannot free itself from its chief flaw: a belief in the infallibility of its past commandments. Laboring under tradition, it grows weak, its "doctrine" sucking it dry and depriving it of the lifeblood that would enable it to open out independently onto a new path with a wide-open vista before it.

3

We must differentiate between two cycles of "unified anarchism": the Moscow cycle and the Ukrainian cycle. Superficially, they seem to represent different types of anarchism, but essentially, and especially from the point of view of thought, they are intrinsically connected enough for each one to seem merely one part of a single, organic whole.

The Moscow cycle covers a period of agitation and propaganda. This was the period of anarchist rhetoric, which, owing to the Revolution, received wide publicity through public speeches and newspaper columns. This was also a period when the Soviet regime was verbally criticized. It is true that, at that time, verbal criticism and propaganda went hand in hand with corresponding action. Although action was not of central importance, it was an integral part of rhetoric.

The liquidation of the Moscow unified anarchist organizations certainly did not mean the liquidation of the ideas and actions of united anarchism per se. Although it proved unsuccessful in Moscow, unified anarchism spread to Ukraine, where it became part of the petty bourgeois movement, which was particularly receptive to the anarchist experiment. Whereas in Russia its character was primarily rhetorical, in Ukraine it became active. The idea behind it remained the same, however. It is a utopian project to immediately establish the "kingdom of freedom."

4

Moscow's "unified anarchism" immediately revealed all the characteristics of anarchist thought, including its internal weaknesses and a slavish subordination to doctrine. In October it emerged from a period of silence and proceeded down the path prescribed by the doctrine of the founding fathers. It did not stop to investigate the reality in which it had to act. It was not that there was no time to think, but rather that there was no need. In fact, thinking betrayed an inadmissible lack of trust in the doctrine. It did not come to independently and intelligently analyze and build—taking time and place into consideration. Instead, it came with a ready-made set of principles and anachronistic measures as well as the determination to act according to its dictates. This is why there was no room for independent criticism. It was, in fact, the doctrinaires themselves who criticized the Soviet authorities by rehashing appropriate passages from Bakunin and Kropotkin, rather than exercising any form of independent judgment.[1]

The fathers maintained that, when revolution came, everything would fall neatly into place due to man's natural sense of solidarity (Kropotkin), or justice (Proudhon), or because he had clarified the meaning of universal gain (Fourier). Everything should be left to its own devices and anarchy would automatically emerge triumphant from the maelstrom of revolution, like a powerful and merciful queen, ultimately gaining a foothold on Earth. The fathers remained true to Manilov's way of thinking, and it was the same for their obedient servant.[2] She did not realize that the situation demanded different ways of thinking and acting and failed to grasp the obvious truth that any attempt to change the existing order would cause those who were committed to its preservation to react and that, therefore, any rhetoric concerning humanity's natural solidarity and universal love—and this at a time of a decisive struggle between two worlds—was tantamount to the most harmful illusion. Weak and subservient to tradition, she was incapable of independently assessing reality and questioning the relevance of past teachings.

The fact that the founding fathers were opposed to dictatorship meant that dictatorship was both unnecessary and harmful. The fact that they rejected any form of authority also meant that revolutionary power was automatically put on par with any other power. The anarchists, who adhered to their principles to the letter, rejected any measures taken by the Soviet regime. They opposed the revolutionary discipline of work, the organization of the village poor and the army, showing a complete lack of understanding of the aims of the Revolution.

And so the anarchists remained true to form. At that time, there was not a single person capable either of reflecting independently on the new reality, or able to assess whether the old doctrines suited it. The doctrinal pressure was such that it squashed individuality, so that nothing remained except a tongue singing to the general tune. This is why we never encounter original, independently minded people among the unified anarchists. They are like a flock driven along before us, containing at best only shallow individuals who are almost indistinguishable from the general human masses.

5

It was impossible to reconcile oneself with unified anarchism and to tolerate it patiently in a revolutionary situation, especially when it behaved—intentionally or unintentionally—as a cover for thugs or white guard elements. But, after it had failed in Russia, it spread to Ukraine, where it was taken to absurd lengths, finally exhausting itself both as an idea and as a course of action.

Unified anarchism in Ukraine was a decisive attempt to put the fathers' doctrine into practice and create an anarchist order. Undoubtedly, it was the bourgeois nature of the social class (the wealthy peasantry) that forced it to cultivate anarchy. The anarchists followed their theoreticians in this respect. Not only did Bakunin show a particular affection for obsolescent forms of Russian communal economy, but so did Proudhon and Reclus. This affection was undoubtedly reactionary.

It is of note here that the experience of anarchy led to its being construed, aptly, and not without a hint of sarcasm, as "powerless power." The experience of anarchism led to a regime of power that contradicted its doctrine's very prophecies and was very decisively at variance with that doctrine. This indicated that that doctrine was null and void because it was unsatisfactory in practice, finally exposing its utopianism. The ship that had been built by Bakunin, Kropotkin, and others, and steered by the anarchist church, was smashed to smithereens on the rocks of anarchism under Nestor Makhno.[3] It was destroyed not by external obstacles, but by its very nature.

The ship was wrecked and the bell of old anarchism sank to the bottom. And so it was that a lone anarchist (neo-nihilist) voice rang out like a dirge in the pages of the anarchist press: "I am deeply convinced that anarchist ideology is splitting at the seams, that there is no one to patch or darn its tattered remains and that it would be pointless anyway."

6

That this critical period was necessary is all too obvious. The failures were too serious, even for thinking that was subordinate to authority. The failure of unified anarchism in Moscow was already cause for this period of critique. When it had begun to unfold in Ukraine, it was already being criticized in Moscow, and the fact that these things occurred simultaneously had a negative impact on this criticism. Thinking that was tottering shakily down a revisionist path could not avoid following what was happening in Ukraine. This was why, when the death knell to Makhnovism had been sounded, more resolute voices began to be heard among its critics.

In the first period, anarchist thought is characterized principally by its stubborn adherence to doctrine, subordination to authority, and inert fanaticism, and, in the second period, by the manifestation of its internal weakness and impotence. In the first period, it is resolute in its actions, and, in the second, paralyzed by criticism—becoming diffident, cowardly, and devoid of creative impetus.

Anarchist thought took the path of criticism not because of a deep-seated disillusionment concerning the rightness of its ideology, but because of pressure from external circumstances. The ideological cracks in unified anarchism caused by its failure in Moscow did not form without a hope for their repair. Further setbacks were necessary before a few individuals finally concluded that "anarchist ideology was splitting at the seams." However, when the final setbacks had occurred, anarchist thought still did not manage to summon the strength it needed. Realizing that the old ideology had collapsed—at least as far as a few individuals were concerned—anarchist thought remains in a state of impasse to this day.

7

Attempts at criticism can be divided into two groups according to their starting points. The first is in favor of retaining the old ideology, with any criticism focusing on tactical revision. The second covers a number of opinions based on the need not only for substantial tactical revision, but also calling for a complete overhaul of the old ideology. The ideas of both groups proved unworkable. The first demonstrated that its critical assumptions were ineffectual, and the second pointed out the worthlessness of its conclusions.

8

The syndicalists were the first to abandon the empty rhetoric of unified anarchism. They decided to embark on a positive course of action to build a new society and initiate a mass workers' movement. But in order to do this, they believed that they should remain faithful "to the precepts of their mentors, Mikhail Bakunin and Pyotr Kropotkin."

This led to contradiction. The positive building of a new society required an important premise: the acceptance of a dictatorship that could secure this building process. But the founding fathers believed that dictatorship was totally unacceptable.

This contradiction could have been resolved by acknowledging that their mentors belonged to an era when they could scarcely have had any objective knowledge of how a new society should be built. Instead, the syndicalists resolved the opposition by agreeing to adhere to their mentors' precepts, which the events in Ukraine merely served to reinforce.

Their fathers' word reigned supreme both in theory and in practice, and their good intentions came to nothing. The enterprise was doomed since, in its attempt at criticism, anarchist thought chose to ignore the very question that it had raised.

9

The universalists went a little further. They understood that there should be "a different approach to the Soviet state," and, because of this, they asked the question: "What is the purpose of anarchism in a socialist state, and what should its methods be?" They acknowledged that the old form of anarchism had neither tried to find, nor clarified, "a course of anarchist action and anarchist practice within a socialist society," and that this was why anarchism, with its empty universal slogans, seemed defenseless in the current revolution. The question was, then, how to find a new "method" that "would not duplicate the old method, because there was a different environment, different circumstances, and a different power structure." Rather than "pinning its hopes on foreign comrades" or seeking a solution to the problem in "former literature," it had to decide on an independent course of action.[4]

These questions were formulated fairly clearly, but their terms were insufficiently defined for any satisfactory answers to emerge. For example, a bare statement such as "the method must be synthetic" or "its concomitant elements potentially consisting of syndicalism, cooperativism, class struggle, and communism" did not constitute a positive answer. How and on what basis can the elements of such a "hodgepodge" be reconciled, and do they not smack of "unified anarchism"? It was the same with "the approach to the Soviet state." A necessary approach was not formulated ideologically.

Universalist thought revealed itself as weak because its essential point of departure was the same as the syndicalists': the doctrine of the fathers first and foremost. The universalists answered the question as to why the anarchists were weak and getting nowhere by stating: "At any rate, it is not because anarchist ideology has reached the crisis point." Terrified of introducing anything new, the universalists declared that universalism was definitely not a new doctrine and that the old ideology would remain.

The doctrine of the fathers prevailed, and any attempts to remedy the situation proved fruitless. The universalists could not find a new "method," nor were they able to negotiate a satisfactory relationship with the Soviet authorities or, indeed, play a valid part in the creation of a new life. Their method seemed naive and their relationship with the government indecisive. As a minority in the universalist organization, we—the Biocosmists—have been at pains to point out that only a new ideology can provide precise answers to the questions raised by experience. The old way of thinking remained, however, essentially redundant and mesmerized by tradition, and its response to our affirmations was purely hostile.

10

The first of the critical attempts of the second type belongs to the aforementioned neo-nihilist, and the second to the anarchist Darani.

The neo-nihilist thought long and hard about the theory and practice of anarchism, eventually coming to the conclusion that anarchism-communism "is closing its eyes to practical existence and its approach to it is irrational," that syndicalism "is on a downward spiral ... is squandering anarchism's last resources," and that individualism is utopian. Under Makhno's leadership and "powerless power," anarchism was united "as a synthesis of these different strands left anarchism in a vacuum." As a result, the neo-nihilist "was deeply convinced" that "anarchist ideology was splitting at the seams." The old anarchist's confessions are of the utmost significance.

This is a reasonable basis for rejecting the fathers and building a new ideology on the original foundation of anarchist thought—namely, individuality. But, even then, anarchist thought remained true to itself. Having ascertained that "there was no one to patch or darn its tattered remains and that it would be pointless anyway," the neo-nihilist immediately slid into a vulgar form of Stirner's ideas, rekindling interest in them by employing the prefix "neo." The lack of creative potential in this type of thought is already apparent in its prefix; its qualities exist only in its grandiloquent title.

11

Darani's attempt to resolve the situation was more serious. Clearly, in his view, "the present moment had completely uncovered all the flaws in the old form of anarchism" so that "every area of anarchism needs to be revisited, including its theory, practice, and organizational matters." Theoretically speaking, there is, to this day, no "balanced, unified anarchist worldview." "The most recent facts from the sociological and economic sciences, and social psychology," "are apparently completely useless to us." "The scientific and philosophical foundations of political anarchism are therefore particularly shaky. Theories concerning the class nature of anarchism are undeveloped, leading to a complete lack of clarity concerning the position of anarchism among the other sociological sciences." "The criticism of contemporary reality alone, without any clear idea of the work involved, is therefore inadequate." "The lack of agreement concerning the position of an anarchist society within the historical development of human society and the objective conditions of its implementation mean that a clear formulation of particular and urgent problems, and questions of social and economic order, is impossible." Matters were every bit as bad from the point of view of anarchist attitudes toward organization. Such were "the universal flaws in the old form of anarchism." These had to be clearly emphasized so that they could be overcome, said Darani, otherwise "we will have a poor, pathetic substitute for anarchism."[5]

Darani did not just emphasize anarchism's flaws. He believed that, since they were predominantly theoretical, he had to plan a suitable exit strategy. The most important thing was to underpin anarchism with proper philosophical foundations. In fact, the old form of anarchism is no stranger to philosophy, but it still adheres to the legacy of eighteenth-century rationalism. Darani believed that this legacy should be discarded and replaced by contemporary intuitive philosophy.

Of course, he was right: it *was* absurd to still be living according to eighteenth-century philosophy. But isn't an escape into intuitivism the same as entering the sphere that is presently occupied by the modern Western spiritual quest—a sign of the destruction of the foundations of an old order shaken by the spirit of revolution? The old ideals are disintegrating and the minds that professed them are unable to accept anything new and robust, striving for spiritual deliverance and a fusion with the absolute.

This modern spiritual quest fits nicely with philosophical intuitivism, and is supported by it. Seeing intuitivism as anarchism's way of getting out of its impasse definitely means coming down on the side that is oppositional to the revolutionary class with its shrewd, vigorous, realistic, and positive type of consciousness.

The impotence of anarchist thought surfaces once again in Darani's quest, which, contaminated by a blend of intuitive mysticism, bears all the hallmarks of the moribund generation of intelligentsia.

12

The quarrel between anarchist thought and the Revolution was essentially one between utopianism and realism. That utopianism lost is only natural. The Revolution dealt a blow to those who supported the doctrine of the fathers, primarily from a tactical point of view. But as they had their doubts about tactics, it was only natural that they should also have their doubts about theory. Anarchist thought went one step further by embarking on an ideological revision, and was ultimately forced to admit that its doctrine was "splitting at the seams." Restoration and reform would, therefore, be useless. However, anarchist thought was too dependent on authority to allow for any independent creativity. It found a lifeline in its doctrine, which saved it from its inherent weaknesses. Because it was weak and subordinate to authority, it was unable to escape from its state of impasse.

The Revolution meant the collapse of modern anarchist thought and the end of historic anarchism; the new spirit was disillusioned with old concepts that were narrow and backward. The Revolution also meant the need for a new form of anarchism (both in theory and in practice). But only someone who is independent, free from tradition and authority, who is able to bring revolutionary courage to creativity and offer a correct appraisal of the situation, can resolve the crisis, create a new concept, and, thus, resolve the current impasse.

We believe that Biocosmism is a decisive, courageous, and sound way of thinking. It is an antidote to cowardly and weak-willed contemporary anarchist thought, and represents a new concept to replace the doctrine of the past. Of course, we dare not hope that weak anarchist thought, despite the fact that it questions the founding fathers, will actually turn to us—to

Biocosmism. It is too cowardly and pathetically self-involved for that! But we have grounds to hope that fresh, strong, optimistic anarchist forces that have experienced the Revolution will turn to Biocosmism and are, in fact, already doing so.

13

In the heat of the Revolution, the old anarchist structure did not withstand scrutiny. But its essential core—the living human individual—was not reduced to ashes, and never will be. Even if the ideological structures built on this foundation crumbled when exposed to fire, the foundation itself will always remain in place for new structures. More spacious and impressive buildings replace the old, demolished buildings to suit the times and, more importantly, the individual (and society).

14

New structures require the expansion of existing foundations. All the abstract concepts in the old form of anarchism define the individual too narrowly. This restricted notion is a fundamental flaw in the anarchist doctrines, rendering them intrinsically unsound from their inception. It has taken time to prove that they are, in fact, essentially illusory.

The old form of anarchism never properly resolved the problem of the individual. Its concepts were based on an idea of the individual that was too one-sided and superficial. A sociopolitical figure, an egoist (Stirner), and an altruist (Godwin) were substitutes for the living individual. Kropotkin reduced the individual, as though scientifically, to an "insignificant man," or he was construed as a rebel, a destroyer, and his positive side—his creative potential—downplayed. In short, anarchism did not take the full individual into account, but rather produced its one-sided abstraction.

The individual was understood in his static form within a narrowly defined cycle from birth to death, and not in his dynamic sense or in terms of his creative forces. Death became firmly established in all the anarchist doctrines (it is odd that anarchist thought, which protested against all authorities, did not take up arms against the authority of "natural death"). The individual was considered outside his unquenchable thirst for immortality and, thus, outside of genuine creativity.

The old form of anarchism took an essentially negative view of the individual. It appeared to affirm individuality but, in reality, denied it, suggested a bad opinion of it, left it in the shadows, and replaced it with an abstraction. Anarchism belittled man and, at the same time, left him too much to his own destiny, ultimately bringing him to individual and social catastrophe.

This is a fundamental flaw in all anarchist ideas. Its core was too weak and its ideas correspondingly weak, one-sided, abstract, lifeless, and utopian.

15

We do not believe in the naked individual consciousness, the sociopolitical figure, the egoist or the altruist, the mask or the abstraction, but in the living human individual. We cannot settle the matter entirely by resorting to egoism or altruism, or by placing the individual within any abstract framework. The instinct for immortality and the thirst for eternal life and creativity are the individual's basic characteristics. The individual will develop his creative forces until he establishes himself in immortality and in the cosmos. This new concept must equate to the discovery and affirmation not of an abstraction, but of a real living human being.

Man is not an insignificant being with amusing pretensions to all-embracing endlessness, which was what Kropotkin believed in his time, proving it quasi-scientifically with ideas based on the Copernican revolution in astronomy (the Slavophile Nikolai Danilevsky[6] believed the same thing, as does, nowadays, the much-talked-of Oswald Spengler). New horizons are opening out in front of humanity; they are vast and unprecedented. The struggle with death is, in principle, no longer impossible (as confirmed by Steinach, Andreev, Kravkov, et al.).[7] We can already prove the possibility of individual immortality (*immortalism*) scientifically, and achievements in physics and technology give scientific credence to the problem of cosmic space (*interplanetarism*).

16

The supreme good is immortal life in the cosmos. The supreme evil is death. We mean real life and real death here. All other goods belong to life, and every evil is rooted in death. Biocosmism, which proclaims freedom from "natural necessity" and humanity's right to eternal existence in the cosmos, manifests the supreme freedom and supreme right of the individual.

The supreme good should be realized by the maximum in creativity. We place particular emphasis on the creative moment in Biocosmism. Personal immortality is not a given, but must be won, realized, created. It is not the restoration of what is lost, as in the Bible, but the creation of what is yet to be. It is not a matter of renewal, but of creativity. The same is true for conquering the cosmos. *Immortalism* and *interplanetarism* are the maximal—but not the ultimate—aim. They represent stages and means to an immeasurably great creativity. But this goal lies before us and is, for this reason, the greatest of all.

Our goal (the realization of personal immortality, life in the cosmos, resurrection) precludes mysticism, which throws everything into chaos, into a void. It involves the realization of rational consciousness. But we do not identify our goals with reality, nor do we base our ideas entirely on what is given; otherwise we would be forced to abandon freedom, creativity, and individuality.

Biocosmism also precludes skepticism and unleashes human creativity, giving it incredible power and a mighty scope. This beacon toward which humanity is moving is the foundation and guiding thread for both individual and social activity. It covers the whole breadth of human action. It is Biocosmism, and only Biocosmism, that is capable of defining and regulating a perfect society.

17

The old society is disintegrating. It is experiencing an "Indian summer" and retreating into the shadows, with the horror of night awaiting it. Our task is to build a new life, a new existence, and a new culture founded on the great goals of Biocosmism.

Modern (bourgeois) society leads to death and is based on it. Because the individual is essentially mortal, it proclaims death as the individual's ultimate fate. Bourgeois society is deeply corrupted by the conviction that "death is inevitable." Religion and old scientific consciousness sanction this conviction, stifling man's spirit of revolt against death. Modern society sanctions all the evils by affirming death and localizing space. If this continues, a complete moral and physical degeneration threatens mankind. Such a society must be destroyed right down to its very foundations.

Society must be built on Biocosmist foundations. By supporting the basic right of every one of us to eternal life, Biocosmist society rules out any division into exploiters and exploited, into slaves and masters. It will guarantee supreme individual development and self-fulfillment. It will become supremely harmonious through the unified ideal of its members. When Biocosmist ideas become the conviction of each one of us (another option is impossible), there will be no need for force, and everyone will willingly carry out the ideas that govern society.

We affirm the unity of all in respect to our great aim. The struggle for individual immortality—for life in the cosmos—manifests the universal will. Restriction in time (death) and space cannot be overcome through individual effort; therefore, collective effort is required. Only solidarity for the sake of our great aim will guarantee victory over death and cosmic space. The struggle for immortality and life in the cosmos is the true basis of the new social order.

18

In the new society, people will unite not because of coercion, but rather because achieving society's great aims gives them a sense of community. A society that tries to achieve *interplanetarism*, individual immortality, and the resurrection of the dead is universally accepted because it works toward the greatest common good. This shared, supreme goal precludes any individual betrayal on behalf of another goal, since it is bound to be a lesser one. There is therefore no need to negotiate loyalty to this society contractually (Proudhon et al.), since individual will and action are infinitely repeated in comradeship and, at the same time, individual strength is enhanced by every step taken toward achieving Biocosmism. This society is "the tool and sword with which you hone your natural strength." We support the individual and the sense of community more than anyone else. A pendulum's swing on one side is as great as the corresponding pendulum swing on the other, so that the more resolutely individualist we are, the more socially active we become.

19

The new society is not made up of small communities or groups, which "do not feel the need to expand their boundaries" (Godwin et al.). The old, erroneous bias toward small units must be rejected in order to overcome atavism and the legacy of the Dark Ages. Maximal space comes first and foremost (or else it's the petty bourgeoisie). The union of all people can only carry out its tasks in large units. Biocosmist society encompasses the whole world and is interplanetary.

20

Biocosmist society is supremely free. Our task requires terrifying freedom for man. Man (humanity) is never left to his own devices as he is in Biocosmism. He does not pin his hopes on God or on life after death. He faces death as a commonplace reality and must conquer this evil alone without external help (from above), by taking his own completely authentic path.

21

In Biocosmism, people unite as coworkers, and the work collective is the most creative form of relationship. The work collective is the opposite of brotherhood since the latter is an uncreative relationship. In brotherhood, relationships are arranged in advance and are naturally predetermined, so there is no creativity involved. In the work collective nothing is arranged, but everything is achieved and created. Brotherhood is conservative, uncreative, and historically obsolete. In our energetic thrust forward into immortality and space, we support not brotherhood but the work collective.*

* Ignorant people, who have secondhand knowledge of Nikolai Fedorov's "philosophy," and our enemies, criticize us for our proximity to Fedorov. Leaving Fedorov's "philosophy" aside for a special analysis, suffice it to say here that Biocosmism came into being entirely independently without any knowledge of this "philosophy" and that, later on, when we did become acquainted with it, we saw that it was totally different.

Fedorov, who adheres to a religious and platonic dualism that is alien to us, affirms the existence of two worlds: a perfect, divine world, and a human world, into which—according to the Bible—death entered, with man's task involving a struggle with evil and death, which takes the form of resurrecting the dust of our

22

Our journey toward Biocosmism is dependent on the Revolution itself, and the courage shown by the revolutionary class. Biocosmism was spawned in

---

forefathers. But recognizing one, real, infinite world, we start by realizing the personal immortality of the living and *interplanetarism,* on which our "common task" is based, with resurrection being relegated to third place. *As far as Fedorov is concerned, the problems of realizing personal immortality (central to Biocosmism) do not exist*—everything is centered around resurrection, and is reduced to and governed by it.

Resurrection is the only area where we overlap, but it is really only a matter of *superficial terminology,* and essentially we have about as much in common with Fedorov as with any priest talking *in his own way* about immortality, which is to say, absolutely nothing. His understanding of resurrection is very naive and takes on a very crude form of materialism—atomism—an arch-utopian collection of scattered atoms "in the bodies of our forefathers, which they possessed at the time of death" (an idea that does not essentially rule out the death of the resurrected bodies, the reconstruction of which is his Sisyphean task). It involves a mechanical, rather than a creative, reconstruction. Our ideas of creativity are entirely different from Fedorov's. Biocosmism, which is not restricted to working within the confines of existing laws and material properties, aims at a change to the very laws of existence and material through man's creative powers (without Solovyov's, Trubetskoy's, and Bely's grace from above).[9] Because it is devoid of any ideas concerning creativity, Fedorov's utopia is organically alien to us. This difference is also reflected in our rejection of the "brotherhood" so dear to Fedorov, essentially an uncreative relationship between people, and in our espousal of *the work collective.*

His vision of two worlds—divine and human—led Fedorov to a complete justification of tsarism. His "philosophy" is the last (fairly archaic) attempt to save tsarism and the Orthodox Church. Fedorov's ideas, which are derived from the Orthodox Church and tsarism, took the form of a simple and muddled local teacher's program. He based his entire "philosophy" on this program, which included provincial school theology and a slim acquaintance with the natural sciences. The divine and the human were blended into an insoluble contradiction and anomaly, of which he remained unaware.

The Revolution has revealed all the absurdity of Fedorov's attempt to rescue tsarism and the Orthodox Church. Nothing would have remained of his "philosophy" if it had not included among its followers living corpses from the intelligentsia dismally playing on the pipe of national-cadet "philosophy" and a few "Fedorovites." Whereas, for the former, Fedorov's ideas were used as only one of the arguments to support their "program," for others, as his imitators, he represented a shaky bible condemning them to a hopeless balancing act between the Orthodox Church and atomism.

the storm of revolution; the Revolution is integral to our beliefs and we rely on its support. The Biocosmist order will emerge from the victory of the Revolution. The aim of the Revolution is the destruction of class inequality, which is a necessary prerequisite to the formulation of questions related to Biocosmism in their totality. But Biocosmism, as the maximum program, can already now promote the unity, fervor, and victory of the revolutionary class.[8]

23

While we believe that the state will be eliminated on the way to Biocosmism, we would also emphasize the current need for a positive relationship with the Soviet system. The Soviet state should not be confused with the bourgeois state. The Soviets are a necessary organization within the revolutionary struggle against the old world. They are also instruments in the struggle with nature; that is to say, they have a natural tendency toward Biocosmism.

Of course, in a period of transition, the Soviets cannot act purely as organs of struggle against oppression by nature; they must fulfill their function within the struggle with the old world by assuming the form of a dictatorship (in a transitional phase, dictatorship is both necessary and expedient). Some form of coercion is therefore inevitable, but is completely different from the coercion practiced by a bourgeois state. Any objections to the Soviet state as an oppressive system acting to suppress individual freedoms and the like are therefore nonsensical.

The old form of the state is a thing of the past. The new Soviet state has different aims and methods. The Soviet system, which in principle guarantees man's freedom from the yoke of external nature, is even now encouraging the growth of individual awareness by freeing the individual from the yoke of tradition. There is growing awareness of personal freedom and responsibility and, as a result of Sovietization, of new ties between people. The people taking part in the Soviet system are closely linked through their awareness of the importance of the struggle that is taking place—a struggle that requires self-possession and discipline. Men are learning to respect each other and themselves by taking part in the Soviet system whereas bourgeois society—a society of masters and slaves—precludes the need for mutual respect.

We believe that, as the struggle with the old world recedes owing to the victory of the Revolution, the Soviet state will increase its struggle against the natural yoke. Both these forms of struggle opening the path to Biocosmism suggest that the questions of *immortalism* and space travel should already be on the current agenda.

Translated by Caroline Rees

Notes

1. Pyotr Alexeyevich Kropotkin (1842–1921) was a revolutionary anarchist, scientist, and philosopher. Born into a family of high Russian nobility, Kropotkin gave up his princely title early on to endorse republican ideas and advocate for the emancipation of serfs. An important member of European anarchist circles, he lived in exile for a considerable part of his life, his activism often leading to his arrest and imprisonment. Upon his return to Russia after the 1917 Revolution, Kropotkin remained critical of the authoritarian socialism he attributed to the Bolsheviks, all the while promoting his notion of an ethically oriented anarchist philosophy.—Ed.

2. Manilov, a character from Gogol's *Dead Souls* (1842), is portrayed as a sentimental serf owner whose self-esteemed, noble, and well-educated nature disguises a profound lack of personality and willfulness. Manilov stands as a caricature of a European-influenced Russian nobility lost to superficial philosophizing and mere obliviousness.—Ed.

3. Nestor Ivanovych Makhno (1888–1934) was a Ukrainian anarcho-communist who commanded the independent Revolutionary Insurrectionary Army of Ukraine (also known as the Black Army) during the Russian Civil War of 1917–1922. Maintaining a stateless anarchist society organized around libertarian communes of workers and peasants, the Makhnovists defended the Free Territory of southern Ukraine against Imperial German and Austro-German occupants and Ukrainian nationalists. In opposing the Bolshevik regime, which he deemed dictatorial, Makhno was forced into exile soon after siding with the Red Army in 1920 to defeat the White Army. He joined a group of Russian anarchists in Paris, contributing to the journal *Delo Truda* (Workers' cause) and copublishing the pamphlet "The Organizational Platform of the Libertarian Communists" in 1926.—Ed.

4. The anarchists-universalists (also known as inter-individualists) organization evolved out of the Moscow Federation of Anarchists in 1920, under the leadership of theorist Abba Gordin. Espousing a pan-anarchist view, the universalists aimed at the establishment of a worldwide and transnational anarchist society united under the banner of an international communist revolution. Gordin and his followers stood against all national-level parliamentary and democratic systems of government, promoting cosmo-politism and cosmo-economism.—Ed.

5. Svyatogor's citations come from an article by an anarchist-universalist named Darani, published in 1921 in *Универсал* [Universal], the journal of the anarchists-universalists, under the title "V chem krizis anarkhizma?" ["Why is anarchism in crisis?"].—Ed.

6. Nikola Jakovlevic Danilevsky (1822–1885) was a naturalist and cultural philosopher. A representative of Pan-Slavism, he designed a biology-oriented cultural theory in his work *Rossija i Evropa* (In Russia and in Europe, 1869), which anticipated the ideas of Oswald Spengler.—Ed.

7. Eugen Steinach (1861–1944), an Austrian physiologist, was on the board of the physiological department of the Biological Experimental Institute of the Academy of Sciences in Vienna. Steinach attracted worldwide attention for his attempts to "artificially rejuvenate" testes and ovaries, and for his use of x-rays and vasoligature, which he carried out on animals and humans. In addition to Tsiolkovsky, Steinach was the most important hope-bearer for the Biocosmists.

Nikola Pavlovic Kravkov (1865–1924), a pharmacologist, and a professor at the Military Medical Academy in Petrograd, operated experiments to revive dead tissue.—Ed.

8. Svyatogor is recasting the "maximum program" previously raised by the anarchists-maximalists, active under the Union of Socialists-Revolutionaries Maximalists until its expulsion from the SR Party after the first Revolution of 1905. The anarchists-maximalists formed an independent political party up until the Revolution of 1917, notoriously resorting to terror and expropriation in the interest of the "maximum" or full socialization of all lands, factories, and means of production.—Ed.

9. Vladimir Sergeyevic Solovyov (1853–1900), Russian religious philosopher and publicist; Prince Sergej Nikolaevic Trubeckoj (1862–1905), Russian philosopher, representative of "concrete idealism," pupil and friend of V. Solovyov; Andrey Bely (actually Boris Nikolaevic Bugaev, 1880–1934), Russian symbolist poet and writer.—Ed.

6 Biocosmist Poetics

Alexander Svyatogor

Prologue, or The First Step

We have important tasks ahead of us, and this is why we are overturning current beliefs and ideas. The future is already indebted to us in our struggle to overcome prejudices. For us, deference simply doesn't exist and the majesty of natural necessity doesn't impress us one jot. The current balance within the natural order is, in fact, our first and last enemy. Should we, like Judas, betray our existence to the power of necessity for the sake of a few silver coins, and the world, too—a bunch of flowers, whose scent we inhale?

Now let's get down to the question of how to realize personal immortality!

It is time for us to dispense with the necessity of death and the balance that includes natural death. Every law is indeed only an expression of the temporary balance of particular powers. You have only to introduce new forces or remove some of the existing forces to destroy a given balance (harmony). If we set the forces of immortality in motion, then, even in the face of opposition, these forces will be able to destroy the balance that includes death, replacing it with immortality. Indeed, every life strives for immortality above all else.

Our agenda also includes "victory over space." Let's not refer to it as aeronautics—it is not enough—but rather space travel. Our Earth must become a spaceship steered by the wise will of the Biocosmist. It is a horrifying fact that from time immemorial the Earth has orbited the Sun, like a goat tethered to its shepherd. It's time for us to instruct the Earth to take another course. In fact, it is also time to intervene in the course taken by other planets too. We should not remain mere spectators, but must play an active role in the life of the cosmos!

Our third task is the resurrection of the dead. What concerns us here is the immortality of the individual in the fullness of his spiritual and physical powers. The resurrection of the dead involves the full reconstruction of those who are already dead and buried. That said, the quagmire of religion or mysticism is not for us. We are too grounded for that and are in fact in the process of waging war on religion and mysticism.

These are, then, our Biocosmist ideas. Biocosmism is, undoubtedly, extremely daring. But everything great or audacious is offensive to others and we can already detect a vague but obvious aversion to it, since Biocosmism denigrates every idea and every ideology. But we are optimists, not madmen. Madmen are those who want to make men free and excellent without recourse to Biocosmism. They resemble Robespierre, who wanted to make mankind happy but ended with the idea to destroy it. Every idyll that promises "happiness on Earth" without Biocosmism is the most harmful of illusions and is at the root of the most monstrous tyranny.

Supremely important tasks lie before us. But do we really look as sanctimonious and dour as monks or dictators? No, we have an altogether different psyche. We feel extremely unpretentious and happy as we travel along the path of Biocosmism, in this respect surpassing even Aristippus of Cyrene, the happiest of men. We are creating Biocosmism like a little boy who merrily rolls his hoop along, singing. We are realizing immortality joyfully, happily, smilingly, beckoned by the cemeteries and ready to go to the docks where the Biocosmist ships are waiting for us.

We are creators. We have already founded a "Creatorium of Biocosmists." Ignoramuses think that "creatorium" sounds like "crematorium," and they are probably right. Indeed, we need to incinerate an awful lot—if not everything. Biocosmism is the start of a totally new era. All previous history, from the emergence of organic life on Earth to the massive upheavals of the past few years, constitutes one age: the age of death and petty deeds. We are in the process of embarking on a new age—the age of immortality and infinity.

And what about our aesthetics?

Our aesthetics does not stem from observation and the registering and analysis of already-existing forms. In spite of its importance, descriptive aesthetics cannot also be prescriptive. All its attempts in this direction constitute an ill-founded departure from its essential domain and a usurpation of rights that do not belong to it. Indeed, it is impossible to define what is desired or might be by establishing what actually is.

Our essential ideas concerning style derive from the Biocosmist ideal. It is our method and the criterion of our analysis. We cannot accept the aesthetics of the symbolists or futurists, not only because they are obsolete and out of date but because we have our own criteria. We don't want to fall into any philological or stylistic mousetrap: Potebnya, Veselovsky, Pogodin, or others like them do not interest us. Rather than historical or psychological aesthetics, teleological aesthetics is of central importance to us. We care even less about today's semiliterate compositions than we care about the old prejudices.

There is also the question of form and content. What should come first and which is more important? We cannot say that content means everything and form nothing. Attaching meaning to form alone betrays a lack of elementary scientific and philosophical education. Idea is immanent to form, but form is not always equivalent to it. Form often contradicts the idea, and the idea may have more than one form. But this isn't the point. We aren't really interested in the age-old debate (about form and content) from the era of German idealism, which is trotted out all too readily nowadays. We have an entirely new axiom.

It's not a question of the primacy of form or content, but of my attitude to ward them. What we are concerned with here is the proud independence of creativity.

And what about our style?

Our style does not start from an isolated word, even if it is artistically defined, but from series of words.[1] Instead of individual words, series of words are of central importance to us—not so much etymologically as syntactically. And, for this reason, creating these word series involves various combinations of their constituent elements.

We do not create images, but organisms. The image of a word is based on external visual perception, on surface. An image is only an impression, only a description, and is therefore inadequate. Images that do not occur in combination only equal chaos. A sound creative path passes from image to series. For the poet, making the image of paramount importance is tantamount to taking a step backward rather than forward. The series is the beginning of the cosmos. We are not bearers of images, but creators of series.

Do we really scorn words or are they all the same to us? Some words are dead, there is a glimmer of life in others; but only rarely do we find words that are really rosy-cheeked. We love words with a degree of punch and breathe life into dead ones. But the resurrection of words is not a matter of revealing the original image; rather, it lies in the skillful choice of prefixes and suffixes. We are also interested in the various guises words can assume; we are attracted to words with the ability to transform themselves, like werewolves or people at a masked ball.

The word escapes its original meaning, breaks away and puts on a mask. In fact, the word is like a mask: it comes to life in a series of words, and the more ingenious the series, the more expressive the words. A series makes words more colorful, emphatic, elastic, and varied. The creator's artistic will forces words in a series to take on a different role. Words in a series are form that changes its scope and content, with the very same word ending up in different layers. In a series, words play, as though with balls, with what is concrete. The creation of series of words represents the transformation and resurrection of words.

We are, in fact, pregnant with new words. Thus, we are able to intuit the exclamation uttered by a man as he rises from his tomb. A million exclamations are waiting for us on Mars, as well as on other planets. We believe that these Biocosmist exclamations (in the broad sense of the word) will give rise to a Biocosmist language, shared by the whole world and the entire cosmos. (It goes without saying that this isn't Esperanto, which is nothing but a pointless joke. The language of barbarians is of an immeasurably higher order, since it is organic). We believe that the expressive quality of verbs is the most important thing. Should we really limit ourselves to the indefinite mood, like the futurists? We are too concrete, too contemporary for that, and with four moods, even we have too few. Tens and hundreds of moods are still too few! We need a mood for the cosmos and a mood for immortality!

Our style begins with the series. The series is either straight or curved, and is traced by the movement of the creative spirit. But it does not really equate to meter. Meter is an external scheme, and the Biocosmist spirit is by no means restricted by it. The Biocosmist spirit traces another sort of scheme altogether. As poets, we have in mind series composed to accord with the rhythm of Biocosmism, which is teleological, to be in tune with its movement, intonation, expression, weight, tempo, and temperature. We are hostile to any given linguistic stabilization in language. We need a new syntax built around the parallelism, intersections, and parabolism of Biocosmist series. We need sentences created to accord with geometric principles. Grammar is, after all, only failed mathematics. We are determined to become the Lobachevskies of grammar!

We are series creators, but as far as we are concerned, series are only living cells for organisms to create. The artistic organism is our ultimate goal. It is not only an aggregate of series, but also a living whole in which particular parts cooperate with others. Apart from its content and the content it acquires according to its position within the series, a word in a series is fertilized and blossoms forth as a more complex organism—through the weight of the whole artistic organism. All the characteristic attributes of a series can be completely understood and interpreted only within this context, within the artistic organism. The latter pulsates and breathes, smiles and laughs like the most perfect creation. It represents our supreme goal and deepest meaning.

Death is tireless. It devotes every second to its vile task: the execution of living creatures. A poet—a Biocosmist poet, that is—is both an activist and a singer in a band in revolt against death and the dictatorship of space. A Biocosmist poet creates his living organisms on the subjects of immortality, space travel, and the resurrection of the dead. How can he become an idolater when he destroys every temple and altar? Should he wade through a mire of petty deeds, sit out office hours, or trade in trinkets when he should be tearing half-witted brains apart in order to sow the seeds of Biocosmism within them? How can he saunter peaceably along with his eyes shut when he should, in fact, be armed to the teeth with telescopes? Should he nod off whimpering miserably when he is being summoned by the supreme creation of which no creator, no enthusiastic brain, has as yet even dreamed?

As Biocosmists, we are united in our movement. But as comrades, we agree chiefly on what constitutes our great aim. Each one of us has his own individual path. In Biocosmism alone is the creator able to reveal his own personal depth. For me, this involves the restructuring of types that have come down to us over millennia (through adaptation), namely, types of animal. Types of animal are superior to types of man. Thus, it was more appropriate for a deity to be portrayed as an animal, rather than as a man. A god personified as an animal is superior to a god with a human form, with Apis being superior to Jesus. Central among beasts, the Rooster represents Sabaoth, the Lord of Hosts.[2] It comes as no surprise, then, that Socrates's last words contained a reference to a Rooster. The Horse is also great as is shown in my poem "Gospel According to the Mare," which is superior to the Gospel according to John. For man there is no greater praise than being likened to a horse. So, in "Yeruslan Lazarevich," we find "Ivashko, the gray horse." I introduce my collection of poems *Stallion* (1919) as follows:

Zikeev,[3] my friend and chestnut horse,
Into your manger I pour these little rhymes
In token of the times
We spent whinnying together
Accompanied by the snickers
Of coarse pygmy ninnies.
No less great is the intuitive sage, the Dog:
... And what of Bergson? As blind as a bat,
His philosophy's nothing but rot.
My advice, then, is "learn from the Dog."
Indeed he is known to be wise.
For him is the bag of secrets untied,
Mysterious and undefined.
Turn to the dog for a lesson,
Free, gratis, and for nothing.
Down on all fours then,
And let out a bark.
Or, the image of the Pig, spat on and despised:
Is not the pregnant Pig
A marvelous phenomenon?
Her udder's as tender and pink
As the vessel of dawn ...
...
... And is not her udder a cup,
Bright like the stars and celestial?
Whether down or up
Her udder's pink and perpetual.

Note that the duplication device characteristic of Biocosmist organisms is being used here. This is an example from the poem "Moon":

... And only now,
With a different yeast
In a different dough
Did he see
The ball of the Earth as small and much too narrow,
That the spirit on the Biocosmist path ...

Suffice it to say that the series of words offered here reflect eternity (lines 1 and 4). They can be limited to a single sound and multiplied infinitely.

The richness of series of words depends primarily on the individual talent of the creator, in whom sprachgefühl is highly developed. Our goal is beyond the confines of language, but for the time being we are allowing Biocosmist language to remain within current linguistic boundaries. We are, however, already in the process of creating series of words as a cosmic leap—a leap into immortality, with series of words, as linguistic leaps, constituting a departure from language as we know it.

In conclusion to this prologue, I think that, unfortunately, vulgarization is unavoidable in Biocosmism. Corrupted by theoreticians of "proletarian art," inferior poets with no dignity or integrity are appropriating our great ideas and distorting them. It is true that, for the purposes of Biocosmist propaganda, such rhymesters are not entirely useless, treating "syllables as soldiers—fit for muster."[4] But ... in a word, the gates of "Biocosmist Creatoria" are open to all, and to become a Biocosmist poet, one needs an honest, original, and exceptional talent.

Translated by Caroline Rees

Notes

1. The isolated word or "The Word as Such" (samovitoe slovo/"slovo kak takovoe") is Velimir Khlebnikov's conceptualization of poetic language, as expressed in the eponymous publication from 1913, coauthored with Kruchenykh and illustrated by Kasimir Malevich and Olga Rozanova. Khlebnikov conceived of "the word" as necessarily unconstrained and opposed to its ordinary, purposeful, and universal usage. He did this by experimenting with Russian as well as other Slavic languages whose roots it shares, through sound symbolism arising from the Cyrillic alphabet and its letters, as well as a profuse invention of neologisms.—Ed.

2. It is worth noting here that Svyatogor referred to himself as "the Rooster of Revolution." See George M. Young, *The Russian Cosmists* (New York: Oxford University Press, 2012), 197.—Trans.

3. Zikeev was also a Biocosmist. He is mentioned by George M. Young as being a "now forgotten figure." Young, *The Russian Cosmists*, 198–199.—Trans.

4. The quote used by Svyatogor here is from Pushkin's poem "Domik v Kolomne." The translation is by Antony Wood, from a collection of translations of Pushkin's verse forthcoming from Penguin.—Trans.

7 A Universal Productive Mathematics

Valerian Muravyev

The desire to create and build is typical of modern life. Questions of labor and production confront us forcefully in all fields, and as we tackle them, we seek ever more real ways of creating. We demand ever more positive outcomes from human endeavors, outcomes that would actually change the world.

The more we throw ourselves into these tasks, however, and the more flexibly we try to conceive them, the more clearly we see our endeavors as not only work but also as struggle. We have been rebelling against nature's inert, blind forces, attempting to replace them with the action of our will, which implements the goals of our intelligence instead of their senseless dictates. Armed with science and technology, humanity has long been waging this worldwide war against the destructive power of the natural elements, which devastate not only man's endeavors but also man himself. It is clear this struggle, whose aim is mastering and managing nature, is the real objective of all economic management, whether it is a matter of managing natural forces, manufacturing, or transforming the material world. Man's final liberation from the slavery binding him to nature and the establishment of his creative power over the latter emerges in connection with this slogan of modern productive activity, as the latter is a synthesis of human creative processes. When we speak of the new culture's coming age, we can outline its main features: the movement of different kinds of human endeavor in this direction. Alongside first nature, which was bestowed upon us, the outcome of blind, senseless spontaneity, we must labor to create a second nature, built in keeping with the projects of our intelligence. It is telling, by the way, that our language has seemingly anticipated the need for a complete identification of natural causality's dictates with the rules laid down by man: in our language, both are called laws. The transformation of nature's laws into laws prescribed to her by intelligence is the goal of culture's productive endeavors. As Herzen taught us, nature must become history.[1]

2

This definition of the basic task of all human productive endeavor implies the special significance of consciousness as a force that transforms primitive elements into culture. First nature is nature bereft of human intelligence; second nature is nature conditioned by intelligence. We are thus faced with the question of the role played by conscious human effort, as expressed in mental labor, and of the methods it uses in the creative process.

However, these methods are quite different, just as the viewpoints that emerge when consciousness is applied are very diverse. There is no doubt, though, that in all instances the mind operates in a similar way when it is applied to practical problems. First, thought draws an image, symbol, or sign corresponding to the perceived impression. Then the mind independently analyzes and critiques these symbols, and by combining them generates a project of reality as altered by the intelligence. This project is applied to the matter at hand, which is correspondingly processed and transformed into a new, improved reality.

All these phases of mental labor produce more or less certain or accurate results, thus establishing degrees of comprehending reality and dominating it. Yet the history of culture has shown that the ultimate degree of such comprehension and the greatest power has had to do with the mind's capacity to formulate its projects and findings in the most precise form, in the guise of numbers or mathematically.

As the individual sciences have improved, this has stemmed from the predominant application of quantitative values and methods of measurement. Currently, all the sciences are increasingly concerned with studying sets of different elements. This research is always affected by the method of calculation, that is, by finding the numbers that characterize the combinations of these elements. Such, for example, are the tasks and techniques of the so-called exact sciences. Mechanics, astronomy, physics, and electrodynamics decompose the world into different elements and look for the laws of their combination in the shape of mathematical formulas. Modern chemistry has been evolving in this same direction, increasingly becoming physical chemistry. Modern quantum theory most clearly emphasizes the numerical basis of chemical laws. There is also no doubt that the so-called natural sciences—biology, physiology, zoology, botany, and mineralogy—are closely bound up with physics and chemistry, and will also have to opt for the application of mathematical techniques. Thus, we see that crystallography has become an entirely mathematical science. On the other hand, the science dealing with living organisms has increasingly been dominated by a belief in the cell's structural complexity. Presumably, the cell consists of numerous primary elements, which will eventually be reduced to chemical elements. On the other hand, statistical methods, likewise based on the properties of numerical combinations, have become increasingly important in these sciences. We can go further and predict, in view of the new biophysical theories—the theory of ion excitation, for example—that mathematical findings will gradually spread to the entire realm of physiology, biology, and even psychology. This will lay a solid foundation for the transfer of quantitative methods to the anthropological sciences. Experimental psychology, sociology, and economics already use statistical methods. But we can hope that eventually we will discover the transitional stage between statistics, or the science describing the set of visible objects in numbers, and the calculation of the invisible sets constituting the nature of things. Then, perhaps, we will succeed in constructing a hierarchy of all the known sets that make up the world, and we will be capable of applying the same laws to phenomena occurring in various areas of life. The laws of sets will become, generally, the laws of nature, and people will draw on this set theory whether they are acting to alter matter, transform man, or constitute new social relations.

In any case, the secret of expanding our power over nature obviously lies in extending this method to the entire environment. The idea of a universal mathematics was prefigured in many ancient theories that shaped the science of numbers. Since the most ancient times, we find traces of this science among the Chaldeans and Babylonians, the Egyptians and Pythagoreans. Via the Neoplatonists, the Neo-Pythagoreans and, partly, the Gnostics, this research in numerical symbolism was transmitted to medieval philosophy and elaborated in the Jewish Kabbalah, the teachings of the Arabs, and the works of Agrippa, Lully, Pico della Mirandola, and so on. Finally, in modern times, the theory of numbers was resurrected as the new mathematics, whose foundations were laid down by Descartes, Leibniz, Newton, Kepler,

Lagrange, and Laplace. In the nineteenth century, mathematics enjoyed an unprecedented heyday: in its countless applications, it became the basis of all modern technology and man's real power over nature. Its meaning was the same as in the ancient teachings about numbers: the desire to express all things by means of numbers and the conviction that knowing the formula of a process or thing gave us the power to change and guide the process and thus create the thing.

This viewpoint found its expression in later attempts at generalizations, namely, in Leibniz's work in mathematics and philosophy and later, in the nineteenth century, in Auguste Comte's efforts to derive the model for all the sciences from mathematics.

Modern mathematics has also taken this path, taking into account the aspiration of the sciences. Accordingly, it has evolved into a theoretical discipline engaged in elaborating a universal set theory. So far much has been done in this direction in terms of developing a special theory, which cannot yet lay claim to universal significance, but which, theoretically speaking, is undoubtedly the basis of a future mathematics. This is set theory, first posited by Georg Cantor, which has now gradually become the basis of all higher mathematics. Set theory, however, has met with a series of paradoxes whose solution by means of the usual logical and mathematical methods is, apparently, impossible. Nevertheless, set theory has continued to progress, influencing not only all of mathematics but also the neighboring fields of logic and philosophy. The latter has been increasingly compelled to employ mathematical methods, thus generating the grounds for attempts to generate a new *mathesis universalis* as a general philosophical algebra. It is the focus of the so-called logical analysts, who have attempted to restructure logic on this basis.

Advances in theory have been followed by similar advances in applied mathematics. Mathematical theory reveals numbers in their essential nature and relationships, while applied mathematics finds the numbers of existing things in the shape of real-world relationships. Technology applies this knowledge to material conditions and makes it possible for man to actually transfigure reality. Yet we should note that this way of influencing things through mathematics is not an exclusive form of action, typical of instances in which mathematics has obviously been applied. The very same techniques are generally used in every conscious action, for the role of the mind in action has always been the role of a calculating or computing organ, that is, seeking the laws that govern how things are combined and how their combinations can be altered. Where there are no clear numbers and explicit mathematics, there are concepts and names and operations produced by logical thought over the latter. We can thus acknowledge that the mind always functions mathematically, and that rather than being a deficiency in our thinking, consequently incapable of grasping life's fluidity as it were, as the irrationalist Bergson has argued, on the contrary, it points to the precise correspondence of consciousness and reality, and to the significance in them of multiplicity rather than fluidity.

To this we may add that the mind's effect on the real, material world can be likened to certain processes known to us from chemistry, namely, the catalytic processes. The power of an intelligent being is always manifested not as physical force, commensurate with the clearly expended energy of the latter, nor as a chemical reaction, commensurate with the atomic weight of the elements involved, but as the action of an enzyme that produces colossal transformations through insignificant movements and, sometimes, simply by its presence. This does not mean, of course, that no energy is expended in these cases, but, apparently, this energy is of a different order than the external changes it produces. It has now been proven that biochemical processes are produced by enzymes without the involvement of the cells, which considerably enlarges the realm of catalysis, extending it to the whole of nature, both organic and inorganic. At the same time, the catalyst has come to be seen as an energy transformer, turning one form of energy into another and thus contributing to changing the system. If we assume a conscious being acts like a catalyst, it is thus as it were an energy transformer. In this case, nervous energy is nothing but a special state of cosmic energy, operating in instances in which consciousness manifests itself in the environment through symbols and words, numerals and names.

3

Such are the general conditions of the work of human consciousness and the human mind's projective role in the business of mastering nature. It is obvious that productive endeavors and all manner of creation must reckon with the work of consciousness to a supreme degree, and that the organization of collective cultural efforts should likewise encourage the creation of projects and symbols, and their application to material processes.

Historical practice, however, has shown us that these two forms of cultural work have not always progressed uniformly and harmoniously with each other. On the one hand, since people have devoted themselves to material creation in the guise of economic construction and production, they have often tended to underestimate the role in these processes of mental labor and the symbolism it employs. On the other hand, ancient tradition has long taken human culture to be overly theoretical and symbolic, neglecting the actual transformation of the world by altering the physical world and creating material objects. In the first case, we have attended exclusively to organizing technology and the material conditions of production. In the second case, transformative work has involved only developing ideas and elaborating artistic images at the expense of a real impact on all of nature.

It is not hard to prove the first viewpoint's one-sidedness.

If we pose the question of productivity in its full breadth—something that both human thought and productive practice have been seeking to do nowadays in most countries—it becomes clear that organizing the work in this manner requires organizing mental labor as well as physical labor.

The value of intellectual work must be taken into account the more so because science has now uncovered the intimate connections between mental and physical events, and therefore the division of labor into physical and mental can no longer be effected with full precision and rigor. All mental labor is simultaneously a particular alteration of physiological states, and all movement is ineluctably accompanied by the relevant operations of the brain. This is strikingly displayed, for example, in the recently discovered close link between hand movements and the work of the brain's speech center. Thanks to the labors of eminent physiologists and experimental psychologists, it has been revealed that the predominant development of one side of the human body is due solely to a normally functioning speech center. But by means of certain exercises, namely, motion exercises, the atrophied center in the brain's other hemisphere can be spurred into action. The complete correspondence between speech and external movement has thus been established. There is no motion without meaning, and no words or names without motion. Pronouncing a word means performing an action. It follows that, in terms of their physiological bases, the organization of movement and the organization of thought and its expression in speech are inextricably linked.

But the need to organize mental labor stems from another source, not individual physiology but the collective and sociological nature of all work. Since the individual can never for an instant be separated from the historical social whole he inhabits, all individual work must also be the common cause of a human group and, ultimately, of all people to be meaningful. This common action can arise when people have been brought together by irrational motives acting blindly upon them, which has often occurred in history under mass movements. But since we seek to rationalize and organize human endeavor, we cannot, of course, be satisfied with this natural means of streamlining it. In fact, more often it is not unity that has been generated in this way, as a consequence of subordination to blind instinct, but, on the contrary, discord. What is revealed is not the primordial relationship among people, but their selfish unrelatedness. Under this regime, the social links among people mostly abide in a state of pernicious dispersion. It is clear that if this state is maintained, however well these people's physical labor is organized, the edifice built in this manner will be left without a roof, because the different forms of labor have not been bound by a rational common goal and meaning. This meaning can emerge only when all individual efforts are carrying out a single common project related to the universal cause. Establishing such a project is tantamount to organizing mental labor.

The project is communicated to other people by the language of symbols and names, which are like the crystallized reserves of human culture's past collective products. The collectivization of this stock—its use by all people—encourages the coordination of their thoughts and efforts, and fashions them into an organic whole, a social body, the *egregore* mentioned by ancient writers.

As we have seen, however, there is the danger of getting carried away with the creation of signs and symbols, and neglecting, for the sake of generating them, the struggle against material nature. This bias has been inherited from the outgoing historical age's incorrect notion of culture's essence.

Until now, during all known periods of human history, a thousandth part of culture was created by man's conscious will, according to the projects of his intelligence, but for the most part it grew as a natural process, beyond the supervision of rational consciousness. Culture's spontaneous emergence and growth sometimes led to its stunted development, sometimes, on the contrary, to its riotous flourishing. But it was always dominated by irrational elements, and humanity moved on without knowing where it was going, yielding to passive faith, fatalism, and indolent contemplation, states complemented by the crystallization of a stagnant, immobile everyday life.

This narrowing of the human mind's role has distorted notions of culture's essence. According to this incorrect view, culture is the totality of the branches of human endeavor, which are situated as it were just outside life and represent a kind of luxury for it. In this view, culture is limited to theoretical knowledge and artistic creativity. It generates not reality but only formulas, signs, images, and likenesses. It is seen, therefore, as complicating life and decorating it in a way that imparts fullness to it, but as something we could do without in a pinch. "First we'll put our lives together," we hear people saying, "and then we'll worry about culture."

Constructing life, however, is undoubtedly tantamount to producing culture. The life that man constructs consciously is, in fact, culture. Culture is the totality of man's advances in transfiguring the world. Culture is the world, altered by man according to his mind's ideals.

But culture, in this case, includes not only theoretical and symbolic endeavors, as encapsulated in science and art. A significant and essential part of culture are those modes of work that actually change the world around us, not merely in thought and imagination. They include economics, manufacturing, agriculture, engineering, medicine, eugenics, applied biology, education, and so on. Indeed, an overview of all the current research and trends makes plain that culture is revealed as the things people actually do to change reality using these means. Culture is not only pure science and pure art, but certainly consists in applying them to production, the mining and processing industry, labor, and technology. Hence, we can say that the ultimate meaning and goal of culture is actually to improve and transform the world through the rational management of nature.

The new culture of the future involves nothing other than identifying this universal culture, revealing it as the work of transforming the world.

It follows that the first task, which precedes all construction and organization, is expanding the common notion of culture to include the modes of human endeavor that have previously been regarded as outside its scope. In other words, what must vanish is the current disjunction between culture and life, and the consequent separation of theoretical and symbolic work—which generates expressions of knowledge and ideal patterns—from work that, by means of action, really changes our environment.

To this end, we must first clearly understand the source of this pernicious disjunction. Its roots undoubtedly lie in the ancient division of the world into the supernatural world, accessible only to the mind and imagination, and the earthly, material world, where human action takes place.

Owing to the limitations of his outlook and the feebleness of his power over nature, man was unable to effect a real, comprehensive transformation of the environment, and so he marked off a special field of endeavor where he found it relatively easier to enact the kingdom of his reason and his moral and aesthetic ideals. This was the realm of pure knowledge and the similar realm of pure art. Here, in a special world generated by the mind and imagination, man produced the ideas and images he wanted while passively contemplating external reality and acting on it only within his own inner world by enriching his intellect and furthering his aesthetic powers. In this segregated realm, he scored victories over unreasonable, vicious nature, but what these successes lacked was the fact that they led to no changes in real life except for producing generations of especially sophisticated, accomplished people quite remote from the mass of humanity, who continued to languish in the grip of a life that was impoverished, meaningless, and misshapen. Thus did passive contemplation and abstract philosophizing evolve. They were joined by pure science and pure art. Scientists have engaged in pure theory, forgetting that their work makes sense only insofar as it truly transfigures the world, and that they, accordingly, are not a self-sufficient corporation, but merely a committee of sorts, appointed by humanity to accomplish a particular goal: drafting a project for the world's transformation. For their part, artists have yielded to the symbolism of images and forgotten that they make sense only insofar as they are linked to reality, and that art's purpose is to provide people with an ideal of a better world and assist in actually converting the present into this future. Consequently, culture has become detached from life and enclosed in the narrow confines of pure creativity, remote from reality.

The outcome of the disjunction between symbolic and theoretical endeavors and real cultural work has been equally detrimental to both. Without thought, action is meaningless; thought without movement is ineffective, while knowledge, since it is applied to nothing, degenerates into abstract intellectualizing; science that has no practical end ultimately turns into an exposition of methods that have no purpose; and art that produces only dead likenesses becomes a harmful amusement. On the other hand, lawmaking and economics, as endeavors that change the material world; medicine and eugenics, which change the nature of living beings; and education, which changes their mental nature, are likewise bereft of a particular purpose and come to serve private and individual interests instead of pursuing the task of transforming the world.

The outcome is humanity's atomization into a number of warring centers. Culture is no longer produced as the common cause of human efforts, while the latter develop, each in its own field, as self-contained strivings. Hence the birth of the destructive particularism we find at the heart of cultural liberalism, which was proclaimed during the Renaissance and has evolved into modern cultural chaos. In this state, people's common conscious action, instead of blazing a course for itself through history as a single, powerful stream, has trickled away into a thousand rivulets, which have mostly ended up as standing puddles of fetid water. Each man lives only for his selfish purposes. A number of dead ends arise, discrete lives fenced off from the rest. An idol in the guise of personal prejudice or passion is erected in each such dead end. Mutual bloody war erupts in the name of the idols, tearing humanity apart with strife. However, at the same time, people are united by irrational factors, but this unity is usually based on narrow-mindedness and passivity, and crumbles when it encounters consciousness, even in its primary selfish, individual form.

These events have caused the crisis now experienced by European culture. It is clear it cannot abide in a state of modern individual atomization, and just as clear that the way open to past attempts at unification, based on extinguishing consciousness, is now forbidden to it owing to its hypertrophied modern evolution. The only way left is to produce a culture in which consciousness would not be removed from life but would projectively manage it—not in the sense of separating people from each other, but, on the contrary, in the sense of uniting them as completely as possible on the basis of a common cause.

5

The need to put an end to this decay and confusion requires that the mind have a unifying and shaping effect on all forms of human endeavor. We have seen that the role of consciousness in each discrete action consists in clarifying the action's project. Inasmuch as all actions are generalized in joint efforts to master nature, collective consciousness must find this action's common project and produce a master plan for the universal cause.

Thus the task of organizing all forms of human endeavor or culture consists in organizing life's symbolism and its practice simultaneously.

Since culture grows spontaneously, the germ of this kind of organization is generated, naturally, in the quite elementary, imperfect guise of the sum of natural forces facilitating or hindering man's transfigurative or cultural endeavors. When the balance of this action is set to favor creativity, the outcome is a historical culture; when, on the contrary, the forces of confusion and mindless causality prevail, the world plunges into the darkness of a primitive era, in which man is enslaved to the blind elements. But always, even in cases of cultural creativity, this natural means of its growth is fraught with an immense extravagance of effort. The individual and collective mind's obvious problem involves introducing the comprehending, organizing principle of the conscious human will into this natural process. In other words, culture must be organized identically in its symbolic manifestations, that is, science and art, and their application to life, that is, the practical forms of human endeavor, namely, economics, production, medicine, technology, education, and the like.

This organization requires that collective consciousness produce a comprehensive synthesis of cultural advances in all fields. The synthesis must bring together all the findings of the separate sciences, as encapsulated in the relevant research. Thus, the outcomes achieved by the special branches of knowledge will be gathered into a single, harmonious whole. Similar work should be produced vis-à-vis art's various manifestations, which should likewise be brought together in a synthesis of its best achievements. Then a total synthesis of science's latest findings in the shape of its greatest generalizations and art's most valuable revelations should be made. Together, these products of art and science will constitute the cultural ideal of the age. Yet when organizing them, we must always have in mind not a theoretical or aesthetical purpose, but an effective purpose, actually transforming the world by implementing this ideal in it. The ideal must be a project for joint action on the part of all people, a project that guides the action toward the highest achievements accessible to man. In terms of its structure, the project must be complex, for it will contain as its components all partial projects for transforming reality, as produced by the individual sciences and arts. Each of these sciences and arts will have its own special purpose, and each scientific discovery and each artwork will have a similar specific purpose. But all these partial purposes will be harmonized in the single common goal of the entire culture embracing them. This happens at the dawn of every cultural era, when its different manifestations seemingly emerge from a common word that generates it. Thus it must be in the new era unfolding before us, in which the general character of culture must be changed by turning it into the universal transfigurative cause of all living beings. This new, common root must give rise to new shoots and offspring in the guise of a new, comprehensive science that knows why it creates and what it serves, ceasing to be an irresponsible game by becoming duty and sacrament.

The main problem of organizing culture—producing its common ideal and project—is connected with the next problem: applying the project to life, actually implementing it. For this to happen, culture must infiltrate life through the relevant institutions and conquer all branches of human endeavor.

Special aspects of the common project must encompass special branches of practical action. Thus, the common project must provide the bodies that implement social forms and fashion the law with a picture of the society these bodies are meant to produce. The bodies maintaining or improving living beings through eugenics need a project or image of the perfect man, who is the object of these endeavors. Finally, the common project must give examples of improved living conditions and a physical environment corresponding to the rational idea, to the bodies that transfigure reality through the creation of material goods by means of the economy, production, and labor. Taken together, all these endeavors would implement the world's transformation as a whole—first the planetary world, and then the cosmic world.

Since, as we have seen above, the most perfect species of thought is thought encapsulated in numbers, the project and all its departments and units must consist of a system of formulas or numbers, each providing a key to a process performed by action. Just as analytical geometry gives us formulas of curves, mechanics gives us formulas of movements, and the applied sciences, such as optics and hydraulics, give us formulas of specific phenomena, so science in general must provide the formula of any and all possible actions in its theoretical and practical modes. Science's projects are thus turned into a universal productive mathematics, including all accurate human knowledge of the world in terms of transfiguring it. It is the same thing as Leibniz's *mathesis universalis*, but as a system of not only symbolic but also effective numbers. However, numbers can be replaced with similarly effective signs or names, whose knowledge gives us dominion over nature.

All these tasks clearly involve transforming nature, altering and improving what was heretofore produced by the spontaneous actions of its powers. Certain changes concern living beings and man himself, others focus on the transformation of matter, while still others produce new forms of communication and movement.

The first group of transformations has acquired particular significance nowadays. We have emerged from the periods of human history when we could only imagine altering man's psyche, cultivating certain ideas or moral inclinations in him. Alongside the essential task of perfecting man internally, we are faced with the problem of transforming and renewing him in a more integral way, of altering him as a natural type. Man must become not only *Homo sapiens*, but nature's real ruler, *Homo creator*. This raises the question of improving man biologically and turning him into a physically more powerful, hardy, and viable being. This raises the need for a special art related to improved anthropology—an anthropotechnics or even anthropourgy. We already have a number of applied sciences that have developed practical approaches to the problem: first and foremost, medicine and hygiene, which have revolutionized our living conditions by eliminating certain diseases and considerably neutralizing others. Medicine has gone further. Surgery alters the human body, eliminates infected organs, replaces them with others, and artificially compensates the body's imperfections. The pinnacle of such advances is the discovery of rejuvenation, which is a very real step in science's campaign for longevity. But medicine is complemented by experimental biology, which has gone even further. In various experiments, albeit still partial, the way to conquering death has been outlined by revitalizing organs, resurrecting the body after suspended animation, and so on. The ultimate goal of biological research is the creation of living protoplasm: experiments on colloids seem to be approaching this goal. We can make out the laboratory creation of real life, the consummation of Paracelsus's old experiments in fashioning homunculi, in the misty distance beyond these achievements. It would be a real and total victory over death, and naturally, anthropotechnics would be supported by anastasis, the art of resurrecting lost lives. While biology and chemistry have not yet reached the point of carrying out these tasks, another science has now raised the practical issue of improving living beings and man through the deliberate cultivation of inherited traits. Eugenics seeks to create a new human breed, to grow *Homo creator* by means of artificial selection. However, the science is still in its initial stage, but its prospects are enormous, touching equally on the improvement of individual and social conditions, sexual and family relations, and finally, the reformation of morals and life.

No less important, however, than the task of altering the nature of living things is the problem of the conscious human will's impact on transformations of matter.

The latest discoveries in the field of physical chemistry not only pose a series of theoretical questions to humanity but also put forward two practical problems in which the application of calculation can bring about advances of colossal importance for altering nature. The first is none other than the revival in scientific guise of the old medieval dream of transforming matter. The alchemists thought such a transformation was possible. They even sought the basic substance, which they called the philosopher's stone, that was the origin of all other substances. They assumed that if a substance was kept in certain conditions, for instance, in the ground, for a certain period, it could be changed into another substance. The idea was rejected when the theory of modern scientific chemistry took shape, and it was discovered that the chemical elements were not subject to decomposition by conventional chemical means. As early as 1815, however, William Prout hypothesized that all the elements were polymers of a single primary element, hydrogen. The idea has now been advanced again in the wake of experiments by Thomson, Bohr, and Rutherford, and brilliantly confirmed in a number of experimental works. At present, the irrefutable scientific truth is that the atomic nuclei of all elements are composed of hydrogen and helium nuclei and electrons. In addition, the undeniable evolution of the chemical elements has been discovered, having to do with their breakdown, as caused by radioactive processes. Ionium is thus obtained from uranium, radium from ionium, polonium from radium, and finally, lead from polonium.

It follows that the question of transforming substances has been theoretically solved in a positive way, and an unbounded domain for altering matter has been opened to human endeavor.

A no less important outcome of the latest advances in chemistry is the discovery of colossal reserves of energy within atoms. The radius of the nucleus is 2,000 times smaller than the radius of the electron, whereas the mass of the nucleus is 2,000 times greater than the mass of the electron. From this it follows that the atom's positively charged inert part (and, hence, its weighty part) is concentrated in an extremely small volume. The question arises as to whether it would be possible to harness this intra-atomic energy and release it by decaying matter in such quantities that would supply useful energy. A positive solution of this problem would undoubtedly produce an unprecedented revolution in technology and production, giving people the power to alter the world on a scale completely incommensurate with our modern ideas.

Alongside the scientific fields we have mentioned, we can mention yet another in which scientific mathematical calculation, as applied to productive endeavors, opens up unprecedented opportunities for human action. This is the field of mastering space by producing new means of communication and motion. Here we should first point out the conquest of the air, a problem that has been considerably solved, producing over several decades advances that have exceeded the wildest expectations and hopes of previous centuries. Aeronautics now needs only certain improvements, mainly in terms of increasing the carrying capacity of aircraft. In parallel, however, arises the incomparably more majestic problem of flights in empty space and, as its ultimate goal, interplanetary travel. Dizzying perspectives have opened up here that with each passing year are ever more defined, at least in terms of preliminary theoretical assumptions and calculations. Scientific thinking is inclined to acknowledge that a rocket, propelled by internal explosions, might be capable of such travel if certain improvements were made. Therefore, just as in the fifteenth and sixteenth centuries people were seized by the hope of discovering Earth's unexplored continents, we can dream of imminently discovering and visiting planets, and translocating our endeavors to the vastness of space. And who knows whether this problem would lead to the question of how to guide the movement of the planets and whether the ideas of the Russian thinker Nikolai Fedorov would be realized. He foresaw that people would one day become masters of Earth to such an extent that it would become a ship obedient to them, and that they would steer it through space.

In any case, while these distant prospects remain the realm of daydreams and fantastic suppositions, great advances have been made in a related field—mastering space by action at a distance. Wireless technology has become particularly advanced. Next in line is inventing means for focusing energy in a single direction, energy usually dispersed through space by the usual means of wireless telegraphy. When we have the capacity to transmit energy without weakening it, we will be able not only to send messages over enormous distances, perhaps to other planets or even stars, but we will also be capable of using electric waves to transmit destructive or constructive force over a distance.

We could list a number of similar prospects in science and technology, but what we have said suffices to give an idea of human action's projective power when it is guided by scientific and mathematical calculation.

To complete the picture, we should mention one more scientific task, involving as it were a synthesis of all the other modes and means of mastering nature. It is the task of mastering all the processes of movement and change by conquering their common root—time.

Overcoming time is not only a possibility that follows from modern physical and mathematical theories. Conquering and mastering time is possible in practice, as a result of deliberate human endeavor. We can go further and claim that we already have actual partial mastery of time in a number of fields and constantly implement it, despite the fact that we are unaware of the meaning of our actions. Indeed, if we paused to consider it, we would realize that there is an example of mastering time in the freely and consciously produced know-how of each and every human being. Every day, in limited areas, we alter time and effect its reversal. This happens, for example, in every scientific experiment. When I produce water from two gasses, and then decompose it and reproduce it again, repeating the process as I wish, each time I am constituting or decomposing a combination of elements in a particular set. In other words, I am repeating the phenomenon's sequence or destroying and resurrecting water. The question arises, however: can we speak in this instance of resurrecting water? It is no longer the same water, but different water, for everything in the vicinity has changed, and the water itself has changed imperceptibly. But this does not diminish the value of the resurrection process. Of course, from the perspective of Earth's movement or even my life, there is no full resurrection in this case, for each new drop of water has new links with a new milieu at each particular moment. We can therefore argue, paraphrasing Heraclitus, that the reconstituted water is not the same water. If, however, we reject such a broad perspective and artificially restrict the experiment to a particular set of relationships—if we deliberately take our mind off all the connections with the environment—we obtain a complete mastery of time and the resurrection of particular events in this limited field. The restriction is manifested in this case in the fact that water is important to us only if it corresponds to the formula H_2O, to a certain combination of particular chemical elements. For this to be the case, there is no requirement that the water be the same water, that is, water consisting of the very same atoms as the old water. When I say "water is resurrected," I mean only that a certain amount of H_2O obtains, albeit from completely different atoms. The notion of individuality is completely limited to correspondence to the formula or number, and nothing other than the number or indicator of a unique combination can be found in any individual.

All deliberately and rationally effected alterations of nature that generate or re-create reality, according to a given formula, are neither more nor less than mastery of time.

So such experiments show us that time has been partly conquered, mastered within a limited field, and that partial resurrection has been accomplished. Experiments in rejuvenation represent a similar victory over time, but within a more complex set of relations. But in this case we can argue that overcoming time or reversing it is conceivable, that its possibility has been proven and depends on our conscious will, inasmuch as the environment mounts no obstacles to it, for to prove that time is reversible generally, I hardly need to try and prove that all time is reversible. It suffices to prove it is possible to repeat a small part of it to be able to say that the fundamental capacity for resurrection exists. Since controlling time is possible in a restricted realm, it is possible in essence, and the question comes down to expanding that realm's limits, that is, the magnitude of the action. If we imagine an experiment in which we, instead of two particular quantities of a gas, wielded a large number of elements, we might also master time with respect to them. By imagining such an action on an even larger, cosmic scale, we get a picture of mastering all of time. This generates colossal consequences. It transpires that deliberate projective action is capable not only of changing things in particular fields, but that changing the world in general is within the grasp of such action. We can conquer any and all time, and we are on our way to this conquest in every consciously conducted experiment.

7

So far, we have been considering relatively long-term perspectives for human projective and productive action. If we move from these complex and broad assumptions to the immediate tasks of productive activity, having practical value now, we can draw up an impressive list of urgent tasks.

The first question in this case is rational use of the reserves located in the Earth's depths and on its surface: minerals, coal, petroleum, metals, gems, timber, plants, and animals. Rapaciously consumed by man, these reserves are rapidly dwindling. In this sense, man's endeavors have already pushed nature toward depletion and deterioration. If this destruction continues, nature will gradually suffer what has happened to many desertified woodlands and extinct species of animals. Indeed, Malthus's law might become a terrible reality for humanity. In light of this, we must, on the one hand, introduce economic methods of use instead of the predatory squandering of resources that prevails now. This can already be seen in artificial fertilization, reforestation, and the cultivation of valuable species of plants and animals. But these methods should be disseminated ubiquitously and in an organized way. They should be complemented by increased exploration of new sources of usable energy that could compensate for the lack of current reserves until the mastery of intra-atomic energy radically revolutionizes all production technology. New sources of energy, available to people to some extent now, include the power of river currents and waterfalls, so-called white coal, and solar energy, for whose capture devices are now being built. We can also point out another problem of colossal importance to the future of agriculture: regulating the weather. There is no doubt that meteorology must become an exact science; regardless of this, people must learn to control the weather and generate the necessary climatic conditions for their lives. In the work of the Russian thinker Nikolai Fedorov we find a number of valuable ideas related to the experiments of the outstanding nineteenth-century Russian scientist Vasily Karazin. At the moment, attempts to generate or eliminate clouds by firing into the air point to the beginnings of this regulation, but true progress in the field will have to do, apparently, not with such relatively primitive know-how, but with the latest advances in the theory and technology of electrical events influencing the atmosphere.

Finally, culture is faced with the general task of guiding and organizing production and labor in all branches of economic life, especially in the field of manufacturing. Instead of the mindless waste of manpower and resources in creating useless things, luxury items, and weapons of mutual extermination, the latter should be tasked with supplying humanity with the items truly necessary for bettering life. Production goals should not be dictated to culture by spontaneous and reckless market trends, but should be assigned to organized industry as a consequence of the special projective work performed by supreme cultural and economic institutions.

8

The organization of culture we have described is a reliable remedy to the atomization of people and the lack of coordination of their efforts, as noted above. The unity of humanity sought by all the best political and social projects would be secured primarily by a unity of productive and transformative purpose that embraces all fields of human thought and endeavor. This would foster the conditions for the genuine birth of a new culture, which must replace the modern Western European culture that has gradually faded before our eyes. Whereas the old culture was based on biological rivalry raised to a dogma—the individual's selfish struggle for physical self-preservation, often in the teeth of other people's and society's interest—the new culture should come from an awareness of a much deeper principle as the engine of life: the symbiosis or cooperation of living beings. The need for such joint efforts follows from people's primeval affinity, as revealed in their common origin as an organic type. But this kinship, given by nature, must become effective labor in its secondary, conscious phase, turning the world into one great family that works collectively.

Created in this way and guided by the united efforts of humanity, who for the first time would genuinely enact the common cause of all living things, the cause of life against death, the new culture, bestowed with such a fusion of aspiration and action, would ultimately attain the broad human basis absent in earlier symbolic and aristocratic cultures. For the first time, humanity would be fully involved in the business of creating culture, and all people would take part in this creative work. Scientific experiments would be carried out not by certain people in certain places, as individual attempts by individual scientists or their corporations, but everywhere and always by everyone, through the mass action of broad sections of humanity, just as the most significant historical and sociological experiments, those that transform human society, are carried out nowadays. And the culture that grows on such social foundations would flourish many times more greatly and richly than the stunted blossoming of the hothouse flowers that were past cultures, dying in the harsh winds of historical and social struggles, consequences of the narrowness of these cultures and their unsuitability for all humanity.

Along with a social basis, the new culture would be given with a comprehensive political basis. It would be not only a national culture of individual peoples but also a universal culture, humanity's common cause, the prelude to a future world society to be constructed on the culture's principles. The organization of culture promotes the idea of uniting humanity not around the vague, past ideals of universal peace, as preached by pacifists, but around the joint interaction of all people working for the sake of attaining a particular goal that can be achieved by common effort. Perhaps when this task has been formulated, the slogan of disarming the nations can be advanced again—but in a new way: not in the sense of a total rejection of weapons and universal conscription, but in the sense of a new armament, directed not against people of other nations, but against nature's blind force, which by that time would be the human mind's sole enemy. Then, after the disarmament of Europe and America in their present form, cannons that shoot for hundreds of miles would be aimed at the clouds to scatter accumulations of hail or cause beneficent rainfall in the United States of the World. Chemical inventions would be used not to kill people, but to revive and resurrect them. And compulsory military service, which in a post-Versailles Europe divided by corridors, occupations, and national enmity functions as a weapon of international violence and oppression, would be turned into a great worldwide labor army, whose courage and craft would be turned against death, time, poverty, and disease. Its object would be the conquest not of regions and kingdoms, but the whole world, with the goal of transforming it entirely.

These are the ultimate goals that humanity must now set itself. Transforming outer space, and establishing real cosmocracy and pantocracy, making it possible for man to live throughout the world, in all environments, by quickening and vitalizing all nature, changing it from the spontaneous, chaotic, irrational modern world, filled with strife, into a world as a consummate whole, permeated by the mind and fully subordinate to it, is the main task for all humanity, liberated from the internal strife that oppresses it.

—Moscow, December 1923

Translated by Thomas Campbell

Note

1. Aleksandr Ivanovich Herzen (1812–1870) was a socialist thinker, publisher, and critic of the Russian imperial regime. Exiled in Europe shortly before the Revolutions of 1848, Herzen collaborated closely with the Proudhonian anarchists-socialists in Paris; along with Bakunin and Marx, he organized the International Workingmen's Association in London. In 1853, Herzen founded the Free Russian Press, a significant contribution from abroad to the liberal discourse that led in 1861 to the abolition of serfdom in Russia.—Ed.

8 The Future of Earth and Mankind

Konstantin Tsiolkovsky

Our Sun shines on more than a thousand planets. There are no fewer than a billion such solar-planetary systems in the Milky Way. Around a million milky ways like ours have been found in the Ethereal Island. Astronomy has so far gone no further. What follows is philosophy, which considers the universe as infinite as space and time. Limiting ourselves to reality, we must accept that the number of planets in the world is a thousand million billion, that is, a one followed by eighteen zeroes (a trillion).

Of the thousand planets in each solar system, at least one is situated at a favorable distance from its sun. It receives warmth, has an atmosphere and oceans, and is habitable. There are thus no fewer than a million billion habitable planets, that is, a one followed by fifteen zeroes (1,000 billion). If we divided up these habitable planets equally among people, each person would receive more than 500,000 Earth-like habitable planets.

What is the plight of these innumerable planets and their beings? We can judge only by the possible fate of Earth and mankind.

Man has recently mastered the atmosphere as a means of transport. It is still in a period of growth, especially with regard to gas-filled airships. The airplane has reached an altitude of nearly 13 kilometers. Higher altitudes will be attainable when the airplane motor has been replaced with a jet engine (a rifle- or gun-ecoil-like mechanism) and the passenger cabin has been sealed, that is, it no longer releases gas (oxygen) into thin air or the vacuum. Experiments are underway in this field or anticipated. We must hope they will not only penetrate the stratosphere (above 12 kilometers), but fly beyond the atmosphere. A projectile would remain there at a certain distance from Earth like a tiny moon. The centrifugal force produced by its velocity and the curvature of its trajectory would render the projectile constant with respect to its position, like any celestial body. It would no longer have to consume energy, since it would be moving in a vacuum, and its motion, in keeping with the laws of inertia, could never be lost or even weakened. Thence, from a lunar position, the projectile would blaze a path into the ether, the interplanetary environment and beyond. Man would acquire all the energy of the Sun, which is two billion times greater than what he now receives on Earth.

Little by little, man would build homes in the ether. They would encircle the Sun, and people's wealth would increase billions of time. All this is so, but we cannot abandon the Earth entirely. First, it is the cradle of mankind. Second, it would be overrun by irresponsible beings who would turn it into a house of agony. Even now, we see that hell reigns not only among animals, but also among most people.

Earth and the other planets would have to be cleaned up so that they ceased being a source of torment to the atoms dwelling in imperfect beings. In addition, we need Earth as a support, as a base for disseminating and solidifying man's might in the solar system and its planets.

Hence we will take up the plight of Earth and its population. Its future destiny is the destiny of the universe, which has been consummated long ago, since the time for it has sufficed. Among people, there are not many children who are one second old. (There is only such infant on the entire globe.) Likewise, there are not many planets the age of Earth: one in a billion or fewer. So nearly the entire universe is immersed in the perfection we anticipate for Earth as well. So let us talk about what we can anticipate for Earth. We cannot imagine everything, however. The planets of other solar systems have probably produced much more.

Earth is currently a desert. There are 55 hectares of land and sea per person, 14 hectares of which is land alone. No fewer than four hectares of this land have a paradise-like, winterless climate with wonderful, fertile soil. There is no need in such places for shoes, clothing, expensive dwellings, or laboring to feed oneself. The only misfortune is humidity, infectious bacteria, harmful insects, harmful animals, and hostile vegetation of mighty proportions.

The inhabitants of countries with temperate climates cannot fight these conditions alone. Natives are aided in coping with them by their own bodies, which have been adapted to the conditions. But they are unable to make use of the paradise bestowed on them and lead pitiful, impoverished lives.

A hundred square meters of soil is enough to feed a person in tropical countries. Planted with bananas, root crops, bread trees, coconut and date palms, or other plants, this little patch of land (an are or 100 square meters) is quite sufficient for a single person to live well.

Hence, I call Earth a desert. Four hectares or 400 ares of fertile tropical soil is available per person, but even one are (the foundation of a house 25 meters per side) is a lot for one individual. How is Earth not a desert if there is 400 times more soil than necessary?

Only when Earth's population has increased a thousand times will man become master of the soil, ocean, air, weather, plants, and himself.

Therefore, reason tells us that reproduction and the simultaneous conquest of fertile and carefree tropical lands must be foregrounded.

This is no easy task: it would require all of humanity to mount a united struggle against nature. The best lands of South America and Central America should be the next step.

Land must be declared common property, and there should be no one who has no right to it.

But what would a person do by himself with his four hectares of fertile land? They would swallow him up with the force of tropical nature.

Fever, insects, downpours, storms, poisonous snakes, vegetation, and so forth would not let him survive for even a year. What is the use of abundance when it is hostile in its particulars?

To combat the equatorial elements, we would need a multimillion-man voluntary army and all the technological means at our disposal. Then the individual would survive, healthy and happy on his tiny plot. He could then reproduce, filling Earth and spreading his dominion over it.

A labor-army front should launch its operations from the very shore of the ocean and be several thousand kilometers long. But let us say it is only 1,000 kilometers long. Then we would need approximately 10 million men, if the width of the front were 10 meters and the soldiers were spaced one meter apart from each other. (Ten million men is less than 1 percent of the Earth's total population.)

What would these soldiers have to do, and how would they be armed?

They would have to move between two large rivers, which to a certain extent would shield the workers from the hostile forces of vegetation and animals.

The first strip, 10 meters wide, would be cleaned without a mesh net. After that, the entire front of workers would be covered with a tight metallic mesh net that would keep out insects, snakes, and beasts, thus protecting the workers from diseases and pests. The net would have the shape of a long canopy or box, partitioned by similar nets at certain intervals. Individual canopies, constituting a single line of the front, would be preferable. It would be 1,000 kilometers long, and the canopy would be 10 meters wide and 10 meters high. The base of the box—a sturdy, flexible metal cage—would move as required on wheels along with the people inside it. It would have no bottom. The people would stand on the ground, but could exit the net and go outside through doors. It would be like a diving bell or caisson. The area under the net would be tilled and planted with suitable crops.

Then the workers would again completely eradicate all plant and animal life for several dozen meters in front of the net, moving their cages to this clean spot. Here the soil would be planted with the purest varieties of the plants most beneficial to man and typical of the climate. After that, the soldiers would exit the cage and eradicate the organic life on the next strip of soil. Then they would move their mobile cage to the clean spot and do their previous work inside it—planting the space inside it with the most prolific crops. As the workers' cage took each step forward, the free strip of soil behind it, already sown and planted, would immediately be covered with a more simply constructed immobile cage, since it would not need to move. Its dimensions would be the same as those of the mobile cage. The processed strip of soil would provide available, safe housing for 100,000 settler-farmers. There would be 100 square meters of soil for each of them. The fruits and root vegetables would feed them abundantly.

Would this net-covered dwelling, with Earth as its perennial breadwinner, be expensive? Ignoring the occasional partitions, we would have to supply each person with 300 square meters of mesh netting. Even with a light frame it would cost nothing. But it must not rust, and thus should be nickel-plated or covered with a rust-resistant compound.

How would the plants thrive under this net, which would baffle the Sun's rays a bit? With a thin nickel-wire ceiling (100 square meters), no more than 25 percent of the solar energy would be absorbed, and the loss to the plants would not be appreciable, for solar energy is not what would matter, but fertilizer, humidity, and atmosphere.

And so the movable canopy would travel along, liberating approximately enough land for 100,000 people per day. This would be possible, since one worker, armed with the best possible means for extermination and regeneration, would handle one square meter of tillable soil per day.

The workers should be able to cultivate enough land for 10 million people in a year. In fact, they would be able to do a lot more. Would a worker equipped with the most modern tools be able to till and plant only one square meter of soil per day? But we have in mind the net, its expansion, and its appendages, which we have not yet mentioned. And yet even if the work were moderately successfully, within forty years Earth's entire population would enjoy a luxurious haven, sustenance, and leisure. The tilled area would amount to 1.6 billion ares or 16 million hectares. This is 3,200 times less than Earth's entire surface, 900 times less than the total land area, and 400 times less than the total area of manageable tropical soil. All that would be left would be to reproduce, fill Earth, and dominate nature.

But a mesh home cannot be considered a sufficient home for man. It would also need a covering to shield it from tropical downpours, dampness, and the cold of the night (if the dwellings were located a certain distance from the tropics). Insects and snakes would no doubt infiltrate the cells from time to time, so measures would sometimes have to be taken to exterminate them in one section or other. However, the larger the space that would be cultivated, the fewer chances there would be for insects and other animals to infiltrate it, since there would generally be fewer of them roaming around relative to the total area.

In fact, the net would shield flora and farmer only during sowing or rest. Outside work, on the contrary, could also be done during cooler times of the day, in the morning or even at night if electric lighting were used. Finally, it could be done by natives, who are more accustomed to the climate and suffer from it less. When free from labor or engaged in mental work and other activities, the individual, especially a settler from cold climes, would need a special dwelling. Protection from pests and fevers would not be enough for him. Initially, a roof and a dry, raised floor would suffice. Later, he would need a home with a constant, not very high temperature. A barefoot individual wearing a light skirt or apron would not be burdened by the average equatorial temperatures, not to mention extratropical climes. But the house should have an average, adjustable temperature. The continents are sometimes subject to unbearable daytime heat and cool nights. The average temperature between the tropics, which ranges from 20 to 28 degrees Celsius, is quite suitable for naked people. The ocean's surface and soil at the approximate depth of a meter are always at the average temperature in places where there is no winter.

When the best houses would be built in the equatorial belt, they would need to have not only the average temperature, but higher and lower temperatures, depending on necessity. It is easy to obtain the average temperature if you filter the air from a house through several underground pipes or a grid work of stones. It would then cool off when the weather is hot, and warm up when it is cold. But the average temperature of a house and the soil below it could be lowered, especially if it were a large dormitory and its foundations covered a large patch of ground. To this end, the house's roof would be made shiny. It would reflect the Sun's rays without heating up the house. Only heated air that penetrated the doors and windows would heat it up. This heat would be easily adjusted and moderated. At night, to the same end, the roof's mirrored surface would be changed on both sides to a black surface. It would cool off under the clear sky, cooling the air below it, which would be let into the rooms or through underground pipes and cool the house down. Thus, one could adjust not only the temperature but also reduce it in a large house and the ground on which it stands. In large houses, this decrease would be quite significant.

In the tropics and at higher latitudes, the Sun's warmth on the roofs of houses could be used in different ways. Mirrored roof panels, curved slightly cylindrically in the focal surface, could heat water in boilers and provide hot water and steam to power engines. (The details are to be found in my special work on the topic.) It would be a source of electrical energy, stored in batteries and used for a variety of needs.

We could, on the contrary, raise the average temperature if it were not enough for an unclothed person. For example, the average temperature at 45 degrees latitude is 10 to 15 degrees Celsius. That is too low. The average temperature of the house and ground beneath it should be higher in this case. There would be no need to wear clothes if the temperature could be raised. Only workers laboring outside would need clothing. In fact, you can work in warm weather when the Sun is shining and do without clothes.

To increase the average temperature, the roof of the house would have to be shielded with a shiny, nonconductive thermal layer when it was cold and at night, while in warm, daytime weather when the Sun was shining, the black surface would be uncovered. The air beneath would be warmed by the Sun. The current of this air would have to be sent into the house or subterranean pipes, thus storing the heat in the house or the soil. In cold weather, aside from shielding the roof with a protective thermal layer, air that had passed through the warm soil could be vented into the house. A temperature higher than the average temperature, typical of the natural climate, would obtained in the house and the area beneath it. Eighty-two percent of Earth's entire surface is located below 45 degrees latitude, and it could be inhabited, thanks to temperature regulation, by individuals not wearing clothing. The air in homes would not only have to be clean, which would be achieved by ventilation, but also fairly dry, a bit drier than the air outside. Such air would be healthier for the majority of people. Indeed, dryness hinders the occurrence of different microbes and fungi that destroy organic materials and even metals. When we cool the ground in the equatorial zone, it would be moister than the outside air. The excess moisture would have to be extracted from this air in the house. This could be done with substances—alkalis—that absorb the vapor from the air. The alkalis would then have to be calcinated at special factories to restore their capacity for absorbing water.

Purifying the air of dust and bacteria would be accomplished by running it through special filters made of fabrics, mesh, powders, and liquids.

What would the outcome be? People would be masters of the air and temperature in their houses, thus ridding themselves of the need to wear clothes and shoes. This is likewise a wealth and comfort not yet accessible to anyone. Nearly the entire surface of the Earth, 82 percent of the land, would become a paradise, except for deserts, mountains, and reservoirs of water.

How could we cope with the waterless, hot deserts? How could we deal with the mountainous areas, the oceans and the seas? What could we do with the remaining 18 percent of the Earth's surface, situated above 45 degrees latitude?

Man shall slowly overcome everything, but for this to happen he needs to multiply, make technological advances, and better the species. Complex structures, mesh nets, mirrors, and subterranean pipes should not frighten us, because with respect to a single worker and his technological capacity, these facilities would cover an insignificant area, less than one are (100 square meters).

Let us turn to the hot deserts, such as the Sahara, the Atacama, and the Australian deserts. Their main shortcoming is a lack of water. There is no water at all or very little even in the depths of the soil, in the deepest (artesian) wells. There are not enough wells generally. On the contrary, all the water we need is above our heads, trapped in the desert air. Only its high temperature keeps it from precipitating in the guise of rain or dew.

This, however, can be done with special devices. The desert would have to be covered with special inhabitable greenhouses to become a paradise on Earth. We have seen that several dozen square meters of fertile soil would be enough to feed one person. A greenhouse several square meters in size is something a person could build. The perennially bright Sun of the desert, the limpid air, the absence of clouds, and the continuous daytime lighting would nearly quadruple the yields of well-selected plants. This would reduce even further the dimensions of the greenhouse or plantation needed to feed a single person.

How would it have to be organized?

The individual dwelling would have to be covered at night with a nonconductive thermal layer, over which a sheet of black metal would be laid. At night, which in the desert can be clear and cloudless, this layer would cool off considerably and be covered with drops of dew extracted from the air. The water would trickle down the pitched roof into gutters, and from there into a special water storage container. Along with the water, cold air would flow down the roof, turning warm and moist on top. This cold air could penetrate the subsoil recesses and cool the red-hot soil. If needed, it could store the coldness. As calculations show, the quantity of water obtained would be quite sufficient to irrigate an area several times the area of the roof. The fields and tall palm tree around the house would be well watered. The trees would protect the house from wind, thus also facilitating the precipitation of heavy dew and the accumulation of water overnight. If the fields were covered with a layer of glass, like greenhouses, the evaporation of water could be significantly decreased. The same thing could be achieved by selecting plants that do not succumb to dryness, such as different varieties of fecund cacti. The humidity emitted by plants could also be collected by running the greenhouse air through the cooled soil, using the method I have described. How would we protect the house from the daytime heat? Our black roof would become incandescent, but the heat would not penetrate the house, because there would be a nonconducting thermal layer under the metal sheet. However, the air surrounding the house would be heated by the black roof and burn nearby plants unless they were protected. To avoid this, during the day the shiny underside of the black sheet of metal would have to be turned over to face the Sun and deflect its rays, which, leaving the air almost unheated, would dissipate irretrievably into the sky. Thus we might even be able to lower the average temperature and cause rainfall.

We could also use the Sun's rays to heat boilers and generate electrical energy, as I have indicated above, and it would be more practical as it would not involve an overall lowering of the desert's temperature. We would end up with a temperature a bit higher than usual, which is typical of the desert. But the appropriate plants would render the heat harmless if they were lightly irrigated.

Given a sufficient number of buildings and trees surrounding them, the wind in the lower atmosphere would slow, and sand drifts would become impossible, not taking into account the borders of the arable lands, where we would continue to struggle with sand drifts.

The drawback of elevated areas and upland deserts is their low temperature. Indeed, for every kilometer of elevation, the temperature decreases by 5 to 6 degrees Celsius.

If it were not for the cold air, the daytime Sun at all heights would heat all dark bodies to a very high temperature, up to 150 degrees Celsius. At night, on the contrary, it would be quite cold. But the air spoils everything. It cools more than necessary during the day and heats things insufficiently at night.

Closed houses and greenhouses could protect themselves from the air's impact and accumulate heat using the methods I have indicated. During the day, ceilings would have to be exposed to the Sun but closed to the winds, that is, they would have to be made of transparent glass to let in as many rays as possible. They would severely heat the air in the greenhouses, owing to the greenery, and the houses, owing to the black floors and walls. The heat would be unbearable were the air not vented into basement pipes or piles of stones. There would be no need to ventilate buildings abundantly and cool them excessively with cold air from the outside, since air spoiled by man's waste, once it has been run through the leaves, soil, and roots of plants, is completely purged of all contaminants. We could say that man and his industry nourish plants, while plants nourish man and supply him with a healthy atmosphere.

The amount of carbon dioxide in the atmosphere is quite small (0.03 percent), which does not facilitate crop yields. Its quantity could be increased 30 times (to 1 percent) with great benefit to plants and no harm whatsoever to man. The gas is not poisonous, and an abundance of it in the atmosphere would only hinder its secretion from the lungs. One percent would cause almost no bother, even if we were talking about human lungs.

I am not speaking of excessive heights, perpetually covered in snow. Such heights are located on the equator at an altitude in excess of five kilometers, and at a latitude of 45 degrees at an altitude in excess of two to three kilometers. There are few such places and they occupy an insignificant amount of land. They could be used to host meteorological and other stations, such as bases for launching sky ships.

Let us turn to the seas and oceans. Can man tame this savage environment, turning it into agricultural country?

When the time comes to deal with the oceans, the population would have reached the enormous number of 400 billion people, 300 times greater than the current population. Its technical might would have increased many thousands of times. Taking this into account, I shall show how man would conquer the seas and oceans.

Initially, we would have to make great efforts, starting with smaller bodies of water. A front in the shape of a raft stretching the entire length of the shore of the sea or lake in question would be erected. For the time being, it would have to be narrow, a few meters wide. Its edges, turned toward the waves, would have engines that would feed on the ocean's turbulence and tame the waves.

The front would have to be built very solidly. As it advanced over the water, the gap between it and the shore would be filled with another, less sturdy raft, covered with soil, plants, and dwellings. Thus, as people reproduced, the front would advance further and further, until it filled the entire lake or sea.

It would be covered on top by a smooth, transparent roof so that the winds would be unable to exert strong horizontal pressures on the raft while the Sun's rays would be able penetrate it. The raft would thus constitute an enormous greenhouse, partitioned into sections to make it easier to make adjustments and combat pests.

The roof could be kept aloft by a slight excess of air pressure within the buildings as long as they were lightly secured. Of course, attaching it to the raft could not be avoided, and the partitions could serve this purpose. This would greatly facilitate construction and make it possible to raise the transparent roof high.

Calculations show that not only lakes and inland seas could be used, but even entire oceans. The rafts would be supported by the shores of the continents, islands, and shallow areas in the oceans. (And, in extreme cases, deep areas.) This would be enough to keep the wind from destroying the roofs and blowing away the rafts, as it would slide over the smooth roofs.

Gaps or channels would be left between them for navigation.

The evaporation of water would be regulated at will, and man would partly conquer the climate. What would be the advantage of regulating the climate and conquering the oceans? First, aquatic animals, who would no longer have access to sunlight, would necessarily vanish or be reduced to a minimum. This would be a source of tremendous moral satisfaction, for beings would cease to suffer from predatory fish, birds, and beasts that make the aquatic abode hellish. Next, man would be able to control cloud cover, which has an enormous impact on Earth's temperature and the growth of plants beneficial to man. Third, Earth's human population would be able to grow four times, thus increasing man's power over Earth. (Earth is three and a half times larger than its total land area.) The most successful thing of all would be farming on oceanic rafts: indeed, compared with the land, there would be an abundance of moisture, an even, ideal temperature, a perfectly flat locale, and cheap transport. The absorption of carbon dioxide by aquatic animals would either stop or slow down, thus greatly enriching the atmosphere with the gas and encouraging an increase in the mass of vegetation, the stocks of fiber, sugar, fruits, and other vegetable produce, as well as the mass of mankind, which also needs carbon. An excess of it in the atmosphere of the dwellings could always be absorbed by a sufficient quantity of plants. One way or another, the atmosphere's makeup would be in man's hands.

Most important, however, would be controlling water evaporation. Currently, Earth irrevocably deflects from 50 percent to 70 percent of all the Sun's rays that reach it. This greatly decreases its average temperature and the energy of the rays, which man could use to grow plants or in future solar-powered machines.

We could use part of this energy, now reflected back into space, if we slowed the evaporation of the oceans and slightly cleansed the atmosphere of fog, clouds, and storm clouds. The extent of purification would depend on us. But would it be possible? Would it not provoke terrible, devastating consequences for Earth's population?

The surface of water would be gradually covered by rafts. There would be no drastic changes. Moreover, the rate at which the oceans evaporated would always be in our hands. Opening the transparent cover over the plants could even intensify the evaporation of water and cause the reverse phenomenon, decreasing Earth's average temperature and, consequently, increasing cloud cover and precipitation. In the first case, the temperature on Earth would be uneven, that is, the difference in warmth between the tropical climes and the polar climes would be even greater than before. In the second case, vice versa. Indeed, a decrease in precipitation along with a decrease of vapor in the air would trigger a smaller transfer of warmth from the hot climes to the cold ones, causing an acute leveling among the temperatures at different latitudes. A clear night sky could also increase the difference between the warmth of the day and the night. But reducing cloud cover would be more beneficial because it would trigger an overall increase in Earth's temperature. Moreover, not only the temperate climes but also the polar climes would enjoy a tolerable temperature and be rid of their ice and winters. The only trouble would be that the tropical climes would be impossibly hot.

Assuming that Earth's light reflectivity or albedo is 65 percent and its average temperature is 17 degrees Celsius, as based on known laws, we can calculate the following temperature table if its albedo were decreased by purifying the atmosphere of clouds.

Albedo (in percentages):						
0	10	30	40	50	65	80
Earth's average temperature (in degrees Celsius):						
104	92	72	58	45	17	21

Hence, it is clear that if we completely destroyed the albedo, which is impossible, Earth's average temperature would climb to 104 degrees Celsius. But even a slight decrease in the albedo, to 50 percent, would produce a high temperature of 45 degrees, that is, it would raise it by 28 degrees.

If the temperature difference remained the same, the average temperature at the poles would be +10 degrees, instead of –18 degrees, and it would be +56 degrees at the equator instead of +28 degrees.

Heating the air would bring about an increase in wind velocity, so the temperature difference would not be so great, perhaps.

This would be all right for the temperate and polar regions, but what about the equator, where the temperature would be unbearable for man? If the average temperature were +56 degrees, what would the daytime temperature be? Moreover, the albedo could be further reduced to the albedo of the Moon or Mars. The average temperature would then climb to between +70 and +80 degrees Celsius.

We think we could eventually eliminate this trouble. As we have seen, the temperature of the housing, which would occupy a vast area, could be decreased at will using shiny roofs. This would not work for the vast area of vegetation, since plants will not grow and bear fruit without sunlight. However, this could be accomplished by using mirrors to reflect sunlight into space. Only this would be wasteful, as the plants would bear less fruit and, in addition, Earth's average temperature would decrease, and the polar regions would be cold as before.

But plants themselves absorb solar energy, accumulating it in fruits and the other fibers of their bodies. The already-existing plants absorb very little energy, no more than 210 percent (e.g., bananas, Burbank cacti). But man will be able to produce plants or processes capable of storing 50 percent or more of the solar energy. The temperature would thus depend on the type of plants and the machines that would store the Sun's spare (potential) energy. This energy, in the form of fruits and other substance, would be transferred to where it was needed, for example, to colder regions and production sites. Emitting it in such places would be the best way to equalize Earth's temperature. The Sun's energy would not be wasted, deflected by clouds or mirrors, but would be released on Earth to heat it evenly and amass resources. It could be used to carry out useful work on Earth, for example, leveling its surface and improving transportation routes. Moreover, Earth's insufficiently warm regions would also be heated.

This would also solve the issue of the areas, on either side of the equator, located above 45 degrees latitude. Constituting 18 percent of the Earth's surface, they would be as warm and populated as the tropical regions. People there would also have no need for clothing and shoes. The polar ice would melt, and the oceans would be cleansed of them and covered with rafts, like the exotic seas.

Earth's population would increase to five billion people, that is, 3,200 times. Everyone would have an are (100 square meters) at his or her disposal.

Although we would be left with a quite transparent atmosphere, it would, nevertheless, not be a lesser evil. First, it would absorb more solar energy. Second, its strong currents, though better than cloudy skies, would produce enormous friction and pressure that would not be easy to combat. Its makeup would be suitable for neither planets nor people. Too much nitrogen harms plants, and animals do not need it, while a lack of carbon dioxide inhibits the productivity of plants. A large quantity of oxygen is likewise not only harmful to plants but is also too much for man, especially if nitrogen has been almost eliminated. The resistance of the atmosphere and its winds would prevent rapid travel on Earth, slowing down the transportation of goods and people. The atmosphere produces very different temperatures at high altitudes. In the highest mountains, it is colder than at sea level by a whole 40 to 50 degrees Celsius. This is no small minus, either. Were it not for the atmosphere, a place's temperature would depend only its distance from the equator. It would not depend in the slightest on its altitude above sea level. It is not so easy to cope with the impact of air temperature, especially in view of its rapid, continuous movement.

After the Sun's warmth has been conquered, the population and its power would be so enormous that it would have ample capacity to adjust the makeup of the air. Indeed, under a cloudless sky, solar engines, utilizing 50 percent of the Sun's energy, would on average supply around 12 kilogram-meters of continuous output per square meter of soil. This is greater than the output of a hardy worker. If we factor in the circumstance that he works eight hours a day, the Sun's energy per square meter would be equal to three or four workers. On his are, each individual would have around 1,200 kilogram-meters of output, that is, 16 horsepower or 12 metric horsepower. Part of this energy, of course, would be expended on nourishment and other human needs. But if only half remained free, every inhabitant would have 8 horsepower of continuous output per are at his disposal. It could be spent transfiguring the atmosphere, land, and so on.

There would be about a thousand tons of atmosphere per person, with his 100 square meters of soil. Such would be the weight of the air above him or, rather, over his are. How could one get rid of this weight while leaving what would be required by plants and people?

First, we shall decide what and how much plants and people need. Since nitrogen is unnecessary for human respiration, the individual could safely settle for half the portion of oxygen he currently takes into his lungs. Indeed, an 80 percent admixture of nitrogen cools the lungs and therefore requires increased oxygen intake. So 10 percent is enough. As it is now, he breathes freely on five-kilometer-high mountains, where the oxygen level (10 percent) is half as much as at sea level (20 percent). He would be able to endure even a 5 percent level of oxygen, although it would take some doing. Children would be able to adapt even to this small portion in view of the oxygen's purity (the absence of nitrogen), the ideal temperature, the splendid living conditions, and the adaptive capacities of young bodies. But let us leave the oxygen at 10 percent. The atmospheric pressure would be 100 grams per square centimeter, which would be offset by a layer of glass or quartz 40 centimeters thick. Consequently, if the ceilings of the human dwellings are approximately 40 centimeters thick, their weight would nicely offset the air pressure. There would be an airless space over the ceiling. If each person required 10 square meters of floor space, the ceiling would have to weigh 10 tons. Would it be economical to spend so much on each being? But there is an innumerable quantity of quartz and other raw materials from which glass is made, and manufacturing would be at its peak, so I think this would be quite possible. Even at a thickness of 40 centimeters, glass can be quite transparent and thus supply a fair amount of light. It could circumfuse (or contain) a solid metal grille and be tremendously sturdy, although this would not be required of it.

Eventually, a breed of creatures would evolve that needed ever-smaller amounts of oxygen, even up to 1 percent, and then the glass would have to be only four centimeters thick. There are creatures with quite grueling lives who get by with a paltry amount of oxygen. I am talking about the big fish. Given the atmospheric pressure and a temperature of zero degrees Celsius, seawater contains 0.34 percent of oxygen per volume, that is, around 1/300 the volume of water. This is three times less than we have assumed man would need and 60 times less than the air contains.

Nevertheless, this paltry quantity of life-giving gas in no way keeps sea creatures from evolving and thinking in their own way.

The ceiling would be at an identical height as on the ocean rafts, approximately 10 meters; if there were tall trees in the vicinity, then in proportion to their height. In this case, the lateral stabilizers would take up little material. It would be the same on large plateaus or large areas at high altitudes. In small areas, the lateral stabilizers would require a greater mass, but there would not be many small areas. Clearly, the air compartments would be isolated from each other where there were large differences in altitude. The temperature in this case would not depend on altitude, which would be quite convenient.

Let us move on to plants. They need very little water vapor, nitrogen, oxygen, and carbon dioxide. Currently, the amount of carbon dioxide relative to the air is one thirtieth of a percent, that is, its pressure is 3,000 times less than the atmospheric pressure at sea level. The levels of water vapor, oxygen, and nitrogen could be just as small. In short, the most favorable atmosphere for plants would supply no more than one hundredth of an atmosphere (10 grams per square centimeter). The transparent cover offsetting this pressure would be four centimeters thick. Given the right makeup, it would deflect almost no solar energy. A greenhouse like this would have a ceiling weighing 10 tons per one are (100 square meters).

So both people and plants would need an atmosphere of negligible height, with a low density and therefore a very small mass. Atmospheric pressure would be equalized by the weight of the hard transparent cover, which would prevent the dispersal of the thin layer of air enveloping the whole Earth, parallel to its solid or liquid surface.

So almost the entire current air mass would have to be eliminated. This could be done in different ways. It would be possible, for example, to compound gasses chemically with other substances and thus convert the atmosphere into solids or liquids.

The latter would be accomplished little by little of its own accord. Indeed, we have seen that man, before filling Earth's entire surface to the extreme, would have flown beyond the atmosphere, settled there on artificial moons or rings, set up industry, left the Earth for a particular orbit, say, between Earth and Mars, expanded industry there, and so forth.

But raw material would be needed for all this. Part of it, especially the construction material, we would borrow from bolides and tiny planets. The other part, organic raw material, required by plants and people, would need a great deal of nitrogen, hydrogen, carbon, and the like. Initially, this raw material could be borrowed from the atmosphere, the water, and Earth's crust.

Populating solar space could be so enormous a task that all this material could be expended on it and it would still be far from enough.

In fact, sunlight's total energy is two billion times in excess of what reaches Earth's surface. But the latter can sustain five billion people, assuming each of them occupies one are of land. So the Sun's entire energy could sustain no fewer than 10^{22} people, a population of no fewer than ten thousand trillion.

How much gas, water, and so on would this population need? Let us consider water. On average, a person, if his total weight is 40 kilograms, contains around 30 kilograms of water. On Earth, there are 300,000 tons of ocean water per inhabitant. So this water would suffice for only 10 million people. The solar system's potential population is two billion times larger than Earth's. Consequently, the waters of the oceans would be enough for only one two-hundredth of the solar system's population. Obviously, we would have to borrow oxygen and hydrogen from Earth's crust—the hydrated and inherent moisture contained in boulders, for example—or other sources.

Let us also examine nitrogen. The average person, weighing 40 kilograms, needs around 1.5 kilograms of nitrogen. The Earth's atmosphere contains 800 tons of nitrogen per are for the future man. Consequently, it would be enough for 530,000 people, that is, not only would all the nitrogen in the atmosphere be expended, but we would have to give serious thought about where to get it to satisfy the solar system's population.

The same can be said of carbon and other elements necessary to living beings. It is possible that, owing to the lack of some elements, we would have to limit the Sun's population, using its energy for other purposes, such as the supreme comfort of beings.

However, more sources would be found, or the means would be sought to convert certain elements into others. Iron, gold, and silver would thus be regenerated, for they would be used to produce organisms. We should note that Earth's crust contains large quantities of carbon in the form of metal carbonates, for example, limestone.

When the limits of reproduction (one are per person) have been reached on Earth, the population would still be quite imperfect. There would have been no time to take care of this. People would have been badly needed for cultivating and conquering Earth. Reproduction would continue just as intensely, but many would be left without offspring, namely, people with various deficiencies. Yet population growth would outpace mortality, and so the surplus of the better part of the population would travel beyond the atmosphere and fill the solar system.

It would be populated partly from Earth and partly independently, that is, people would be reproduced in the heavens, in the ether. So raw materials from the atmosphere, water, and crust would be turned into organisms on Earth and in the ether. Initially, there would be more of this on Earth, but then more in the ether when the population there would be larger than Earth's.

The Earth's waters and atmosphere would soon vanish into the heavens. Earth would be left with only the bare essentials: a layer of air, that is, a nutrient mix of gasses and vapors only several meters high. It would be kept from dispersing by a thin, transparent roof. Its weight would be close to the pressure exerted by this artificial atmosphere.

Clearly, the more populated the ether would be, the more raw (non-organic, dead) matter would have to be sent to satisfy the needs of the population beyond Earth. One would not have to expend the solar energy reaching Earth on obtaining organisms, except for the mechanical energy needed for overcoming Earth and the Sun's gravity when dispatching materials. On the contrary, this force would also be partly borrowed from the total solar energy. In one way or another, it would be delivered from the sky to Earth. This would greatly speed things up, since Earth's energy is relatively insignificant, whereas the total solar energy is two billion times greater than Earth's.

Why should we bother with such a large population? The fact of the matter is that the greater the population, the more perfect its members, and the more advanced its social system. This point could be explained properly only in a separate work.

But let us return to Earth. It would decompose, that is, parts of it would be gradually removed to ethereal space, and dead matter would reanimate it. In fact, theoretically, large portions of our planet could be reanimated with the power of total solar energy. Indeed, the Earth's mass is 6.10^{21}

tons, while the solar system's potential population is 10^{21} people. That would be 0.6 tons or 600 kilograms per each potential inhabitant. That would be just enough for sheltering, equipping, and feeding the creature's living body.

However, there is no need for such a complete transformation of Earth's mass. The goal is different: to achieve perfection and banish all possibility of evil and suffering in the solar system. At present it is hard to imagine how this could be achieved, especially on its large planets.

Translated by Thomas Campbell

9 Panpsychism, or Everything Feels

Konstantin Tsiolkovsky

Foreword

The Universe's Monism

At my age, people die, and I am afraid you will leave this life with bitterness in your heart if you do not learn from me, a pure source of knowledge, that continuous joy awaits you.

Hence I am writing this summary without having finished many major works.

I would want this life of yours to be a bright dream of the future, a future where happiness never ends.

The way I see it, my sermon is not even a daydream, but a strictly mathematical conclusion based on precise knowledge.

I want to guide you to the delight of contemplating the universe, the destiny awaiting us all, and the wonderful story of each and every atom's past and future. It will increase your health, lengthen your life, and give you the strength to bear life's vicissitudes. You will die joyfully, convinced that happiness, perfection, infinity, and the subjective continuity of rich organic life lie in store for you.

My conclusions are more comforting than the promises made by the most life-affirming religions.

Not a single positivist could be soberer than I am. Compared to me, even Spinoza was a mystic. If my wine makes you drunk, at least it is natural.

To understand me you must utterly abandon all things obscure, such as the occult, spiritualism, dark philosophies, and all authorities except that of hard science, that is, mathematics, geometry, mechanics, physics, biology, and their practical applications. [...]

Panpsychism, or Everything Feels

(Abstract) I am a pure materialist. I acknowledge nothing but matter. I see only mechanics at work in physics, chemistry, and biology. The entire cosmos is merely an endless, complex machine. Its complexity is so great that it borders on the arbitrary, the unexpected, and the accidental. It generates the illusion of free will among conscious beings. Although, as we shall see, everything is periodical, strictly speaking, nothing is ever repeated.

The ability of organisms to feel pain and pleasure I call sensitivity. We should note that this word often connotes responsiveness (in living beings, they are called reflexes). Responsiveness is something else. All bodies in the cosmos are responsive. Likewise, all bodies change in terms of size, shape, color, strength, transparency, and all other properties, depending on the temperature, pressure, light, and impact of other bodies.

Dead bodies are sometimes more responsive than living bodies. Likewise, thermometers, barometers, hygroscopes, and other scientific instruments are much more responsive than man.

Each and every particle of the universe is responsive. I think they are also sensitive. Let me explain what I mean.

Man is the most sensitive of the animals we know. The other animals are less sensitive the lower their organization. Plants are even less sensitive. It is a continuous ladder. It does not end at the frontier of living matter, because there is no frontier. It is artificial, like all frontiers.

We call the sensitivity of the superior animals joy and sorrow, suffering and excitement, pleasure and pain. The feelings of the inferior animals are not so intense. We do not know their names and have no notion of them. We are even more ignorant of the feelings of plants and inorganic bodies. The intensity of their sensitivity is close to nil. I say this based on the fact that when death comes or organic matter becomes inorganic, sensitivity ends. If it ceases when someone faints because of a cardiac arrest, it vanishes all the more so when a living thing is totally destroyed.

Feeling disappears, but even a dead body retains responsiveness. It only becomes less intense, and the scientist has more access to it than does the average person.

Man can describe his joys and agonies. We believe him. We believe he feels just as we feel, although there is no hard proof of this: an interesting example of faith in something unscientific. By crying and moving, the higher animals make us guess that their feelings are like ours. But lower beings are incapable even of this. They only escape from what threatens them: that is, they engage in tropism. Plants are often incapable of doing even this. Does this mean they feel nothing? The inorganic world is also incapable of telling us about itself, but this does not mean it has no inferior form of sensitivity.

Various parts of the universe differ only in the degree of their sensitivity, which varies continuously from zero to an indefinitely large magnitude in supreme beings, that is, in beings more perfect than people. They have evolved from people or live on different planets.

Everything is continuous; everything is one. Matter is one, as is its responsiveness and sensitivity. The degree of sensitivity depends on combinations of matter. Just as the living world, in terms of its complexity and perfection, represents a continuous ladder that descends to "dead" matter, so too does the power of feeling represent a similar ladder that does not vanish even at the frontier of life. If a mechanical event like responsiveness does not cease, why should sensitivity—a phenomenon incorrectly identified as mental, that is, having nothing in common with matter—cease? (We ascribe materiality to this word.) Both sets of phenomena occur simultaneously and harmoniously, never abandoning either the living or the dead. Although, on the other hand, the dead have so few sensations that theoretically or roughly speaking we could say they are absent. If a white speck of dust lands on a black piece of paper, it would not be grounds for calling it white. The white speck is like the sensitivity of the dead.

In terms of mathematics, the entire universe is alive, but the power of its sensitivity is manifested in all its brilliance only among the higher animals. All atoms of matter feel in keeping with the environment. Finding itself in highly organized beings, atoms live their lives and feel their pleasure and pain. If they find themselves in the inorganic world, they sleep, as it were, immersed in a deep state of unconsciousness, in nothingness.

Even in a single animal, as they wander around its body, the atoms live the life now of the brain, now of the bones, hair, nails, epithelium, and so on. Meaning that atoms now think, now live like atoms imprisoned in stone, water, or air. Now they sleep, with no awareness of time; now they live for the moment, like the lower beings; now they are aware of the past and paint a picture of the future. The more organized the being, the farther this notion of future and past extends.

I am not only a materialist but also a panpsychist who acknowledges the sensitivity of the entire universe. I consider this property inalienable from matter. Everything is alive, but conventionally we regard as living only what demonstrates a sufficiently intense power of feeling. Since all material, under favorable conditions, can always go into an organic state, theoretically we can say that inorganic matter is potentially alive.

The Three Bases of the Argument

Our argument is based on three principles or elements: time, space, and energy. Everything else is derived from them, even sensitivity. These three notions are typical only of superior intelligence and are its products, that is, the structure of the brain.

The simplest notion is time. It has two directions, past and future, and a certain magnitude, that is, it is measurable like any magnitude. Like any magnitude, it is infinite, that is, it has neither beginning nor end. I mean to say that there is an indefinite amount of time in the universe. All atoms are generously endowed with time. All enormous spans of time, both known and imagined, are absolutely nil compared with the reserves of time in nature. Never-ending time is the cosmos's supreme gift to all of its parts, and thus to man as well.

The notion of space is more complicated. It not only has numerous directions but we also attribute different shapes, volumes, and so on to it.

In nature, space is boundless. It is as abundant as time.

So atoms are also endowed with inexhaustible and boundless space.

Energy is a more complicated notion. It derives from the notions of time and space.

These three elements of the argument are abstract, that is, they do not exist discretely in the universe. But they all merge in the notion of matter. They define it. Without matter, neither time nor space nor energy would exist. On the contrary, everywhere we find one of these notions, we find matter as well. It is defined by these three notions. They are quite subjective, of course. We believe there is little point in going into their essence.

The Law of Recurrence

Some deny infinity altogether. But it is either one or the other: finitude or infinity. There can be no opinion in between. Limiting any magnitude is something that cannot be allowed. So we are left to accept the only thing we can accept: infinity.

It used to be thought that Earth was unique. The heavens were the only other thing, but they had nothing to do with Earth. The stars, the Sun, and the Moon were all gods.

Then science discovered that our unique Sun harbors more than a thousand planets like Earth. The Sun was likewise considered unique. It had mainly passed for the chief god. But then several thousand million suns, none of them a whit worse than our Sun, were found. And since they are ringed by hundreds of planets, just like our Sun, the number of earths has increased by hundreds of billions. The group of suns, along with their retinues of planets, is called the Milky Way, a so-called spiral nebula. From a sufficient distance, this multitude of suns would indeed resemble a barely visible hazy spot.

Currently, we have identified around a million such nebulae.

Hence it is clear that the number of planets in the cosmos has increased a million times and has reached the hundreds of millions of billions (10^{17}). This means 100 million planets for every inhabitant of Earth.

The facts take us no further. But the imagination and the mind suggest that the million spiral nebulae or milky ways we have discovered also constitute a single group, an astronomical entity of the fourth order. I have grounds for calling it an ethereal island. But is it possible that it is unique in nature, for it takes up an infinitely small part of total space? Is the other infinite part of space really empty? Where there is space, there must be matter as well. And since space is boundless, the extent of matter cannot be limited either.

We conclude that the number of ethereal islands is endless. The group of these islands constitutes an entity of the fifth order. The number of astronomical entities is probably as boundless as time and space; that is, there exists a sixth order, and a seventh order, ad infinitum.

Cosmic Events Are Frequent: The Universe Has Generally Always Had the Same Shape

People tend to think everything dies the way they themselves die. By death, they mean the eternal extinction of life or a particular condition. This is one of the mind's illusions, so-called anthropomorphism or likening the environment to human life. The anthropomorphist thinks a stick, hill, blade of glass, and insect think and do as he himself thinks and does. For example, a stone is born, grows, and dies. A hill ponders. A bacterium figures things out. An amoeba is cunning, and so forth.

But it is impossible not to believe in the reverse process: regeneration. Is not the birth of plants, animals, and people a process that reverses dying? Do we see only the destruction of organisms? Creation, the opposite event, is just as prevalent. It is even stronger than dying, since the number of organisms on Earth increases continuously. If a supreme state of well-being is maintained, Earth's population could increase a thousand times. If it were not for the limited solar energy allocated to Earth, the whole of it could be turned into a living thing. The entire planet would then come to life from its very depths. After imagining this picture, can we doubt matter's vitality? The brain and soul are mortal. When the end comes, they are destroyed. But atoms or parts of atoms are immortal, and so decomposed matter is regenerated and again provides life, even more perfect life, according to the law of progress.

The planets were shining suns that burnt out. All suns await the same fate. They must burn out. Their radiation, the source of life, ceases, and the living world on the planets dies. The universe should become like a windowless, doorless dungeon. But is this possible? Would it last forever? The universe has existed for an infinite amount of time, and if the suns had faded, the thousands of billions of suns we now see in the milky ways would not exist.

Astronomers rarely observe the fading of suns; new suns emerge more often. Several of them appear in the Milky Way every century. This is true of other spiral nebulae. Eruptions of emerging suns occur there as well.

This is the answer to the riddle of the Milky Way's eternal glow and that of the million other spiral nebulae. Although suns are extinguished, new suns ignite in their place.

So suns shine for billions of years, reviving the matter on frozen planets. Then their surfaces cool and they cease radiating. But the atomic process underway within them do not stop. They amass radioactive matter, which produces a substance that is basic and quite elastic. This issues in an explosion, that is, the advent of a temporary star and the formation of a rarefied gas cloud, which in fact produces a star with planets and their satellites a billion years later.

Spiral nebulae (terribly distant groups of suns or milky ways) also die; that is, their suns fuse and turn into extremely rarefied matter.

The fusion of the stars in each milky way is inevitable according to the theory of relativity, but it takes an enormous amount of time, which can be calculated. It is billions of times longer than the life of a single solar system. The fusion is followed by a period of shining, then cooling. Next there is an explosion, and a nebula, that is, a rudimentary milky way, takes shape. It is resurrected, again generating a milky way consisting of a group of suns. Proof of this occurrence is provided by the hundreds of thousands of nebulae always visible to giant telescopes. If some of them fade away, others are regenerated from the invisible, faded ones. It is the same with a group of milky ways; that is, an ethereal island must have a temporary end. But there are a multitude of ethereal islands. If one of them is transformed into basic matter, another arises from it. All astronomical entities live and die, only to arise again. Rather, they are only transfigured, forming now a complex substance, now a basic substance, and appearing to us now in the shape of the starry sky, now as a cloud of rarefied, mostly invisible gas.

If the lifetime of a solar system is billions (10^{12}) of years, the lifetime of the Milky Way (a third-order astronomical entity) lasts for quadrillions (10^{24}) of years, and the life of an ethereal island lasts sextillions (10^{36}) of years. The more complex the astronomical entity, the higher its class, the longer its recurring life cycle. What is the outcome? The conclusion is that the universe has generally always presented one and the same picture. Although our planetary system was in fact a nebula billions of years ago, the shape of the Milky Way has remained unchanged for quadrillions of years. It was a cluster of hundreds of millions of stars of various ages, from planetary nebulae to dark suns with frozen surfaces. And although the Milky Way was a mass of extremely rarefied matter quadrillions of years ago, other milky ways existed in the ethereal island, milky ways consisting of conglomerations of suns, and its aspect, on average, has changed almost negligibly for sextillions of years. Similarly, the ethereal island was temporarily destroyed, but a group of them, or fifth-order entities, lived as before, consisting of numerous surviving ethereal islands. Each contained millions of milky ways, and each of the latter, in turn, consisted of hundreds of millions of solar systems, and each solar system, of hundreds of planets.

So the universe has always contained a multitude of planets illuminated by solar rays.

The limited human mind cannot encompass cosmic infinity. But let us imagine we could observe one of our ethereal islands over the course of sextillions of years. What would we see? In each of the milky ways that comprise it, suns would fade away time and again, and nebulae would occur, turning into gigantic suns and then into planetary systems. Our planetary system must also have died and emerged many times.

Many billions of years pass again, and we see the suns in all the milky ways gradually merging. They approach unity and, many trillions of years later, extinction, having gone through a preliminary period of unimaginable brilliance caused by the collision and fusion of suns. So we see, after quadrillions of years, the extinction of milky ways, their conversion into nebulae, and their recurrence as clusters of solar systems.

An ethereal island lasts for sextillions of years, and its milky ways are destroyed and emerge many times. Ultimately, however, the milky ways fuse, and the ethereal island is itself destroyed, only to arise once again in the full brilliance of its life.

When did the universe begin? If we limit ourselves to the ethereal island, the beginning of the universe could be regarded as an "island"-like state in the guise of amorphous matter. But we must not forget that this "beginning" is only the beginning of a period and recurs an infinite number of times.

If we regard a milky way as the cosmos, the universe begins as a gaseous state. And this "beginning," of course, is only the beginning of one of an infinite number of recurring periods.

Finally, if we restrict the world to a solar system, then the cosmos begins when it takes on the form of quite rarefied matter.

The Frequency of the Formation of Atoms and Their States in Celestial Bodies

The universe is made up of simple and complex bodies. We know of around ninety simple bodies. There are likely to be many more. There are billions of complex bodies, an unimaginable quantity. They are made up of simple bodies. Before our very eyes, however, the simple bodies are also transfigured into even simpler bodies, that is, with a smaller atomic weight. Science now has a good deal of grounds for arguing that the ninety known chemical elements consist of hydrogen. Astronomy confirms this hypothesis. Embryonic suns, that is, planetary nebulae, contain a very small quantity of the simplest elements. Later, they generate suns, which contain known and unknown simple bodies. Thus, what man has made a supreme effort to see only recently, nature has been producing continuously since time immemorial, albeit slowly.

The whole variety of the so-called chemical elements and their compounds derives from much simpler, possibly uniform matter (substance—essence—origin). On the contrary, when extinct suns explode, forming planetary nebulae, complex matter is turned into simple matter. Moreover, both processes always occur simultaneously, but now one prevails, now the other. Decomposition (analysis) prevails in complex substances, in suns, while composition (synthesis) predominates in elementary, simple matter.

Through the transformations of the astronomical entities we have described, the entire mass of matter not only is dislocated or intermixes, but simple bodies also turn into complex bodies, and vice versa. I mean that gold, lead, and other elements turn into hydrogen and helium, and vice versa, hydrogen, helium, and other simple bodies with a small atomic weight turn into gold, silver, iron, aluminum, and so on. I also want to say that the core parts of celestial bodies end up on their surface, and vice versa. In short, everything continuously and frequently moves and transforms. The process of exchange and transformation among the elements has always been occurring, in addition to catastrophic events. All suns emit and lose matter, but they also absorb matter. Shining suns lose more than they receive, while it is the reverse with dark suns. Planets are, of course, no exception in this case. They always possess at least a small degree of radioactivity.

Monism

We preach monism in the universe, nothing more. The entire scientific process consists in the quest for monism, unity, the elementary principle. Its success depends on the extent to which it achieves unity. Monism in science is due to the structure of the cosmos. Did Darwin and Lamarck not seek monism in biology? Do geologists not want the same thing? Physics and chemistry draw us in the same direction. Astronomy and astrophysics have proven the uniform configuration of the celestial bodies, the similarity between Earth and sky, and the homogeneity of their substance and radiant energy. Even the historical sciences tend toward monism.

In biology, the cells of inferior beings combine to form animals with a single control center (brain—soul), and people combine into societies, seeking to fuse into one powerful body. The entire Earth must come together in this way. This unification must have achieved supreme results on other planets.

I shall add to the known types of unity matter's universal sensitivity, the potential ability of each atom to live in a complex environment. The brain thinks, but it is the atoms, its components, that feel. The brain is destroyed, and the intense feeling of the atoms has disappeared, replaced by the feeling of nothingness, close to nil.

The Timely Advent of Organic Life on Such Large Planets as Earth Cannot Be Denied

The planets in different solar systems have much in common. They are composed of the same substances. If sufficiently large, they have seas and atmospheres. They are lit by the rays of suns, subject to the force of gravity, and have days and seasons. Why could life not be engendered on them as it has been on Earth? True, it is cold on planets distant from their star, and hot on those close to it. But every sun has a number of planets. Like Earth, some of them must be situated at a favorable distance from the star and thus be suitable for life. Theory suggests that all planets originally separated from the Sun, first coming into contact with it and then gradually retreating. So every planet, for a certain period of time, had temperature conditions suitable for life's spontaneous generation and growth. Nevertheless, every planet, including Earth, also lacked these conditions at one time. Likewise, every planet that now has a favorable degree of warmth will eventually forfeit it as it moves away from its star. In addition, this selfsame central star, as it flares up or fades, provides all planets with opportunities to develop life, regardless of their changing distance from it.

Some planets are small and therefore bereft of liquids and atmospheres. Others are gigantic and therefore are still hot. And when they have cooled off, they will have moved far from their sun and ceased to receive enough of its radiation. So neither small nor large planets have generated life.

We should note, however, that these "moments" can last billions of years, which is sufficient for the conception and evolution of organisms.

Conceived at the proper moment, life does not perish when conditions change, since the changes occur gradually, and life manages to adapt to them.

Small planets have no atmosphere. This seemingly interferes with the emergence of life.

We will not argue this point now. The conclusion is still that most large planets or, rather, planets with gaseous membranes either are habitable, were habitable, or will be habitable.

What to Expect from Mankind

It is hard to imagine the process of life's evolution on some planet without turning to Earth. What can we expect from the world's population?

Man has made a great journey from "dead" matter to unicellular beings, and thence to his present semi-animal state. Will he come to the end of his road? If he does, it will not happen now, for we see the giant strides of progress currently being made in science, technology, and with respect to mankind's living conditions and social structure. They point to changes in man himself. At any rate, these changes must occur.

However, for the time being man himself has changed very little, bearing the remnants of animal passions and instincts, and displaying a weakness of mind and a fondness for routine. In terms of social evolution, he even yields to ants and bees. But he has generally surpassed the animals and, consequently, has made huge progress. Nothing stops immediately, nor will man stop in his own development, the more so since the mind has long ago hinted at his moral shortcomings, but the animal propensities are stronger for the time being, and the mind cannot overcome them.

We can soon expect the advent of a rational, moderate social system on Earth that will harmonize with man's qualities and his limitations. Unification will come, leading to the cessation of war, since there will be no one to fight against. The happy social order, as suggested by geniuses, will cause technology and science to advance with incredible rapidity, improving everyday human life with the same rapidity. This will involve increased reproduction. The population will grow a thousand times, and man will become Earth's real master. He will transfigure the dry land, alter the atmosphere's makeup, and make extensive use of the oceans. The climate will change as desired or required. All of Earth will be rendered habitable and made to bear great fruits. [...]

There will be full scope for nurturing man's social and individual traits, as long as they are harmless to others.

It is difficult to imagine the mental world of future man, his security and comfort, his understanding of the universe, his quiet joy and confidence in serene, unending happiness. Not a single billionaire has anything like it now.

Future technology will make it possible to overcome Earth's gravity and travel through the entire solar system. All its planets will be visited and researched. Imperfect worlds will be eliminated and replaced with our own population. The Sun will be ringed with artificial dwellings, built from material borrowed by asteroids, planets, and their satellites. This will allow for the existence of a population two billion times more numerous than Earth's population. In part, Earth will surrender its excess population to the colonies in the heavens, and in part, the resettled cadres will themselves multiply. This reproduction would happen terribly quickly, since an enormous amount of eggs and sperm would be expended on the cause.

Billions of billions of beings will grow and evolve around the Sun near the asteroids. A variety of breeds of perfected beings will be produced: breeds suited for living in different atmospheres, at different gravities, on different planets; breeds suited for living amid the vacuum or rarefied gas, for living with food or without it; breeds living only on solar radiation, capable of withstanding heat, cold, and abrupt, substantial temperature changes.

The most dominant breed, however, will be the most perfect type of organism, dwelling in the ether and nourished directly by solar energy like a plant.

After our solar system has been populated, other solar systems in our Milky Way will be settled. Man will find it hard to separate himself from Earth. It will have been much easier to overcome the Sun's gravity owing to the freedom of movement in the ether and the immensity of the Sun's radiant energy, which man will have been able to use to his benefit. Earth is the starting point for the resettlement of perfect creatures in the Milky Way. When they encounter a desert or immature, ugly world, they will painlessly eliminate it, replacing it with their own world. Where good fruit can be anticipated, they will leave it to ripen. Earth's population has traveled a hard road. Its way has been long and anguished. And there still is plenty of time left for painful progress. This way is undesirable. But by resettling in its own spiral nebula, that is, the Milky Way, Earth can eliminate this hard road for others and replace it with an easy road that excludes suffering and does not take the billions of years required for autogenesis.

Populating the Universe

We have the same right to expect from other planets what we expect from our planet.

The beginnings of life were manifested in their time on all planets endowed with atmospheres. But on some planets, because of their advanced age and conditions, life blossomed more luxuriantly and rapidly, giving beings technological and mental power, and becoming the source of supreme life for other planets in the universe. They were centers for the dissemination of perfect life. These streams encountered each other and settled the Milky Way without hindering each other. All of them had a single goal: populating the universe with a perfect world for the common good. How could anyone be opposed to this? In their travels, they encountered rudimentary cultures, deformed cultures, backward cultures, and normally evolving cultures. In some places, they eliminated life, while in others they left it to evolve and renew itself. In the vast majority of cases, they found life that was backward, in the shape of mollusks, worms, and unicellular or even more primitive animals.

There was no point in waiting billions of years for it to painfully evolve and produce conscious, sentient beings. It is much quicker, simpler, and more painless to reproduce more sophisticated, available breeds. I think we should not wait for wolves and bacteria on Earth to turn into human beings, but had better reproduce its most successful specimens.

The sowers of supreme life reasoned in the same way. In some places, they destroyed embryonic primitive life or monstrously misshapen life; in other places, they waited for good fruit and the renewal of cosmic life.

So the other milky ways (groups of suns or spiral nebulae) were settled without suffering. The same thing happened in all the ethereal islands and throughout the entire boundless universe. From the most favorable, happy locations, life spread to neighboring suns without going through the agonizing process of autogenesis and thus quickly filling the infinite wastes.

Intelligence and supreme forms of social organization have prevailed and will prevail in the universe. Intelligence is what leads to each atom's eternal well-being. Intelligence is supreme egoism or true egoism.

Worlds in a state of infancy, like Earth, are a rare exception in the cosmos. Are there many people on Earth who are one day old? There are even fewer people who have just been born. And infants who are only one second old amount to only one among the one and half billion people on Earth. Similarly, there are few worlds in a state of infancy. There are particularly few of them in the universe owing to the fact that most settling of worlds is carried out through emigration. A ready-made, perfect semblance of mankind colonized the cosmos.

What are our conclusions? We see a boundless universe, populated by an infinite number of decillions of perfect beings, produced by painless reproduction and resettlement. Pockets of life as on Earth are extremely rare exceptions, like an infant who is a third of a second old. So Earth's agonizing life is a rarity, because it was produced by autogenesis, not by resettlement. As the more advantageous process, resettlement prevails in the cosmos. For man cultivates carrots and apples from preexisting organisms. What madness it would be were he to want to produce them through spontaneous generation (autogony).

It would be possible only if he were willing to wait a million years for carrots to emerge.

But spontaneous generation is allowed in the cosmos, albeit extremely rarely, owing to the need to renew or replenish perfect beings. They sometimes degenerate and are eliminated as a result of occasionally occurring regressions. A fresh influx is necessary. Otherwise, perfect life could fade away or be displaced by deformed life.

The role of Earth and a few similar plants, albeit agonizing, is an honorable one. The improved batch of life from Earth is meant to replenish the losses incurred by regressive breeds in the cosmos.

A heavy lot, a tremendous feat, has fallen to Earth's population. Few planets receive it, hardly one in a billion. It could not be otherwise. If it were otherwise, it would contradict the intelligence of perfect beings, that is, the supreme egoism, but they would not work to their own detriment.

Some share of the suffering in the cosmos is a bitter necessity in view of the possibility that beings can devolve, regress, move backward.

But it can be said that organic life in the universe is in brilliant condition. All living beings are happy, and this happiness is hard for man to understand.

Burdened by the eyesore of earthly chaos, you might object. How can you say that when there are so many unfortunates on Earth?

Shall we call snow black because of a few microscopically minuscule black flecks of dust on its surface? For snow glitters in a such a way that it hurts the eyes. Are we afraid to lose a lottery if one ticket in a trillion is a losing ticket? We are not even afraid to die this year, although the likelihood of death is at least 2 to 3 percent.

The Feeling of the Atom or Its Parts

We have seen that each atom, that is, each constituent part of the cosmos, is transformed during upheavals, during the infinitely recurring long and short lifetimes of all astronomical entities, during their disintegration and resurrection. The atom now decays, and its weight or mass decreases; now it is generated, and its atomic weight increases. Heavy (massive) elements turn into light elements, and vice versa. It is a necessary condition of the frequency of suns, milky ways, and other astronomical entities. One thing is bound up with another. If it were not for the transmutation of elements, astronomical entities would not emerge with a particular frequency, and vice versa.

Moreover, the atom moves, for example, from a celestial body's central parts to its edges, from suns to planets, and back. And this recurs endlessly.

This makes it clear that there is not a single atom that has not been involved countless times in higher animal life.

Thus, entering the atmosphere or soil of planets, the atom sometimes becomes part of the brains of higher beings. Then it lives their life and feels the joy of being conscious and serene.

Suppose the realization of this instance requires billions of years. Yet the atom is involved in life countless times. Time is endless, and however colossal the intervals into which we divide it, the number of these intervals is infinitely large. In other words, the time in which the atom is involved in higher life (and there is no other life, in general) is endless in an absolute sense. This involvement never ceases.

But, you say, relatively speaking, it is tiny, since the brief periods of life are divided by billions of years of nonexistence. But oblivion counts for nothing in subjective time; it does not exist, as it were. What exists is a single, supreme, conscious, happy life that never ceases. To understand this better, let us discuss absolute and subjective time and its flow.

Absolute time is what would be observed by a being that is steadily alive, that never dies and never sleeps. This being is imaginary, of course. Absolute time is defined by hours, the rotation of celestial bodies, and man-made chronometers.

Subjective time is something quite different. It is the apparent time experienced by organisms. It flows at different speeds in one and the same being. It flows now quickly, now slowly, depending on the impressions produced by one's environment, mental state, or thoughts. It depends on how the brain functions. It flows faster during sleep. But even in this case its progress depends on the abundance of dreams. In dreamless, heavy slumber, subjective time is nearly imperceptible. It is even more imperceptible when one loses consciousness. But often time flows imperceptibly when one is happy and impressions are many. (Happy people do not notice the hours going by.)

We will not discuss the subjective time of various animals. Among the higher animals, its flow is probably similar to its flow in man, but it is hard to picture among the lower animals. Perhaps their lives are like sleep among humans. They have a feeble conception of time. There is no past or future, only the present moment.

We are not so interested in the subjective time of inferior beings, since the cosmos in general is teeming with life even higher than human life.

There is almost no space left for lower life. And the human condition, as we have seen, is semi-animal, transitional, and infantile, and occupies an inconspicuous place in the cosmos.

Mature life dominates, and it is mature life that interests us most of all.

Likewise, the notion of subjective time among the dead—that is, that of the atom in an inorganic body, in the air, water, and soil—is interesting. This is an even more dominant state of matter.

Here we see more than a loss of consciousness, and so the flow of time is almost completely imperceptible in this case. Not only years but also billions of billions of years fly by like a second for a living being. After realizing this, can we be afraid of "inorganic" time or count it?

So the vast periods of nonbeing do not exist as it were for the atom. The only thing that exists are the periods when it dwells in living organic matter, mainly, in the brains of higher beings.

No matter how brief the life spans, by recurring an infinite number of times, they add up to infinite subjective and absolute time. It never stops and never has stopped. The past is as boundless as the future.

Therefore, the duration of life of any atom is not only unlimited in time but also subjectively continuous. It is also continuous in the sense that the feeling of life never ends, although it experiences an abrupt change with each death or birth. The atom is always alive and always happy, despite the absolutely enormous gaps of nonexistence or being in inorganic substances. But since incarnation is inevitable in view of all the foregoing and time's infinity, all these incarnations subjectively merge into one subjectively continuous, beautiful, endless life.

What can we conclude regarding man, animal, and every atom, whatever the situation it finds itself in?

When the body is destroyed, an atom of the individual, his brain or other body parts (as well as the atom's ejection from the body, which occurs many times during its lifetime), initially ends up in an inorganic environment. Calculations show that, on average, hundreds of millions of years are needed for it to be reincarnated. This time passes for the atom like nothing. Subjectively, it does not exist. But Earth's population will be completely transformed during this time span. The globe will then be covered only with higher forms of life, and our atom would use only them.

So death puts an end to all suffering and provides, subjectively, immediate happiness.

If much more time accidentally passed—billions of billions of years—this would be in no way worse for the atom. Earth would no longer exist, and the atom would be incarnated on another planet or other abodes of life, no less beautiful.

It is extremely improbable that the atom would be incarnated on Earth a few hundred years later and therefore be part of the animals, not yet destroyed, or imperfect man. Life in plants and lower beings does not count, as it is almost insensible. Life in higher organisms is like a dream, but life in higher animals, although it is horrible from man's viewpoint, is subjectively thoughtless. Cows, sheep, horses, and monkeys do not feel its humiliation, just as man does not currently feel the humiliation of his own life. But the superior beings regard man with pity, as we regard dogs and rats.

When people believe in the possibility, however small, of their atoms living in the bodies of animals, they will try harder to eliminate the animal world. It is a slight threat to us for our cruelty to lower earthly beings.

Likewise, the atom's rare potential existence in the body of modern man encourages us to improve and eliminate all backward breeds.

A Picture of the Atom's Sensual Life

Those who have not thought their whole lives about what I have recounted would find it hard to picture the atom's sensual adventures clearly. But I shall offer a comparison so that the reader may understand and appreciate the atom's continuous, boundless life.

We shall neglect only the period of infancy, the emergence of organic matter, whose use and value is as imperceptible in the cosmos as a microscopic fleck of dirt on a mirror or snow-white sheet of paper.

Imagine if our lives consisted of a series of happy dreams. The individual awakens, ponders his beautiful dream for a second, and then hastens to get back to sleep in order to plunge into bliss again. In each dream, he forgets who he is, and he is a new character in each dream. Now he imagines he is Ivanov, now Vasilyev, now someone else. His second dream is not a continuation of the first dream, and the third dream is a not continuation of the second. Neither is any dream linked to the one before it.

But the happiness is obvious. All the dreams are lovely, eliciting joy alone, and they never end. The person has always dreamed them and will go on dreaming them.

What else would you want? You are continuously happy. This easily imagined picture gives us a certain notion of how each atom in the universe lives, wherever it is found. We have given you a rough idea of the sensual life of all and sundry.

When you tell people about it, they are unhappy. They definitely want the second life to be a continuation of the one before it. They want to see friends and relatives. They want to live what they have lived through. "Would I really never see my wife, son, mother, or father?" they bitterly exclaim. "Then it would be better not to live at all. In short, your theory is no consolation to me."

But how would you be able to see your friends when your notion of them has been generated by your brain, which shall definitely be destroyed? Dogs, elephants, and flies will not see their kith and kin for the same reason, and man is no exception. The dying bid an eternal farewell to their environment, for it is situated in their brains, and their brains come undone. It occurs when the atom once again ends up in a brain, someone else's brain. The brain provides it with an environment, but a different one, with no connection to the first.

You were happy with your charming dreams, waking up joyfully each time only to plunge back into them. What is it that you want? Now you want to meet the dead, but death will exterminate this desire as well. Your dissatisfaction is possible only while you are alive. When life goes, dissatisfactions go too.

In a previous life, we had friends, but do we see them in this life? Do we say, I know that fellow well, though I have never seen him and never heard of him?

All that survives in the new life is happiness and pleasure.

How difficult it is to shrug off routine and acknowledge the truth. It is just as hard as feeling the Earth move.

But there is a difference between a number of beautiful but unrelated dreams and the numerous real lives lived by the atom.

These lives are as conscious as the lives of the sages, not vague and confused like dreams. In the intervals between dreams, we feel something, albeit briefly, namely, a single life.

We feel nothing in the intervals between the atom's lives, despite their vastness. They do not exist for us. The atom's life is subjective, continuous, without beginning or end, since all its discrete lives merge into one. Each of the discrete lives can be imagined as a wave in an endless series of waves.

Real life—the wave—has a beginning and an end, and it is a single life span amid a multitude of them.

All these life spans are, in fact, fairly monotonous: happiness, pleasure, awareness of the universe, awareness of one's endless destiny, understanding of the truth that there is a right path to maintaining the cosmos in a brilliant state of perfection.

But each wave has a beginning and an end: emergence and extinction, conception and decay. They recur in the following wave. However, we would be wrong to consider the waves identical. Waves can be quite long, that is, a single life span can be quite great, continuing for hundreds and thousands of years, but it is definitely all the same to the atom, since life's short waves, merging into one, also produce infinity. There will be no death pangs. Only the life of the organism, despite this, should not be short, so that the being can evolve and be abundantly fruitful during its span. What is the point of an expensive machine that breaks down and falls apart in two hours?

Summary

Along with its moons, any planet in the universe is an astronomical entity of the first order, for example, our Earth, Jupiter, and so on.

Any solar system in the cosmos, for example, our planetary system, is an astronomical entity of the second order. (An astronomical unit is something else.)

Any spiral nebula, consisting of hundreds of millions of solar systems, is an entity of the third order. One such entity is our spiral nebula, the Milky Way.

We shall call the "ethereal island," consisting of hundreds of thousands of spiral nebulae, an astronomical entity of the fourth order. But, in keeping with the law of recurring entities, there must be a multitude of them, and their totality is an entity of the fifth order.

According to the same law, just as there are different classes in arithmetic, there should be an endless number of different orders.

Now we shall briefly summarize what seems undeniable.

1. There is no denying the unity or uniformity in the universe's structure and formation: the unity of matter, light, life's gravity, and so on.
2. There is no denying the universe's overall consistency, because new suns arise to replace extinct ones.
3. There is no denying that the number of planets is infinite, because time and space are infinite. Wherever they exist, so too must matter exist.
4. There is no denying that some planets enjoy conditions favorable to life's development. The number of such planets is infinite, because a part of infinity is also an infinity.
5. There is no denying that animal life on certain planets has reached its supreme stage of development, surpassing human development, and that it is ahead of the development of life on other planets.
6. There is no denying that this superior organic life has attained great scientific and technological might, which would allow its population to disseminate not only within its own solar system but also in neighboring solar systems and all other solar systems. (Cf. my essays on airplanes, dirigibles, jet devices, the richness of the universe, and solar energy, among other things.)
7. There is no denying that superior life is disseminated in the vast majority of instances by means of reproduction and resettling, not by means of spontaneous generation, as on Earth, because it eliminates the delays and pangs of gradual evolution, and because the mind of conscious beings understands the advantages of this means of settling the cosmos. Earth will be populated not by transforming wolves and monkeys into men, but by reproducing man himself. We produce vegetables and fruits not by growing bacteria, but by using available, perfected plants.
8. There is thus no denying that the universe is filled with higher consciousness and perfect life.
9. There is no denying that the atom is now simple, now complicated, periodically adopting the guise of all the chemical elements.
10. There is no denying that astronomical entities are cyclical. For example, a sun cools, then it explodes and turns into a rarefied gaseous mass that once again produces a brilliant sun ringed by planets. Then the same

cycle recurs. Yet matter is mixed, and the chemical elements transform into each other.

11. There is no denying that the atom has the inherent capacity to experience life when it is part of an animal's brain. Thus, it must live the lives of different beings consecutively.
12. There is no denying that the atom's experience does not vanish in organic matter, but is close to nil and can be called nothingness.
13. There is no denying, in view of the fact that substances and chemical elements are mixed and transformed, that there is no atom that has not been periodically involved in organic life, that is, has not been in the brains of higher beings from time to time after intervals of billions of years.
14. There is no denying that time is nearly nonexistent to an atom within an inorganic substance, that time in this state is nothing to it, an oblivion, like fainting. This huge amount of time does not exist subjectively.
15. There is no denying that, subjectively, all the atom's relatively brief moments of life in the brains of beings merge into a single continuous life.
16. There is no denying that the existence in the universe of imperfect animals such as our monkeys, cows, wolves, deer, hares, rats, and the like is of no benefit to the atom. Likewise, the existence of imperfect people and similar beings elsewhere in the universe is of no benefit.
17. There is no denying that all sentient beings become aware that imperfection in the cosmos is inadmissible.
18. There is no denying that the perfect is stronger than the imperfect and therefore, impelled by genuine egoism, painlessly eliminates all that is imperfect and anguished. Spontaneous generation should be allowed quite rarely in order to renew and replenish regressive superior life. Such, perhaps, is Earth's martyr-like, honorable role.
19. There is no denying that the painful extinction of imperfect species is advantageous to the atom, that is, to all the living and the dead.
20. There is no denying that, as a consequence of this, the atom can find itself only in a supreme being, for there are no other beings at all. Consequently, its infinite existence can only be serene, intelligent, conscious, and happy.

We do not notice a gray fleck of dust on a snow-white field. So we can also ignore the few planets doomed to the agony of spontaneous generation.

Let us repeat what we have just said in different terms.

1. Can we really doubt that an innumerable number of planets are periodically illuminated by suns?
2. Can we really doubt that life on one of these plants has attained such might and perfection that we humans would find it hard to imagine? It encourages us to overcome the force of gravity and resettle throughout the universe.
3. The outcome will be the dissemination of perfection and the dominion of reason throughout the cosmos.
4. Can we really doubt that this has already occurred endlessly long ago and that it is the universe's perennial natural condition? Spontaneous generation and the agonies it entails are merely a rare exception.
5. Can we really doubt that any atom that finds itself in a brain lives? It does not give orders, it does not rule, but merely feels life like a record feels the air vibrating in the horn of a phonograph. Only no recording is left on the atom.
6. Can we really doubt that matter is mixed and periodically transformed, and that every atom takes part in life an infinite number of times, albeit after enormous spans of time?
7. Can we really doubt that the time an atom dwells in inorganic matter passes like a strong fainting spell and thus does not exist for it?
8. Can we really doubt that the life spans subjectively merge into one seemingly continuous, happy, endless life?

So there is only truth, perfection, might, and satisfaction in the cosmos, leaving so little for everything else that we can regard it like a black fleck of dust on a white sheet of paper.

All my numerous works—finished and unfinished, published and unpublished—have a sole object: to prove the ideas set out briefly here or to conclude, ultimately, that the cosmos generally contains only joy, satisfaction, perfection, and truth. The contrary is small and imperceptible in the universe. We are blinded only by the Earth's proximity.

Translated by Thomas Campbell

10 Theorems of Life (as an Addendum and Clarification on Monism)

Konstantin Tsiolkovsky

I will not stop trying to understand what is most important to a conscious being: (1) the subjective continuity of life; (2) its limitlessness in either direction; and (3) its bliss. All this, it seems, is refuted by biological life on Earth. So as not to succumb to this misconception, we need to look at life from the height of cosmic space. Here I present only sixteen theorems of life. Matter is considered devoid of feeling by the majority of people. I do not agree with this. That is why we call any part of matter *spirit*.

Contents

First Theorem: All matter is alive at its core.
Second Theorem: No atom in the universe can avoid a complicated life.
Third Theorem: A mass of any size can produce spirit.
Fourth Theorem: The simplest spirit is an atom.
Fifth Theorem: The whole universe contains only spirits—simple and complex ones.
Sixth Theorem: An animal is a particular combination of simple spirits.
Seventh Theorem: Every animal or complex spirit consists of a multitude of spirits of varying complexity (atoms, molecules, cells, their aggregate, the whole animal).
Eighth Theorem: The death of an animal is the destruction or discord of this combination, and the creation of more elemental, or even simpler, spirits that feel independently and in their own way.
Ninth Theorem: Inversely, the birth of an animal or a plant is the formation of this combination from elemental spirits.
Tenth Theorem: The richness of spirit depends on its mass and organization.

Eleventh Theorem: The complexity of spirit is, generally, proportional to its mass.

Twelfth Theorem: A particle of matter, of any size, feels.

Thirteenth Theorem: Chemical, physical, and mechanical phenomena determine the life of a spirit.

Fourteenth Theorem: Where there is matter, there is also spirit.

Fifteenth Theorem: Being inside a body from birth to death is an illusion.

Sixteenth Theorem: Unity is an illusion.

First Truth: All matter is alive at its core.

All animals and plants feel. Can I doubt that my brother and my friend feel? The highest of animals express their pain and joy with shouts in their own language, which is incomprehensible to humans. (The language of several monkeys has been decoded, chicken breeders understand the language of chickens, and so on.) The lowest express their pain and joy with body movements. It is impossible to doubt, in general, that animals and plants, even single-celled organisms, have feelings.

Let's provisionally define that part of the world or that body that can feel happiness and sorrow as *spirit*.

Then we can say: where there is an animal or a human, there is spirit.

Therefore, there are many spirits, and will perhaps be even more, because the number of beings on Earth can increase indefinitely.

Moreover, since all matter, by way of an embryo (an egg), turns into an animal, then all matter is alive at its core as long as there is enough enlivening energy (for example, the rays of the Sun or the chemical energy of food).

However, one could object that these earthly animals consist of only twenty to eighty chemical compounds rather than all ninety-two, and that not all parts of matter can therefore be considered alive.

We can respond to this by saying that under different temperature conditions—radial energy, environment composition, and so on—other elements would also successfully take part in building organisms, as those twenty to thirty do (see my "Animal of the Cosmos" and L. L. Andreenko's "Life on Planets" in French).

Moreover, it is known that elements in the universe transform into one another, and that is why atoms of gold, iridium, and so on can form atoms of nitrogen, carbonate, and so on—which, as we well know, contribute to life. Therefore, there should be no doubt that all the elements of matter are able to participate in life.

Second Truth: No atom in the universe can avoid a complicated life.

Planets and suns are destroyed, mixed, created again; all matter (the elements) transforms. Therefore, there is no single particle of matter that wouldn't have been a part of something living and already participated in life an infinite number of times. For example, some time ago, the Earth and all that is on it was part of the Sun. Our bodies were also part of it. But this did not in any way prevent our bodies from becoming alive.

Even now, the origin or source of all elements is considered to be electrons and protons, and with the development of science they may find a single origin for all types of matter.

Here it becomes apparent that all matter is alive at its core, because it is uniform and has one origin (though science for now supposes two origins—protons and electrons, or positive and negative electricity—the conclusion remains the same).

Third Truth: A mass of any size can produce spirit.

Nature creates large animals, such as the elephant and the whale, and small ones, such as ciliates, insects, and so on. They all feel joy and sorrow, and therefore they are all spirits.

Thus, the existence of spirit is not confined to some definite minimal mass of matter. Both large and small masses can produce spirit. From the latter follows:

Fourth Truth: The basic, minimal spirit is a separate element of matter: an atom, an electron, ether, or some other unknown and uniform essence of matter.

This frequently suggests an incorrect conclusion, where the atom is ascribed the qualities of the brain with very complex, animal qualities: memory, reason, consciousness, physical force, and so on. This is a deep misconception.

The atom is only an atom, with all of its scientifically known and unknown mechanical qualities. It can be compared to the solar system. There is no equivalence or likeness here. But I would like to point out its mechanical nature.

An atom is relatively passive and only reflects the influence of its environment. When it is in a nonorganic environment, it can be compared to a still record. When it is in an organic environment, it can be compared to a spinning or playing record. It is also this way in the brain. The record is as passive as an atom. When the record is under the influence of some force, it talks, laughs, sings, barks, sounds as an orchestra, and so on. Likewise, an atom in the brain of an animal experiences the influence of the ethereal oscillations surrounding it in its brain (under the influence of the brain's activity), manifesting in a passive feeling of life.

However, even in the brain, an atom does not control the spirit: it remains passive. It is a brick in a building, or a particle of steel in a working machine. What controls the body and the mechanisms of being is its complex machinery, that is, the aggregate of all atoms in the body.

Fifth Truth: The whole universe consists of elemental and complex spirits.

For example: every sun or every galaxy consists only of elemental spirits, while planets, on their surfaces, have created plants and animals, that is, complex spirits.

Sixth Truth: A living organism is composed of a group of spirits combined in a very particular way.

From this follows:

Seventh Truth: Every animal or complex spirit is composed of a multitude of spirits or different levels of complexity (atoms, molecules, cells, their aggregate, and everything living) that feel in unique and independent ways.

Eighth Truth: The death of an animal or a plant is the disintegration of complex spirits into those that are more simple or elemental.

After the general life of a body stops, its cells still live a little longer and even reproduce. After the cells are destroyed, only molecular and atomic life remains.

Ninth Truth: Birth is the combination of various spirits into a single whole.

This is a union, or association, of elemental and complex spirits into a more or less complex combination.

Birth begins immediately after death with the reproduction of bacteria and other more complex organisms, into which the matter of a body is transformed, that is, atoms of primitive spirits.

In some cases, they are soon destroyed, leaving only atomic life. These primitive spirit-molecules and atoms enter the surface of the Earth and the atmosphere, and even prior to that, enter the composition of plant cells and begin cellular life. Then from grass and other plants they enter the bodies of more complex beings to live the life of unified cells, that is, they transition into the composition of various animals and humans.

Tenth Truth: The power of spirit, or the richness of spirit, depends on its mass and its organization.

For example, in descending order, based on their complexity, the spirits will be: the highest descendant of humans, humans, apes, dogs, fish, insects, infusoria, bacteria, molecules, atoms, and so on.

Eleventh Truth: The greater the mass of an animal, the more complex the spirit (in general, on average).

The more complex the machine, the more matter it requires, even though sometimes the opposite happens. In this way, a watch is more complex than many massive machines.

However, if we tried to achieve maximum complexity, it would generally grow with the additional material we have used to build a machine.

Nature also strives for the greatest perfection, which is possible only with the greatest complexity of an organism for its given mass. The complexity of machines is highly constrained by mass, owing to the large size of human hands and the large tools they use. Nature's creations are much smaller. The scale can become microscopic. However, even nature has limits owing to the particular size of an atom, and especially in the particularities of complex molecules. Therefore, the most insignificant cell has a much more complex substance than all that is produced by man. That is why each mosquito is more complex than our most intricate machines.

It is therefore clear that the larger the mass of an animal, the more opportunity it has to be complex and perfect. Of course, there are exceptions, as there are for human creations: for example, an elephant and a whale are simpler in their design than a human, and are therefore less intelligent. The same is true of the abundance of massive animals (for example, fish).

However, the organ of the mind is not the whole body, but simply the brain, and its size correlates more closely with the perfection of thought, even though here there are also many exceptions. Thus, people of genius frequently have an average-sized brain. Here, the complexity is in the form, the organization of the organ of thought, so to speak—in the quality of the brain.

However, there are still fewer deviations from the above law in the world of animals than there are in the area of human creation.

Thus, an elephant is one of the smartest animals. If it is less smart than a human, it is only because its brain is simpler.

The size of animals, of course, draws attention as the reason for the complexity of the body and the development of the brain. However, to avoid mistakes, one needs to pay attention to the quantity of nerve knots (ganglia) in the brain, which are responsible for memory and thinking. The brain of an elephant can be larger than a human's, but its organization is still simpler.

For creatures with a large body, its central management, of course, also increases the volume of the brain. But the brain's main part goes, apparently, to the mind and its elements: memory, thinking, creativity, and so on.

The scope of an animal's feelings, that is, its ability to suffer and to be happy, is also dependent on the number of nerve knots. We have shown this many times (see my "Mind and Passions").

Single-celled organisms are just chemical plants with complete spiritual equilibrium (when compared to humans). They do not have a nervous system. Insects already feel the sting of life. Fish are capable of feeling more suffering and joy. Overall, the larger the brain of an animal, the higher the amplitude of life's oscillations. A human being, in this respect, as in many other things, seems to represent an apex. The particularities (individuality) of a type have a great deal of influence on the oscillations of well-being.

Twelfth Truth: In a mathematical sense, every particle of matter, in nonorganic and organic form, feels.

Indeed, in the universe we see (1) mammals (for example, humans, dogs, rats, lions), beginning with the most complex (human) and ending with the simplest (mouse, and so on); (2) birds; (3) lizards; (4) amphibians; (5) fish; (6) mollusks; (7) insects; (8) worms; (9) single-celled organisms; (10) bacteria; (11) plants; (12) organic compounds; (13) nonorganic matter; (14) the ninety-two elements; (15) protons and charged particles; (16) hypothetically unified origins of matter (provisionally, ether).

Where in this list does the feeling of life begin and end: at the ability to reason, to feel happiness and sorrow, to respond to nature's influence?

Is it only humans who can think, or does this ability stop with a dog, a rat? Can anyone then deny that in nature we have a continuous chain, the links of which differ only quantitatively?

Likewise, is it possible to determine the boundary of the feeling of life—joy, sorrow? And here various beings differ only quantitatively.

Finally, the response of "dead" nature is exactly the same as that of the living.

Temperature, pressure, movement, electricity, the chemical influence of the environment, and so on—all this, in the qualitative sense, equally influences both dead and living matter. A wealth of material on these events has accumulated, which undoubtedly confirms that external manifestations of "dead" matter are equal to those of the "living."

Thirteenth Truth: Chemical, physical, and mechanical phenomena (in relation to the mechanics of the body) produce life with all its qualities: to feel pleasant and unpleasant, to think, to move.

Perhaps they will say that chemical, physical, and mechanical phenomena exist everywhere. Therefore, according to you, life is everywhere!

Yes, it is truly so, but what kind of life? Where there is no complex mechanism (such as the Sun), life is disorganized, primitive, and represents only the life of spirit-atoms, which is very simple and without any of the brain's influence. Within a chemical process there is the same exact life of separate atoms. In a piece of stone or metal there is also primitive, separate life. In a complex machine—for example, a calculating one—the chemical reaction is lacking, and in bacteria the brain and its intricate activity are absent.

An animal is a combination of a mechanism and chemical reactions. In the simplest of creatures the chemical life is complex, but the mechanism is simple. The higher the animal on the biological ladder, the greater its chemical quality, and the more intricate its mechanism. Both of these are revealed by its feelings of joy and sorrow and by the complex phenomena of memory, thinking, ideas, and muscle activities.

Thus, a complex animal is the combination of a mechanism and its chemical qualities. The latter produces feeling, while the mechanism informs us about it. In the simplest of creatures, the mechanism is so simple that it cannot tell us anything about the feeling of a cell. Neither can an atom tell us anything about itself. In the simplest of our machines the chemical composition is simple, while the mechanism cannot compare to the mechanism of a fly. Also, the life of a machine is weak. The mechanism by itself cannot produce noticeable life, while its chemical composition alone cannot inform us about it.

Fourteenth Truth: Where there is matter, there is feeling.

We have seen that the simplest of spirits is an atom, or a part of it. Its life is unimaginably simple and passive (i.e., it is mechanical, depending mostly not on the atom itself, but on the environment and its influence). Where there is an atom, there is feeling. An atom wanders in space, and with it, the feeling of life also wanders.

The same pertains to a complex spirit: its unified feeling can be found wherever there is an animal. The animal wanders—and its feeling of sorrow and happiness follows it. A bird flies—and with it flies the space of its perceptions.

This is clear as far as an atom is concerned, but it is not clear in relation to the animal. But let's look at the atom first.

How does an atom, or a primitive spirit, wander in the universe? Because of their well-known and incessant movement, atoms—the essence of matter—move into suns, planets, their centers, all celestial bodies, the ether, other milky ways, animals, plants, higher beings, and so on.

In inorganic bodies, the atom is like a wanderer who travels sleepily without any impressions in an unvaried, limitless desert similar to a sea. Here it is in a state of nonbeing.

When it enters the bodies of animals, it is as if it is vacationing in hotels of the most wide-ranging quality. Here it transitions into being and perceives what animals perceive.

It is harder to understand an animal. Matter moves in it throughout its life, as water moves in a river. The river remains the Volga River, but the liquid in it is different each year.

An animal is similar to a building constructed from the simplest of spirit-atoms. But these atoms are constantly leaving the building and going outside, being replaced by new atoms that have just entered from the animal's environment. They become alive when they enter an organism, while the atoms departing from it enter nonbeing—the simplest state. The organism is renewed hundreds of times during the life of an animal, that is, its atoms change a hundred times over. Having lived several days, they leave and are replaced by new ones (metabolism).

Fifteenth Truth: If feeling is to be found where matter is, then anything living, at the very least a human being, considers his feeling to reside in his body throughout his whole life.

He says, "I remember myself from the time I was two years old and I will certainly remain (i.e., will live) until my body is destroyed."

But how can this be, if matter leaves the body hundreds of times and continues to be replaced by new matter? The feeling should also run away.

This is one of the illusions that is similar to the one where the sky with its stars seems to be moving around the Earth.

When my atoms leave my body, I cannot convey this any more than someone else can convey to me his continuous existence within his body.

Memory consists of a part of the brain constructed under the influence of life's events. When foreign spirit-atoms enter the brain, they feel the influence of this part of the brain and remember not what they have experienced, but what the body has at some point experienced, or what was experienced by the atoms that were once part of it, and that have since left—the primitive spirits. Likewise, our thoughts about the future, which comprise a part of the brain, make us think about the unavoidable future and death, which we will probably never experience, for atoms (and together with them our primitive spirit) will leave the body in several months and will not experience the feelings of death or even the near future (for example, the next year). The spirit of childhood will not experience the feelings of adolescence. We needlessly fear the agony of death: it will be experienced by other spirits, and not the atoms of the current body.

It is very hard for a human to abandon these misconceptions, as it is hard for him to abandon the perceptions of the sky, the movement of the stars, and the static state of the Earth.

Sixteenth Truth: We think that in every body there is one being.

The rational organization of an animal demands, as does the good organization of the state, a single management, a single will, to which animals and society will submit themselves. The latter is ruled by a single law; the animal is ruled by a single brain. If the animal had two wills, they would contradict each other and decrease the power of being, as happens with indecisive people. They do not know how to act, and inactivity and weakness result. Likewise, two governments cannot successfully rule the country, for they would not be in accord and would weaken each other. The scourge of humankind is its rule not by one will, but by many, which is why wars and other types of self-destruction happen.

That is why an animal with a singular administration, singular will, is perceived to be unified, as the French king thought himself to be the state.

Translated by Anastasia Skoybedo

11 Goals and Norms of Life

Alexander Bogdanov

1

Only a few thousand years have passed since life for humankind ceased to be a bare "struggle for existence." For thousands of centuries, life's entire meaning, its whole content, was reduced to its simple *preservation,* to defending it against the formidable and hostile forces of the external world. All human efforts were directed toward avoiding death and ruin, to sustaining life *such as it is.* Given life's fragility and instability, the slightest change threatens it with terrible danger—a near-unavoidable destruction. And man feels an insurmountable terror before everything novel and unusual, both in his own life and in the surrounding environment.

All of this is quite natural and justified. When the spark of life is barely flickering, every vibration is dangerous, as it threatens to extinguish it forever. The elemental forces[1] of the external world cannot help but engender, from time to time, spontaneous changes in the nature of men and their mutual relations. However, these changes are often infinitely more devastating for life than they are useful. They disturb the established equilibrium. And if life lacks the elements required to create a new, higher equilibrium, then its demise is inevitable. This is the origin of the *spontaneous conservatism* of primitive life and of the tremendous inner resistance that it marshals against every development and every change. This conservatism and this resistance have held an undivided rule over humanity for so long that the entire movement of history has been unable to erase them. Their traces are felt ubiquitously, even in the psychology of the most progressive groups and classes of contemporary society.

In the epoch of primitive conservatism, the question regarding the "norms" of human life was simplified to the extreme. To be more precise, it did not exist at all. This established form of life is something *absolute and necessary*. Its conservatism is the norm. Nothing should change; everything must remain as it has always been and as it continues to be—such was the "universal norm" of primitive psychology.

However, in fact, it isn't really a norm. A norm presupposes a more or less conscious definition and presumes the hypothetical possibility of its violation. Primitive conservatism is free from any deliberate definition. There is no need for formulations, since there is no concept of the possibility of "disturbing" this conservatism. It *exists* and there is as little need to define it as a norm as there is to justify the instinct of self-preservation, which is its purest form. Everything that disturbs this conservatism for a primitive man is an external and hostile force. And against all of these things man fights instinctively, obeying a direct impulse, and not the voice of his conscience, legal awareness, or even common sense, which presents its demands in the guise of various "norms."

Primitive life is commonly characterized as being ruled by "custom." But the meaning of this "custom" is not at all what we understand in the contemporary world. It is not the old, universally known *norm*; it is not a rule that people follow and try not to go against, but a thousand-year-old *habit*, which has become an inalienable part of human nature. There are instances when this "custom," too, is violated. However, for the primitive consciousness this is an exceptional disturbance of the normal order of things, comparable to the birth of a two-headed monster or a solar eclipse. The monstrous infant gets thrown away, the violator of customs is either killed or exiled, and the dark force that obscured the Sun is attacked with arrows. All of these are psychologically homogeneous actions—manifestations of the unconscious and unconditional conservatism of life, of the instinct for self-preservation in its initial phase of development.

People who belong to the same primitive clan group are as psychologically homogeneous among themselves as they are similar in their physical constitution. Thanks to this, their relations with each other are simple and free of contradictions. Meanwhile, norms become necessary only when relations are complex and contradictory. That is why primitive life knows no norms; that is why it is ignorant of the most basic notions that comprise the necessary content of any regulation. This world, so remote from our own, has no space for ideas of what "ought" and "ought not" to be, of "coercion" and "freedom," of "law" and its "violation." There is only the immediacy of life, which convulsively resists everything that disturbs its uniform and endlessly cyclical flow.

2

The norms of human life express the knowledge of "good and evil." Their rule begins with man's original sin.

This fall from grace did not happen on a single day, or even over a thousand years: it was a long and terribly slow process. It consisted of life becoming less and less faithful to what it used to be—to its own initial, ossified form.

However rare and accidental the *useful* changes in conservative, primitive life, they were preserved as long as they helped to preserve life, while all other changes brought peril to it and perished with it themselves. Through the endless accumulation of infinitesimal values, new and real values are created. Life force increases and prevails in the struggle against the hostile forces of nature.

An excess of energy gives rise to life's growth. With its accumulation, a need emerges for new forms of equilibrium. The faster the accumulation of energy, the stronger the need for new combinations and relations, and as a result the simple preservation of given forms becomes more difficult and less expedient.

In this way, by necessity, life began to transform little by little from the simple repetition of immutable cycles into a development. From the simple struggle to preserve what exists, life changed into the struggle for something greater. *The given* stopped being the sole goal and norm of life.

Incipient development could not have been anything but spontaneous; the nascent struggle for greater life could not have been anything but unconscious. This advancement was involuntary and hostile to the balanced course of things. That's why in every given moment, in every given manifestation, it turned out to be partial and unilateral rather than holistic and shared. It *disturbed* the established harmony of the life-system. This is when the old instinct to *preserve what already exists*—the desire to defend and to restore previous harmony—would enter the stage. However, as the force of development increased, this instinct could no longer triumph. Retreating before progress, the instinct for preservation transformed into the desire to set limits on disturbances of the established harmony. Here we find the point of departure for the emergence of compulsory norms.

It is certain that when, in tribal communes, individual members began seizing tools or other items (weapons, clothes, or jewelry) for their own exclusive use more and more frequently, these rather progressive occurrences—from the historical point of view—profoundly shook the entire order of communal life and prompted a painful reaction. However, the simple form of their suppression, such as was initially practiced, could not succeed. These incidents took place more and more often and their imminence permeated the collective consciousness until it had to adapt to them. Then semi-unconscious creativity led to a certain compromise: "the new" was allowed, but only to a certain extent, past which persecution began. The *customary norm*—"this is allowed, but that is forbidden"—is the embodiment of this compromise. Prohibitions were sanctioned by such norms, which meant social coercion and violence against the perpetrator. Such was the first fruit of collective creativity directed against the contradictions of social development.

3

What was it exactly that drove people into this sinful state, in which deviations from the established norm were no longer seen as absolutely exceptional but became an integral part of the chain of natural events?

Everything began with people of the same group losing their psychological unanimity, when their thinking stopped being "homogenous." The *division of labor*—which simultaneously presupposed the *division of experience*—gradually started to supplant the previous homogeneity. People's labor began to vary more and more widely. Experiential content that stimulated thinking was no longer the same for a peasant as it was for a forest hunter, and that of a hunter differed from that of a fisherman. When dealing with nonidentical material, the cognitive processes of separate given individuals increasingly produced divergent results. Society was transforming into an incrementally more complex combination of elements of increasing heterogeneity. People's ways of expressing life became less and less coordinated. A profound and strong social need emerged to bring these expressions into accord.

The division of labor frequently leads to conflict even when interests are aligned—for instance, when a hunter chasing a deer tramples a peasant's fields, or when a herdsman leading his cattle to the water disturbs a fisherman's work. However, what was more important were the conflicts that emerged between the habits of different workers, their perspectives on life, their abilities to respond to their environment—these tended to be more frequent and profound. The rudeness and carelessness of a warrior agreed very poorly with the gentleness and prudence of his fellow peasant; the refined needs of a skilled artisan provoked perplexity and disgust in a modest fisherman; and so on. An organic similarity in habits was gradually disappearing. They lost their character of absolute stability and spontaneous immutability.

In these circumstances, violations of the old "custom" should have occurred more frequently. As the previous, unconsciously reflexive relation to custom was becoming impossible, such actions no longer seemed monstrously strange and incomprehensible. The work of reason in this sphere was unavoidable and necessary, since the *previous* form of the custom was shown time and time again to be insufficient to restore the disturbed equilibrium of life.

This is where the radical transformation of custom occurs—radical, even when its content remains the same. From the bare immediate fact of life, such a custom becomes its *norm*. An organic tendency receives a definite formulation.

"One must act in a certain way!" ... This imperative not only contains the desire to *preserve* a prehistoric given form of vital connections but also presupposes a possibility that this form could be *disrupted*. It expresses the struggle of two forces—the inner contradiction of life. Both sides of a custom find objective expression when its "norm" is disturbed: this is when "coercion" enters the scene and puts an end to the disturbance. "Custom" manifests itself as a coercive norm with a specific sanction.

This opens a whole new sphere of human development.

4

The growing heterogeneity of elements of the social whole, at a certain stage, leads to its increasing *disorganization*. This is when the world of coercive norms acquires colossal dimensions.

As individual elements of society become increasingly less homogeneous, it becomes increasingly easier for their functions to become discrete. Maintaining a constant connection between them becomes more difficult. In small familial or tribal communes, the activity of the main organizer—the patriarch or the chief—assured the perpetuation of these ties. However, the expansion of production results in a considerable growth in the size of society. Then the common organization of labor is no longer possible. Such a task becomes absolutely insurmountable for a single individual, and the now-heterogeneous society is no longer capable of accomplishing it collectively. Society then disintegrates into smaller separate groups: private households, each of which organizes its own work activity and has no external connections with others.

The material connection between these households remains. They form the links of one gigantic chain—a system for the societal division of labor. Had they been entirely independent they would have certainly perished, since on their own they are powerless to defend themselves against nature. The disorganized character of this connection finds expression in the *exchange relations* between these households. These lead to the anarchic, irrational, and unplanned *distribution* of the products of labor in society.

The disorganization of life results in the inadvertent waste of its forces, the antagonism of its forms, and the contradictoriness of its manifestations. This is true for all areas of life. In the sphere of production, common labor must satisfy social needs fully and accurately. However, when it is disorganized, when its distribution among social units occurs without any plan or control, such strict correlation between results and social demands is no longer possible. Inadvertently, some of this labor dissipates fruitlessly, producing excess social demand in one sphere or another. In the meantime, not having found a sufficient amount of the necessary products of common labor, other demands remain unfulfilled. "Overproduction" accompanies "underproduction."

In the sphere of distribution, the lack of organization produces new and profound discords. Distribution itself acquires the form of struggle and competition—a struggle between buyer and seller, as well as internal competition among buyers and sellers themselves. Everyone is trying to gain more at the other's expense. The result is irregular and disproportionate distribution. Even with a general surplus, the needs of many members of society remain unfulfilled; many households perish or suffer a diminishing quality of life. Crude market power mocks human efforts.

During further development, the same disorganization of the social system results in class struggle, which escalates as the powers of these warring classes increase. This struggle permeates *the entirety of* social life, from its very "material" to its most "idealistic" manifestations. Life's monumental progress and humanity's energies are always accompanied with the massive expansion of social contrasts and contradictions.

It is not hard to understand just how great the significance is of anything that brings a bit of order into this chaos, anything that introduces some organization or contains this disharmony—in other words, the significance of anything that acts as a coercive norm. This is why social creativity in this sphere unfolds with immense energy and gives rise to an immense wealth of forms. It is a result of the harsh necessities of life.

5

As we have seen, the development of the normative world began with the transformation of a custom from the direct expression of organically holistic life into an external, coercive norm. Later, this new, "normative" custom became the source of a whole series of other norms of the same type: common laws, etiquette, and morals. Despite the differences between them, all these species of normative forms are similar in a sense: to members of society, they represent an external and coercive force that is directed at regulating social relations. The meaning of this regulation is to weaken and eliminate the contradictions that development gives rise to—and to instill organization into—an atomized and anarchic social life.

The violence that society enacts against transgressors is the main and primary form of external coercion regulating the enforcement of norms. This sanction is preserved entirely in the sphere of customs and law. The type of coercion that protects etiquette and morality is of a different character: it is limited to social reprobation and contempt. Such a softer form of social opposition to "aberrant" (from the point of view of established customs of relations) human actions remains the sole option when transgressions do not directly and dramatically violate the vital interests of the collective. As a tempered reflection of society's crude material struggle against the "deviant" actions of its members, this second type of coercion, naturally, does not exclude the first kind, and typically accompanies it in cases of "crimes" and "violations" of the norms of inherited custom and law. Such crimes and violations are not only curtailed and punished by society's physical force, but are branded as something immoral and also at times as something indecent.

The perpetrator himself is a child of the society that punishes violations with censure and scorn. He has grown accustomed to this norm; he *acknowledges* it even when, driven by some immediate motive, he violates it. That's why he often self-incriminates and subjects himself to the type of punishment customary in his society—at the very least, such self-incrimination assumes the form of remorse and self-contempt. Such is the objective basis for the torments of a heavy conscience. They are the individual, psychological reflection of the *social* reaction against actions that violate a norm.

Here we find a convenient ground for the individualistic fetishism formulated by Kantian moral philosophy. Moral norms are ascribed the status of an exceptional inner imperative, based on the sole fact that once formed they acquire the power to induce "pangs of conscience." They are presented as the proper and autonomous self-government of an absolute personality, which lies at the foundations of the human self. Such a view completely ignores the genesis of ethics: their direct descent from custom and their subsequent separation from common law (something that has not even been fully accomplished, for instance, in feudal Catholic society). The obviously nonautonomous character of ethical norms is ignored along with their externally coercive character, which becomes distinctly visible in the conflict between moral obligation and the instincts and desires of developing life. Ignoring all of this, Kantian moral philosophy managed to obscure for a long time and for many people the simple fact that "inner" moral conflicts are in essence conflicts between the direct impulses of life and the crystallized force of a society's past, which is external to these impulses despite coexisting with them in the sphere of individual consciousness. In any case, the liberatory struggle of contemporary *amoralism*—both individual and social—alone presents vivid proof that the obligation to heed moral norms is only a historically conditioned form of social coercion.

In this respect, there is no real difference between morality and any other form of normative regulation.

6

The significance of normative forms for organizing humanity's social life—life that is often driven by contradictory impulses—is truly immense. To fully appreciate this significance, we must try to imagine, even if only approximately, what would have happened to society had it not been for these norms. It would have fallen apart, as a barrel without ferrules. It would have decomposed like a human organism without a nervous system regulating and unifying the activity of its parts.

Exchange is a necessary condition of life in historical, cultured societies. Competition and class antagonism are the driving forces of social development. However, exchange assumes the form of a struggle between the buyer and the seller to acquire the greatest possible value. Had this struggle not been limited by the coercion imposed by custom, law, and morality, and had it been allowed to develop naturally, it would have transformed into merciless mutual pillaging. This would have made exchange itself impossible. Analogously, competition would have transformed into the physical extermination of inconvenient competitors, and class struggle would have been unthinkable in any form other than acerbate and bloody internecine war.

And this is what happens in reality when life's contradictions, temporarily aggravated to the extreme, puncture through the sheath of norms and, freed, become raging elemental forces. The tremendous destruction of life-elements—not only of the old and decaying, but also of the nascent ones—reveals the real meaning of "development through contradictions" with astonishing clarity.

The breadth of their significance to life is not equal for all norms. The legislative norm of private appropriation covers and determines the entire life of contemporary society. Meanwhile, many other norms—for instance, etiquette—apply only to some specific cases of human interaction. This does not make norms different in principle. Their essential character *as tools for social organization* remains the same in all instances.

To organize life: for us this means the graceful regulation and harmonious adjustment of all of its manifestations. However, it is from this very point of view that the organizational significance of coercive norms may seem deeply controversial. More than that—in some cases, their role appears as distinctly disruptive and introduces many contradictions into the developmental process. In our time we see how many legislative norms in political life and how many moral laws in domestic life lead to intolerable contradictions, which are deeply detrimental to developing life. In such situations it is possible to clarify matters through historical research into the development of norms. This research makes abundantly clear that their positive role belongs to the *past*. A norm survives long after the conditions that created it have disappeared (and with them, its significance). It remains as a useless atavism and an obstacle on the path of development. Sometimes a norm grows decrepit very quickly, as is frequently the case with many legislative regulations. At other times, a norm does not lose its vital importance for millennia—as with some moral principles. Such a varied, but always historically circumscribed, vitality can be reduced to the same core meaning—the organizational function that it plays in social processes.

Contemporary societies, with the anarchic structure of their collaboration, are held together solely by *coercive norms*. The norms of *property* and *contractual subjugation* comprise the soul of capitalism.

7

In primitive society, the custom-norm encompassed all spheres of people's existence and activity. Following the custom, normative forms acquired, little by little, just as significant a domain. They regulated the technology of social labor along with people's economic relations, their consumption, and their thinking. People began to run into ubiquitous, coercive limitations, to feel the pervasive power of external norms over themselves—norms that these people did not establish and which formed in the social sphere without their consent.

Since every deviation from a norm was "criminal," it was possible to commit "crimes" in all areas of life. Every significant improvement of technology was considered a "criminal innovation" and was severely persecuted until the forces of normative coercion relented in the face of economic necessity. The tragic fate of many inventions and inventors during the Middle Ages and during early modernity provides a vivid illustration of this fact. We can witness a similar attitude of moral repulsion, if only in a diminished form, in the contemporary peasant from a backward region who sees in unusual household innovations some "demonic play"—in other words, something most sinful. In the consumer sphere we also find various forms of characteristic "taboos": common, legislative, ethical, and so forth. Religious customs enshrined in the Pentateuch prohibiting Jews from consuming pork and the blood of animals as well as many other kinds of food, medieval laws punishing the display of luxury beyond one's class stature, contemporary rules of etiquette that prevent us from wearing simpler and more comfortable clothes, certain manners of eating, the moral repulsion that many cultured as well as noncultured people feel against alcoholic beverages—these are typical examples of the "taboo," and many more could be listed.

The all-encompassing force of custom-habit defined not only human *actions*, but also their inner *experiences*. Here coercive norms also followed custom. Ancient Oriental tyrannies knew instances of the death penalty applied for "criminal dreams," when, for instance, a person dreamt of killing a king. The Inquisition considered heretical thoughts to be criminal transgressions, regardless of whether these thoughts were expressed. There was even a case wherein an inquisitor assailed by blasphemous thoughts denounced himself to be rightfully burned at the stake. The notion of "sinful" or even "criminal" thoughts has not entirely vanished, even from our cultured world. The only thing that has disappeared is legislation punishing the "unlawful" association of ideas. However, moral coercion remains, in the shape of social reprobation and pangs of conscience, together with a nearly indistinguishable coercion associated with violations of the norms of civilized behavior.

In this way, the web of external norms—sometimes crude and rigid, and sometimes elastic—entwines all the possible manifestations of human life.

8

Externally coercive norms of all kinds serve to introduce order into the disharmony born out of life's spontaneous development. However, the order that they introduce is not yet a true harmony in the positive sense of the word. The resulting unification and regulation of diverse life-processes is only superficial. For instance, a person may experience an emergent contradiction between immediate egotistical and immediate social drives—between a desire to turn and walk away from other people's sufferings, and a desire to help them at the price of some sacrifice. The dictates of law and moral obligation subjugate some of these motives to others. A person acts in accordance with those motives, which correlate with the "norm." However, within one's psyche the struggle never stops: it may even intensify when a norm compels one to act according to motives that are becoming outdated, and not according to motives that at the moment are organically gaining strength. For example, a man comes to bitterly regret having given part of his money to a pauper after he realizes he might come to really need it himself. In this way, while smoothing and suppressing the manifestations of inner contradictions, the external norm never eliminates the contradictions themselves. It may even add a new contradiction—a contradiction between a specific tendency of life that gets suppressed by this norm, and the norm itself.

Furthermore, external norms are conservative; they form very slowly, and for the most part are very slow to change. They always outlive the necessity that gave rise to them and they die only after a tenacious struggle. Our time is filled with such struggles: the near entirety of the political life of underdeveloped countries and even a considerable part of the political life of leading countries can often be reduced to them. The same holds true for the sphere of normative ideology. A legislative organization or a system of customs and morals that has outlived itself and no longer regulates spontaneous development does not assuage its contradictions, but simply postpones them. Sometimes its resistance causes the massive waste of the best forces of developing life—we have so many examples of this in our country. Here lies a new source of living contradictions.

Undoubtedly, externally coercive norms are necessary for the preservation of life among the contradictions of spontaneous development; however, they accomplish this preservation at the cost of constraining this very development—at the cost of stunting and delaying it. On the other hand, by replacing external crude conflicts with inner contradictions that are born out of coercion, they direct human consciousness toward the production of new forms of life and development all the more strongly—toward forms that would be free from spontaneity, from contradictions and coercion.

It could be considered a common rule that the higher the stage of life, the deeper, wider, and more acute the contradictions that manifest themselves. In the spontaneous development of a human organism, entering the stage of sexual maturity brings many more anxieties and dissonances than it does in the development of a young animal. Similarly, the progress of "cultured" capitalistic societies is acquired at the price of an incomparably greater sum of contradictions than the progress of "precultural" agrarian communities. For higher forms of spontaneously developing life, its accelerated development is accompanied by its accelerated expenditure.

It often happens that this expenditure exceeds the increase in life, that development transitions into degradation, and that "one step forward" is followed by "two steps back." The maladies incurred during early development sometimes result in the deep and prolonged exhaustion of a young and fragile organization, and sometimes in its complete collapse.

What exactly exacerbates, to such a degree, the contradictions created during the spontaneous development of the highest forms of life? The answer is the very peculiarities of these forms—the very things that make them "higher."

This, first of all, has to do with their lesser degree of conservatism, and their increased flexibility and plasticity. Static, conservative, lower forms naturally possess far stronger immediate resilience. This immediate resilience is akin to the resilience of a stone, which is hard to break. But once it is broken, its previous form is lost forever. However, such resilience protects the complex of life from an all-too-speedy deterioration under the influence of moderately strong and harmful factors—that is, the ones that are more common and frequent. Similarly, the contradictions created during the period of sexual maturation are experienced much more painfully and acutely by a city dweller or, for that matter, by a cultural person with his more impressionable and less robust constitution, than by a savage or a peasant.

The rich life-content of the higher forms—the great number of elements and the variety of parts comprising them—is another of their peculiarities. Each transformation born out of spontaneous development naturally encounters, among the mass of existing combinations that comprise a given life-system, many elements with which it finds itself in a vital contradiction. So, a new idea, born in the mind of a given individual, has a higher likelihood of encountering far more resistance and opposition in the sphere of the complex and widely disjointed ideological life of a society than in the narrow and impoverished ideological life of the immediate circle of people to which the author belongs.

Finally, the third particularity of the higher forms of life—a particularity that accentuates the contradictions that arise during their spontaneous development—is found in their internal unity, organization, and the close vital connection of their parts and elements. It is precisely thanks to this connection and unified organization that the atrophy or hypertrophy of some organ or function in a human organism has a more profound impact on the rest of his vital processes and is far more dangerous than, for example, in a ringed worm, whose body's separate segments have a relatively low vital connection and interdependence.

It is evident that all these conditions, exacerbating the disharmony of spontaneous development, must intensify during the course of this very development. Contradictions must necessarily proliferate.

The solution is not found within the limited framework of natural development, but instead in the change of the form of development itself.

10

A new need emerges out of the torturous oscillations of life as it develops spontaneously, and out of its high cost and increasing unreliability: the need to introduce unity and harmony into the developmental process itself, to make it coherent and holistic, to eliminate its spontaneous character. Its oscillations must give way to uninterrupted continuity—its dissonances to full and clear harmonies. Its cost must become equal to its results; the element of unpredictability must disappear. In a word, it is necessary that life must transform from a spontaneous motion into a harmonious one.

Only then can progress find its indestructible foundation in the entire sum of accumulated life forces; only then may the infinity of a vanquished and continuously reconquered nature open before it: *a struggle for more would transform into a struggle for everything.* In this type of conscious and purposeful progression of life, the question of life's goals receives, for the first time, its full meaning and finds its answer free of contradictions: to provide an infinitely increasing sum of happiness. We, the people of a one-sided and disharmonious development, the people of the epoch of contradictions, are incapable of imagining this type of life fully and with any degree of clarity. But we vaguely anticipate it in ecstatic moments of thought or contemplation, when, in a living communion with magnificent nature or a mighty genius, we begin to feel our small existence disappear, merging with infinity.

11

It would, however, have been foolish to speak of a higher type of life, about its harmonious progress, had our experience contained nothing but vague premonitions and indeterminate longing, had it been impossible to notice its embryonic forms in the past and in the present, had we not had the data to outline, even if only in a most schematic manner, its possible further development. Fortunately, such germs and such data exist. And their number suffices to give us the basis for quite determinate conclusions.

First of all, where do we find the conditions that create the very *possibility* of a transition from a spontaneous and contradictory development to a systematic and harmonious one? *In the very same place* where we find the conditions that lead to the progressive intensification of contradictions that characterize life that develops spontaneously: in the increasing plasticity of life forms, in the increasing richness of its content, in their increasing organization.

Only the high plasticity of life allows a rapid and diverse adaptation to its environment. In this regard, compare the flexible character of an urban proletarian worker with the rigid and lumbering psyche of a peasant from a backward village. Only in rich, complex, and diverse life-content can we always find the elements necessary for such an adaptation. Juxtapose, for example, the quick-minded resourcefulness of an experienced and wizened man with the typical, obtuse confusion of a person of meager experience as they are confronted with any change in their habitual environment. Finally, only the increasing organization of forms makes individual, private processes of development less isolated. As a result, each of these given processes is no longer limited to that part of the living whole where it first manifests itself, but is immediately reflected in all other parts, causing a series of transformations in them. In this regard, the opposition between a highly organized thought of a philosopher and a comparatively poorly organized mind of a philistine is very characteristic. While for a philosopher every encounter with a new phenomenon or idea may cause resonant changes and even transform the entirety of his worldview, a philistine files every new discovery into one of the many drawers in his brain and then proceeds to lock it, remaining indifferent to the notion that other drawers contain thoughts and facts that are deeply contradictory or, on the contrary, particularly harmonious with the one that he has just compartmentalized.

In this manner, the transition from lower to higher forms of life, while intensifying the contradictions of spontaneous development, at the same time prepares the ground for the fundamental elimination of these contradictions together with the spontaneity to which they give rise.

12

Development that is sufficiently harmonious and free of contradictions is only a liminal concept that expresses the already-familiar tendency toward emancipating the process of development and the contradictions associated with it. Providing a clear demonstration of this type of harmonious development, therefore, is possible only by juxtaposing the concrete instances that approximate it best against the instances in which the lack of harmony is most glaring.

In contemporary society, a large capitalist enterprise, considered from the point of view of its labor technology, can serve as an example of a highly organized, rich-in-content, and plastic living environment. In this limited sphere, processes of development unfold rather harmoniously. For instance, the introduction of a new technological invention significantly reduces the expenditure of labor power in some given aspect of this production. A series of further changes follows immediately.

Removing old machines and replacing them with new ones alone is insufficient. It is necessary to modify the entire organization of the factory to integrate these machines. For instance, an old building may no longer be suitable for housing them. It may have to be remodeled to accommodate these new requirements. Partial adjustments of other areas of the factory and the spaces communicating between them may have to ensue. The system of gears distributing mechanical force between individual machines must also be adjusted accordingly. A reduced demand in labor power frees up a portion of capital. This labor power may instead be redirected toward a more or less equally distributed expansion of the entire enterprise. Hands, which have been freed up by the introduction of machines, may be used again, though for a considerably different purpose than before. It is in the interest of the business to assign to each worker the most suitable task in the redistribution of labor. Some, perhaps the least capable workers, might have to be removed altogether and replaced by a more careful selection. All of this redistribution of capital and labor is performed quickly and easily thanks to engineers and directors with rich experience and knowledge of management. In this manner, development in one part of the system causes corresponding adjustments in the rest, and the progress of a part becomes the progress of a whole. It is not accompanied by any significant delay or disturbance in the technical life of the company.

However, the matter appears in an entirely different light when we consider this company in connection with others. The capitalist system is characterized overall by *anarchy*. In this respect, even when compared with an individual, highly organized, capitalist business, the system appears overall as a lower form of life, since its development is incomparably more spontaneous and contradictory. The technical progress of some businesses leads to a decline in or even the ruination of others. This deprives many capable workers of their useful role in a common social task together with their means for subsistence. An increase in productivity for some enterprises renders many of their workers superfluous; at the same time, less progressive and therefore failing businesses cannot hire them. At times, technical progress itself produces a general crisis of production—a devastating shock to the entirety of social life. Finally, class contradictions are the offspring of the very same spontaneous progress. And although it is only by living through these contradictions that society may shake off its spontaneous character, this does not diminish the contradictions' torturous disharmony and destructive force.

In this manner, the anarchy of the whole prevails over the organization of its parts, destroying or weakening with its elemental force the outcome of planned, harmonious development at every step. The general character of social development remains profoundly contradictory.

13

The entire meaning of life and the entire positive significance of coercive norms are inextricably bound with the contradictions of spontaneous development. As these contradictions and their spontaneous character retreat in the face of organization and balanced development, the social role of coercive norms changes radically. The meaning of these norms vanishes and their significance becomes perverted. The conservatism of external norms clashes radically with the uninterrupted drive of progress and, in turn, becomes a key or perhaps even the sole source of life's deep contradictions. A need emerges for other norms that would correspond more closely to this new way of life's movement. These new norms, obviously, must be free of the coerciveness and conservatism of the previous ones. Such are the *pragmatic norms*.

Legislative and moral norms, as well as other norms of external coercion, may be "pragmatic," that is, useful to society. Moreover, they occupy their firm place in life only insofar as they are "pragmatic." This, however, does not make these norms truly pragmatic. They coerce without providing a motivation or discriminating between different circumstances. They do not correlate their force of coercion with changing conditions. "You must do this or that and you may not act in that way or another": the dictates of these norms are entirely indifferent to circumstances. They simply state that "you must" or "you should not dare" as a categorical and unconditional imperative.

Pragmatic norms have nothing in common with *such* imperatives. Scientific and technical rules are one typical example of this. These rules do not coerce anyone to do anything. They only point out more useful ways to reach a *specific* goal. They say: "If you would like to accomplish something, you should act in the following advantageous manner." Their imperative is contingent and hypothetical. Externally coercive norms impose on a person his very goals, or, at the very least, the limits of these goals: "Do not covet your neighbor's wife," and the like. Pragmatic norms offer a choice: "If you are covetous of your neighbor's wife, then you may do the following ... and so on."

The connection between these norms and the harmonious course of development is very clear. If development does not give rise to contradictions, then the ensuing norms express its tendencies and do not clash in irresolvable conflicts. Therefore, it is in life's interest that they not be delimited.

To the extent that we are dealing with intermediary and mediating goals, the pragmatic norms may define one's choice of goals: if you would like to achieve some end, you must at first set in front of yourself some smaller, preliminary goals and advance through them toward the desired aim. It is obvious that, in this case, directives have a contingent character: they merely point out the necessary means that temporarily present themselves as goals. So, for a conscious political actor, the strength of his party presents one of the main but far from ultimate goals. When necessary, he must forget the former for the sake of the latter. If the given means are no longer necessary for achieving a set goal, or no longer represent a sure path to it, pragmatic norms dictate that we should reject these means.

Pragmatic norms are fully subject to critique from the perspective of experience and learning, while norms of coercion demand the complete subjugation of this critique. These two tendencies of thinking find their philosophical expression in the primacy of theoretical reason over practical in the first case, and in the primacy of practical reason over theoretical in the second.

14

If pragmatic goals do not prescribe concrete goals to people, wouldn't it then follow that according to these norms the selection of goals is utterly arbitrary?

The answer is both yes and no.

Formally speaking, yes, it would, since we can logically think up any goals at all, the most rational and the most monstrous, along with the pragmatic norms that would correlate with them best. "If one would like to sacrifice his life in a way that would be most beneficial for the development of humankind, it must be done in one way; if one wishes to rob somebody of their life, then these are the means that would help in this task, etc."

Practically speaking, no, it would not. Out of countless logical possibilities only one measures up to reality. Pragmatic norms are not a game of reason, but concrete *forms of life*. They will replace norms of coercion in the sphere of social relations only under specific life conditions, and are historically inextricably bound with these conditions. They are in accord with the harmonious development of life and are premised on it. The universal ultimate goal to which they are subjugated—to achieve the maximum life for society as a whole that, at the same time, would correlate with the maximum life for the individuals who comprise it—is almost entirely defined by this alignment. Without such a correlation, harmonious development is impossible. When this correlation is present, then goals and diverse norms that serve them coalesce in a *socially coordinated struggle for happiness*—a struggle for everything that life and nature can give to humankind.

15

It is only at a very specific phase of humanity's development that pragmatic norms must wrestle their rule over social life away from coercive norms. However, they emerge well before this stage, undergoing a long period of development, little by little spreading over ever-wider spheres of life, all the while *remaining subjugated* in the overall system of life. This is understandable enough: when and where the goals and results of human actions cease to be mutually contradictory, when and where the disharmony of social development disappears, then and there a space opens up for the creation of pragmatic norms.

The sphere that these norms conquer the fastest is the sphere of *labor technology*: the sphere that governs the immediate struggle between people and nature. Here is where human efforts are first unified; here is where the need to defeat the great common enemy first overcomes both the direct conflict of human goals and the life contradictions born indirectly out of their spontaneous combinations.

The system of the pragmatic norms, which systematically organize people's technical experience, is what we call *science*.

We count here not only the technical sciences, which are already understood as systematically listed practical directives about which means are best used to attain a specific technical goal. The natural sciences—from mathematics to astronomy, sociology, and theories of cognition—have, in essence, *the same significance*. They represent a system of pragmatic norms of the highest order—the norms regulating norms and regulating the application of all sorts of practical rules. When, by using mathematical analysis and principles of mechanics, an engineer develops a project for the construction of a building and a bridge, he in effect creates technical pragmatic norms by using scientific norms. When a politician comes up with a program of action for a given historical moment and a given social group, relying on a specific social-philosophical theory and an analysis of the relationship between social forces, he also creates technical pragmatic norms by using scientific norms. In the end, every act of scientific cognition is a creation of pragmatic norms for people's practical activity.

Pragmatic norms prevail in the ideological life of today's society as well; however, they do not rule fully there. In contemporary society, an individual may *believe* that what he thinks is useful for the salvation of his soul; he may *think* in a fashion that he holds to be useful for correct understanding and the evaluation of his surrounding reality; but as soon as he begins *to express* the results of his ideological work, he must immediately take into consideration the norms of coercion—laws, morals, and customs. Primitive societies contain more of these coercive norms than the more advanced ones, where these norms no longer prevail so strongly and are pushed into the background. Here, too, progress leads to the relative weakening of coercive norms and their substitution with pragmatic norms—in other words, *to the emancipation* of human activity.

16

When in one or another sphere of life the emancipation of people from coercive norms is completed, the very memory of the norms vanishes together with the notion of "freedom." In our time, nobody in the advanced countries is concerned with the "freedom" of inner experience—the "freedom" of thoughts and dreams, the "freedom" of technical inventions and improvements, and so on. But the process of improvement itself inevitably assumes the form of coercive relations—moral or legislative, for instance.

Cultured countries have "freedom" of conscience, speech, print, and association. What is it, this freedom? It is a specific *right*. As a legal norm, it must consequently contain in itself all the elements of external coercion. What do they consist of? Of suppressing every attempt to disrupt this freedom with the use of social force. For instance, the legal content of the "freedom of speech" is the following: no one may prevent others from speaking their mind, and those who attempt to do so will be punished. But the very idea of preventing others from expressing their thoughts presupposes that traces of previous coercive regulations of speech still survive—that, at the very least, the memories of earlier censorship have not entirely dissipated. When these traces and memories disappear completely, society will be as little concerned with freedom of speech as it is today about the freedom to breathe or to dream.

Here we observe the common evolutionary law in accordance with which new life-content borrows the elements for its organizational forms from the old content. Only as these elements die down does life create new and original forms to replace them. The new emerges out and through the old. Censorship's legal coercion may be overcome by the legal coercion that protects freedom of speech. And only with this final negative coercion may the legal form disappear from a certain sphere.

In the social sciences, metaphysical idealism construes freedom of conscience, freedom of speech, and the like as a series of "absolute" or "natural" human rights that are immutable and eternally mandatory. It does not understand that actual, realized freedom is not a "law," but rather a rejection of laws. Things have reached a stage wherein metaphysical idealists strive to replace a policeman, whose presence delimits freedom, with a policeman whose task is to protect it. However, metaphysical idealism in its flight of fancy can reach no higher, and naively attempts to make this stage permanent. What makes itself clear here is the influence of a specifically bourgeois, narrow psychology that does not allow an "idealist" to surpass the limitations of the ideological forms (legislative, moral, etc.) that characterize the bourgeois world.

17

In the sphere of technology and cognition, the dominance of pragmatic norms is foreshadowed already in our time. Matters stand differently in the area of economics—of the mutual relations between people that arise in the process of labor.

In contemporary society, such relations are characterized by disorganization and anarchy. Their development is associated with the highest sum of contradictions. As a consequence, here we find objectively the least amount of space for pragmatic norms and the greatest demand for norms of coercion. We have already seen how necessary these norms are for the exchange process—a process that expresses the main economic structure of the present society. The deeply rooted and irremediable contradictions of this process make the presence of coercive norms necessary.

Here, the principle of ownership reigns—the right of possession of specific things by specific people. Other coercive norms (legal, moral, and so forth) are clustered around this principle as its specific instances, variations, or necessary supplements.

A bourgeois economic order is absolutely unthinkable outside of the legal system. It is its skeleton; it provides the necessary unifying framework for its parts and the constant form that clothes them.

18

The transition from an economic system riddled with contradictions, and therefore regulated by external norms, to a harmonious system of collaboration that does not require any such norms may occur only after passing through a specific intermediary phase, during which the new and incompletely formed content is still using old forms. The transformation of the economic order must occur with the assistance of a new type of legal relations—in other words, through politics. It is for this reason that, historically, this transformation is first advanced as a program of a specific *party* and usually gets described by the term "the state of the future."

In investigating this formula through the prism of the Marxian theory of history, which has made it into its slogan, it is easy to conclude that it contains a contradiction. This school of thought teaches us that the "state is an organized class domination" while positing as its ideal the abolition of classes. How are we to reconcile this with the idea of the "state of the future," which is after all still envisioned as a state?

This contradiction, of course, is only an apparent one. Indeed, it is true that the "state of the future" is the organization of class domination; however, the new ruling class should be *the one that strives to abolish all classes.* "The state of the future," therefore, represents an intermediary stage, as it is bound to contain traces of old class ideologies that enter into conflict with the new organization of life and are therefore subject to legal regulation. When these atavistic traces disappear and the psychology of the entire society conforms to the new system of collaboration—universal collaboration for universal development—then the "state of the future" too, having shorn its coercive elements, will no longer be a "state." It will be a society, in which mutual relations between people, as well as their attitudes toward nature and experience, will be defined by pragmatic norms. The socialist world is just such an ideal, of which modern men are aware.

19

A contemporary individual, a child of the epoch of contradictions and coercion, will inevitably ask whether such a society is conceivable. This question will be followed by another one: is its emergence probable?

The first question expresses a demand to point out which elements of social connections may be regulated by pragmatic norms.

The second question is a demand to demonstrate the possibility of expanding these connections to include the whole of society.

The internal relations within a circle of comrades may provide us with an answer to the first question.

How does the distribution of labor occur in groups of this type? Independently from norms of coercion and in accordance with pragmatic norms. People gather and discuss which exact part of the common task each of them will take on. The common goal is the point of origin for all decisions.

It is self-evident that legal coercion has nothing to do with this situation.

Obligation by "conditional agreement" may be excluded from consideration as well. Such an obligation presupposes that a person complies with his group's decisions as long as he remains its participant. If he does not want to comply, he must leave. Comradely relations in their pure and developed form are free of this sort of coercion. If a group member announces that the role suggested for him by others does not suit him and that he cannot fulfill it, this does not lead to his exclusion from the organization.

Moral obligations are also out of the question. No unconditional imperative guides human actions here. A person may take on a task that does not agree well with his habits, or even that he is directly averse to. However, he accepts it simply because none of his comrades can—that is, out of pragmatic considerations—or because he would like to relieve his comrades of work that may be too taxing for them. That is, he would do this out of sheer sympathy for his fellow associates. And this sympathy, as with every immediate feeling, of course does not contain anything normative, formal, or obligatory.

The private goals of individuals, therefore, stem out of their common task and relations. And their actions are defined by pragmatic norms in accordance with these goals.

Such is the highest type of social organization in its *elementary form.*

20

Now we are to face the second, more challenging question: can the comradely organization of labor be expanded to the scale of a whole society and further still—to the whole of humanity?

At first glance, the only possible and natural answer is a negative one. We are faced with such a mass of arguments in favor of the negative answer that we do not know where to begin.

However, upon examining these arguments, it is easy to reduce them to two types. Some stem from a certain understanding of comradely relations themselves (excluding the possibility of their boundless expansion). Others relate to human nature and the nature of society, both of which, supposedly, limit this expansion. Let us consider the first type of argument.

The most common and serious among them is the following: comradely relations are in essence the relations that exist within closed circles. They are founded on the *personal affinities* of individual people toward each other. Where such sympathies do not exist, comradely association is impossible or unsustainable. Meanwhile, the sphere of personal sympathies for every person is finite. As a consequence, the sphere of comradely associations between people must also have its limits: it cannot span the millions and billions of individuals comprising society and humanity.

The entire weight of this argument resides in the confusion of a particular, concrete form of comradely relations—and the lowest form at that—with comradely relations understood broadly, that is, with the specific type of development they represent.

The essence of comradely organization consists of a unity of purpose, which its members formulate freely and without any coercion, and which exceeds each of their individual interests. It is only natural that in a fractured, anarchic society, where the goals of human lives are extremely diverse and so poorly connected that contradictions arise at every juncture, comradely unity of purpose is found early on only in small groups of people who are bound closely by kinship, friendship, general personal sympathies, and other private aspects of life. Such a narrow, intimate emotional bond reinforces this unity of purpose: love for the common task becomes indistinguishable from love for the people who share it and who find in it an external support. However, as the task itself grows, everything changes.

Eventually, personal closeness and tight community bonds not only stop being a secure foundation for common work but often become directly detrimental to it. Having grown accustomed to associating the common goal with specific individuals and assessing these individuals in a limited and subjective manner informed by his immediate sympathy for them, a person of a narrow-social-circle psychology has a hard time putting up with the now inevitable changes to his role in the evolving common task. His discontent becomes a source of conflicts and contradictions in the shared life of the comradely organization. Moreover, at this stage of its development, the comradely bond is not yet free of a certain authoritarian coloring. The positions of comrades who are recognized as leaders appear more "influential" and "respectable" than those of others. It is not infrequent that a member of the circle begins to struggle with those comrades he does not have a personal affinity for, in order to win "positions" in the circle for the people he is closer to and fonder of.

This often happens in the life of professional and political organizations of the comradely type during the transition from operating on the level of a small group to something broader, especially when several separate circles merge that have been working independently from each other for a long time. The resulting picture is rather strange: people who appear to be striving for the same goal, and who do not even disagree about the means of attaining it, enter into a bitter struggle with each other and senselessly waste the energies of the collective whole. Such a struggle ends only when victory is won by the groups that are least suffused with the spirit of the narrow circle and most attuned to the idea of the collective whole. The comradely organization then frees itself from the domination of personal bonds and sympathies and presents itself as a true collectivity, united by genuine solidarity.

However, given the anarchic and disorganized structure of the entire society and, in such conditions, the inevitable prevalence of individualistic psychology, even a comradely association as it expands must adopt impersonal forms of a conventional normative character and adopt formal organizational "statutes." Although they appear to be the same as externally coercive norms—legislative, common, moral, and so on—in essence they are somewhat different. From the beginning their compulsoriness is subjugated to their pragmatic goal. The possibility and even the necessity of violating these norms as soon as they enter into an obvious contradiction with the common goal, in the name of which the organization was created, are recognized in advance. These are not the dictates of personal or impersonal power, demanding submission without providing any motivation. These are the organizational pragmatic norms that establish the most useful forms of collaboration. Under normal conditions they are devoid of the fetishism that is the soul of norms of compulsion and that transforms these norms into laws imposing on people the goals of their activity. These norms simply guide people to choose the most suitable means for attaining their freely determined goals.

It follows that the narrowness of relations within a circle does not presuppose the same narrowness within comradely relations. Quite the contrary. Only by getting rid of the elements specific to relations within narrow circles may comradely relations attain the chance to develop freely. This does not mean that they can be entirely devoid of elements of sympathy and that the bond between comrades should be emotionally cold and entirely businesslike. No. However, sympathy here is not marked by such a narrowly personal and individualistic character as it is, for example, in friendship, kinship, or sexual love. Sympathy grounded in collaboration, in the common struggle and the common goal, can be *no less* deep than sympathy born out of the usual pleasant impressions received from another person. At the same time, this type is more developed in the sense that it is far less sensitive to the accidents of life and far less fragile during the inevitable calamities of life. It is not co-suffering that prevails in it, but co-rejoicing.

A comrade values another comrade as a force that is in harmony with him in the common struggle, as a partial living embodiment of the common goal. Every success in this common struggle serves as a rich source of that shared joy, which is amplified and deepened by mutual expressions of happiness. However, failure or defeat do not provoke an exchange of grief and sorrow to the same extent: the active nature of comradely relations does not allow that. When a comrade leaves the ranks, when a comrade dies, the first thought is how to *replace* him in the name of the common task—how to fill the gap in the system of energies directed toward the common goal. There is no room for despair or funerary sentiments here: all attention is direction toward action and not "feeling." This is the root of the "callousness" to comrades' sufferings, which so impresses the philanthropic philistines, in active political fighters.

So, in essence, the bond between comrades is capable of the same boundless expansion as the conscious collaboration that forms the real foundation of this bond. Affinities of a narrowly individualistic nature are not only unnecessary for comradely relations but, on the contrary, exist in a certain antagonism with its developmental tendency. This feeling, which invariably plays a significant role in the early stages of the development of a comradely organization, becomes an obstacle that must be overcome during the subsequent stages. Affinity is replaced by a different kind of relation that is alien to individualism and pettiness, and capable of encompassing in its development an indefinitely expanding circle of personalities.

21

Let us now consider a different series of arguments raised against our concept. Isn't it the case that human nature and the nature of society are such that they make living contradictions between people, and, as a result, coercive regulation of their relations, inevitable? These conditions are immutable as long as man remains a man and not an angel. Egotistical instincts will always cause clashes between personal interests. And in order that these clashes, as they escalate, not turn people into wolves gnawing at each other's throats, they have to be reined in by the law, morals, and so forth. The norms of expediency are quite powerless to perform such a reining in, for in different circumstances they will point with equal conviction to helping one's neighbor and to cutting his throat. Their conditional imperative dictates means, not goals. Only the categorical imperative is strong enough to ensure unconditional control.

Imagine, those who hold such views tell us, a vast railroad network, traversed simultaneously by thousands of trains. Only through the great precision of each of the countless operators involved in this common task can we evade mortal danger, threatening the lives of thousands of people and a deep shock to the entire social system. What would happen if each of these operators were to act according to pragmatic norms? What would happen if they were to, essentially, pursue their own goals, trying to achieve them with maximal efficiency and with a minimal expenditure of energy? Even if the most experienced specialists were to come up with the very best and the most practical schedule that would outline in thorough detail each worker's responsibility, who can vouch that all these instructions will be followed? Everything will depend on the arbitrary choices of each of the many thousands of workers. Without the threat of coercive force over their heads, without fear of punishment, they may at any moment fall prey to indulgent and arbitrary whims and incorrect calculations. And collective life will become impossible as a result. Today, a tired train conductor will find it expedient to stop the train for a few hours to take a rest. Tomorrow, a stoker will prefer to contemplate an enchanting landscape over the tiresome task of attending to the furnace. The day after tomorrow, a switchman will deem it convenient to direct all trains to the reserve track for them to stand and wait there until he gets back to work after an amorous rendezvous. Only strict control may keep everyone within the exact boundaries of their responsibilities.

Such strong affects as wrath, vengeance, sexual attraction, and jealousy, which in our time so easily rupture the robust boundaries of law and morals, will meet with even less resistance within the framework of lithe and elastic forms of pure pragmatism. This will mean complete freedom for crime. Fear won't save people by preventing them from going to extremes and acting impulsively. Everything social will drown in the anarchic chaos of unbridled instinct. Insanity and fear will reign in place of reason and freedom.

All these arguments originate in the idea that human nature is essentially unchangeable. They are premised on a view of human nature as static, as something that, given any social forms or historical circumstances, remains egotistical and individualistic—just as we see in contemporary society. True to narrow and individualistic interests, human nature is alien to the idea of the whole. Social interests and social goals become ruling principles only through coercion and punishment, through violence and fear that make these social goals become the matters of personal strategies and individual goals. Fortunately, things are not as dire as this in the case of human nature, and the belief that it is unchangeable is a thing of the past.

Contemporary historical theory teaches us that the personality of a man is a derivation of his social environment. If in a given epoch he is an individualist, this is only because our contemporary atomized, anarchic society built on competition and class struggle turns him into one. As he is a reflection of this social structure, a person cannot help but be an individualist. However, he wasn't an individualist in another, differently organized primitive-communistic tribal society. In such a society, personal interest was not divorced from the collective interest. A person merged organically with his entire social environment—his group, his society—in the way that cells merge together in living tissues. Thousands of years of development had to pass before a man distinguished his personal goals from the shared goals of the collective. And this separation occurred only once the primitive unity of society had disintegrated—when from a small, organized system it grew into a large, disorganized aggregate.

There is no doubt that in a new society, in which the disjunctive forces of competition and class war have vanished, the psychology of separation, which holds that a person must oppose his interests to those of other people and society as a whole, will disappear as well. Realizing that he is an integral part of a greater whole, that his life exists in an uninterrupted connection with the life of this whole, a man will lose every notion of egotistical and narrowly individualistic goals. At the same time, coercive norms, regulating the struggle of these goals, will become superfluous.

Even in contemporary society, the bonds of coercion and violence only barely prevail over bonds of sympathy and solidarity. In a whole slew of cases the latter entirely prevails over the former. And it is exactly then that collective action reaches its greatest strength and balance. When two armies meet in battle, and the soldiers of one army are motivated by a coercive military and moral duty while the soldiers of the other act by the living, immediate consciousness of a common goal experienced as a love for their motherland (as was the case when backward Europe struggled against the great French Revolution), it is not hard to imagine which army would be more organized and heroic in action. Just how much more vivid, bright, and deep must the consciousness of the collective goal be in a society wherein this goal becomes apparent not only in exceptional circumstances, but instead permeates the entirety of social life and becomes directly embodied in the organized system of collective labor.

22

This is where the argument premised on "human nature" transforms into an argument based on the *nature of society*. It is precisely the collective organization of labor—the organizational form that alone is allegedly strong enough to eliminate personal, group, and class antagonisms and, by doing this, frees the way for pragmatic norms—that requires a massive development and expansion of coercive norms. Indeed, social production should be ordered in such a way as to fully satisfy all social needs. For this, human labor must be expediently distributed between all areas of production. And how can this distribution be accomplished other than through coercive measures? If everyone were free to choose for himself what type and how much work he would like to perform, then the most interesting areas of production would always be overfilled with workers, while other spheres would experience a dearth of laborers. Therefore, it is necessary to implement a universal workday—perhaps not too lengthy, but mandatory for all—and to deprive individuals of the right to choose their occupation. Such a compulsory workday will clearly involve instances of the complete subjugation of an individual to the external force of the whole, making it impossible for the pragmatic norms to fully prevail.

The fearsome specter of state barracks, where an individual is mercilessly chained to his hated work—the specter of "future slavery"—evokes profound anxiety in the contemporary individualist. The great scientist, who for eight hours each day has to stand by a loom performing mind-numbing labor, the talented artist who spends the same hours toiling in a dark coal mine, the genius novelist hunched over clerical accounting books, and so on and so forth—all these prison labor terrors simultaneously reflect the spontaneous, instinctive revulsion that the contemporary individualist feels for the higher forms nascent in the heart of capitalist society, as well as a profound *misunderstanding* of these forms.

Work is an organic human need. For a society to make people work it is not at all necessary to threaten them with the whip of the state or even with moral coercion. For a normal developing person, a workday is perhaps something more than just x number of hours. Consider a worker who has recently awakened to life: in the years before the Revolution he would, after ten to eleven hours of forced labor, often spend hours engaged in the most intensive self-education. Take a political activist, who often barely has time to eat and sleep after extremely strenuous labor. The psychology of these people of the future, already living in our contemporary society, guarantees that the future social order will have at its disposal a colossal amount of voluntary labor. Even within our present-day social relations, which systematically raise the upper classes to be parasites—even here, representatives of these classes in most instances are not mere idlers. Even pure rentiers work, albeit less than other people. The only difference is that they have the freedom to choose their occupation and, out of class prejudice and other abnormal life conditions, in most cases they settle for a profession that holds the least meaning and use for society. We have every reason to think, therefore, that even without any formal coercion the future society will not lack people willing to work. It is true, though, that perhaps this voluntary labor will not be evenly distributed across all spheres of production and that some areas may experience a shortage of it. Here is where the question of "filling the gaps" by coercive means appears. The *transitional collectivist society*—a society that will still operate within the bounds of state and legal forms and be based on organized class domination (the rule of the proletariat)—will certainly resort to enforcing the workday. However, given the sufficient development of productive forces, already in its early stages mandatory work will comprise only an insignificant part of the necessary collective labor, and this will likely require not an eight-hour but perhaps only a six-hour workday. When distributing this share of labor it is necessary that, whenever possible, society takes into consideration the personal inclinations and tastes of the workers. And only when the voluntary choice of labor does not meet real production needs will social obligation and coercive norm have to be put forth.

However, this pertains only to the transitional stage of such a society. Eventually, a change must occur in regards to two aspects. First, quickly developing production forces themselves will decrease the need for coercively organized labor. Machines will replace man, freeing him from labor, but not robbing him of the means of livelihood as happens in capitalist society. On the other hand, human psychology itself will change under this new type of social organization, becoming something all the more socially adept and all the less individualistic. This in turn will make the voluntary distribution of labor easier. The amount of labor missing from one area or another will be quickly filled by volunteer workers. No force of social coercion will be necessary to attract them, just statistical tables stating the social need. This will be accomplished all the more easily as the progressive development of technology makes transitioning from one kind of work to another less difficult, and as the intensive growth of energy in the human organism begins to give rise to a constant desire to substitute one set of labor processes with the other.

23

To conclude, neither human nature nor the nature of society contains conditions that preclude development from reaching the stage wherein external norms and coercive relations are fully abolished and pragmatic norms and comradely relations are completely ascendant. Only one question remains—a question of the utmost importance: Just how progressive are these higher forms of life? While allowing unlimited space for development, do they provide it with sufficient stimuli? Wouldn't their harmony lead to stagnation and their balance toward stasis? If this were the case, our contemporary world, with its tortured development characterized by multiple contradictions, would appear to be infinitely better than such a "higher" world blossoming harmoniously and painlessly in meaningless cyclical repetitions.

Advocates of individualism adamantly insist that this is exactly the case. To them, social development is born only out of the contradictions of social life. Competition and class struggle alone give impetus to progress. Weren't clan societies, unaware of such conflicts and contradictions, the most stagnant that history has ever known? Isn't it the case that technological advancement—the basis for all other types of progress—brought about precisely the kind of competition that propels capitalists to search for ever-new means of maintaining and protecting markets against their rivals? Isn't the very change of social forms driven by class struggle? And, therefore, isn't it obvious that to eliminate competition and class struggle, to eliminate the social contradictions inherent to spontaneous development, would be to erase technological progress together with the evolution of social forms and development in general?

Not only market competition and direct struggle but even the simplest forms of rivalry must disappear with the abolition of individualistic sentiments, since the former flow entirely out of the latter. When an individual does not place himself in opposition to others, there is no room for rivalry. What would then provide an incentive for growth? The answer is very simple. The struggles between people, competition, and rivalry are all only *derivative* stimuli for development, concealing the *primary* stimuli. The latter appear when man meets nature face to face, and when in direct struggle with it he acts as a productive, creative force. Here is an intrepid explorer in his solitary, desperate battle with arctic nature; here is a consummate hunter risking his life in a deadly war with predators; here a persistent inventor tirelessly strains his thought and imagination to subjugate yet another of the universe's elemental forces to man; here an idealistic scientist struggles with unwavering energy to wrestle its mystery from nature. These people experience the most rapid and intensive development. But could anyone say that it is only competition that drives their will? Of course not. Such motives are the least important to them.

Everywhere that we find new experiential material and everywhere that we find disharmony in its old material, the progressive, creatively harmonizing work of the mind begins. Clan society started to lose its conservatism and to advance technologically not as a result of competition between individuals, but of universal hunger brought by overpopulation. The discovery of America, and the mass of impressions that it brought, could have transformed humanity without the interference of any rivalry. A human enemy does not push us toward the path of progress nearly as forcefully and accurately as our other great and mysteriously enchanted adversary—nature.

Given complete mutual understanding among people, the breadth of comradely communication in the new social system will guarantee a flow of new sensations and experiential content. At the same time, the nuanced and complex harmony of life that will develop over time, and become nearly habitual, will attune sensitivities to every emerging disharmony. These conditions, necessary for the most intensive development, are in direct opposition to those that we observe in our contemporary world. Here the "fragmentation" of man through specialization diminishes the degree of mutual understanding and narrows the scope of communication. At the same time, the *habit* of life-disharmony, which naturally appears wherever a person is surrounded at every step with contradictions, dulls sensitivity to any further new disharmony. Out of our present experience we know all too well what extremes this insensitivity to the most atrocious and maddening manifestations of life-contradictions can reach in periods of social crises.

The internal social struggle that the individualist takes as the only possible and unquestionably necessary engine of progress in reality appears rather as its barrier. It wastes energy and dissipates the creative *attention* of men. The first point is clear all by itself; the latter becomes evident as soon as we recognize that the victory of one man over other people—even if their struggle is of an economic nature—is achieved by means that have nothing to do with social progress. How much thought and ingenuity that could have been put to a better end is wasted on stock market trickery? At the same time, the possibility of implementing machinery for production is becoming more limited, since the key reason for such an implementation is the profitability of these machines, rather than their usefulness—the increase in profit margins instead of care for the workers.

Man's struggle with nature—the *main* and *universal* engine of progress—is entirely devoid of such detrimental side effects.

The degree of progressiveness in comradely organizations depends heavily on the extent of communication that is achieved in them. Narrow circles, with their impoverished content, inevitably fall into conservatism as their members run out of new things to offer to each other. Large comradely organizations, depending on how diverse they are, survive much longer and develop more intensively. After a few years of flowering, communes with several hundred participants begin to decline. At the same time, political parties of an analogous type and counting thousands of members grow and become more robust while generating new forms faster and more energetically, without showing any signs of exhaustion. All this certainly leads us to conclude that progress may be accomplished with the greatest speed and energy, the greatest versatility and harmony, only in a society that would have comradely cooperation as its form and the whole of humanity as its limit. There the forces of development will become infinite.

Translated by Anastasiya Osipova

Note

1. Throughout this text, the Russian word *stikhijnost* is translated as "elemental force" or as "spontaneity," depending on context.—Trans.

12 Tektology of the Struggle against Old Age

Alexander Bogdanov

Let us try to apply our outlined principles to one particular yet essential question—the question of methods for fighting old age. Until now, this question has been a concern only of the applied sciences—of medicine and hygiene—and their insights were founded on the theoretical findings of physiology and pathology. However, if old age is a particular problem of universal organization and is an example of contradictions due to systemic discrepancies, then the problem of how to fight it could also be framed tektologically. Such an approach always involves the broadest generalization, and is therefore most useful for clarifying the *methods* of problem solving.

Previous specialized scientific thinking approached this task in the following manner: it analyzed the manifestations of old age in the same way as it analyzed diseases, and then searched for suitable medicine and a prophylactic diet. Some held that the process of aging began with the deterioration of the circulatory system: with the loss of blood vessels' elasticity and calcification of their walls. Against this they prescribed hygienic and medicinal measures. Others assigned special significance to the decrease of natural secretions having to do with sexual life, and attempted to replenish them with external supplements—extracts from seminal glands, and the like. Others still, taking as their point of departure chronic poisoning of the organism by substances released by the digestive tract, attempted to invent a medicinal diet. Undoubtedly, all of these approaches contain many useful

"Tektology of the Struggle against Old Age" was translated into English and published with permission from the International A. Bogdanov Institute, from *Tektologiya: Vseobschchaya organizatsionnaya nauka* (Moscow: International A. Bogdanov Institute and Finansi, 2003), 242–250.

elements, and many victories have been claimed along each of these paths. However, all of them are insufficient in principle, since *they are not holistic.* Meanwhile, old age is not a partial damage to the organism and not even a simple sum of partial, albeit numerous, damages.

One could call old age a tektological illness that extends to the entire structure of the organism. Partial methods against it are only palliative—they merely address individual symptoms, but do not help fight the underlying illness itself. The authors of such methods by and large admit this themselves and claim rather that they fight against "premature" and for "normal" and "natural" aging, that is, for the latest possible onset of old age in a given environment. And *this* old age is held to be something immutable. Whether consciously or unconsciously, we accept that old age has some metaphysical basis behind it—that some "exhaustion" of the vitality of all elements in an organism is inevitable. It is as if this vitality were some special energy, a specific quantity of which got invested into an organism, rather than a perpetually changing relationship between the organism's active and inactive processes, which gradually leads to its destruction.

This characterization can be extended to the newest and more successful experiments in rejuvenation practiced by Steinach, Voronov, and others. They ascribe the role of the "elixir of life" to internal secretions: the hormones of the so-called puberty gland, located between small vessels of the seminal gland. "Rejuvenation" is achieved by transplanting fresh testicles together with puberty glands from another organism, or by a partial vasectomy that enhances the growth of "puberty" tissue and stimulates the production of hormones in the testicles by slowing down the production of sperm. The frequent but unreliable success of these experiments depends—just as it did in the earlier trials—on the extent to which they are consistent with the "law of the least."[1]

Indeed, all systems of organs in a living organism are inextricably connected and mutually necessary, and must be *mutually sufficient.* Each one provides some living conditions for the rest. As a consequence, the life of the whole is necessarily limited by the level of functioning of the weakest and the least advanced systems. If, for instance, the source of weakness and decline lies in the respiratory system or in the digestive system, then to support these systems would mean to elevate the life of the whole to the level of the next system that has fallen behind. If the hormones of the puberty gland are necessary for the normal functioning of the organism, the entire life of the organism will decrease with the decrease of their secretion. And vice versa: the increased activity of this small organ results in the general increase of all functions. Therefore, to accept that, for the majority of males of the higher species that lead intensive sex lives, the decline begins precisely with that specific organ and function suffices to explain the success of the many experiments undertaken in this direction—a success that, of course, is only partial and temporary.

However, rejuvenation through vasectomy and suppressing the production of semen leads us to think that here we are also dealing with another "least": with weakening the cells of the central nervous system and supporting them by increasing their vital balance. The production of sperm undoubtedly competes with the functioning of the nerve cells, since it requires a relatively large intake of phosphorus, proteins, and nucleoproteins—after all, the largest part of a sperm cell consists of a nucleus, which is rich in these substances. If we take into consideration a difficult (for the depleted nerve cells) struggle with neuroglia, or the connecting tissue cells, and the cells of the brain membrane, then we can easily imagine how even a small deficiency of this precious material may prove to be fatal for the nerve cells, which then get dominated by the lower elements. It is also clear that improving balance by reducing such significant expenditure may improve matters for a while. Transplanting fresh testicles enhances balance in an analogous but somewhat different manner. It instantly introduces into the organism a large store of substances so important for the nerve cells, which, during the regressive transformations of sperm-producing cells of the transplanted gland, are gradually absorbed through the lymph and blood.

It is easier to reconcile this position with an altogether different response of the female organisms to the analogous methods of rejuvenation, as well as to castration. On the one hand, "rejuvenation" itself does not produce the same level of results as with males. On the other, however, removal of ovaries has a far less pronounced effect on the female organism's life and does not precipitate its decline as dramatically as does the removal of a testicle in males. This has to do with the fact that the production of oocytes does not compete with the nerve cells for nucleus-forming substances to the same degree and, as a consequence, has a much smaller influence on their balance. A single oocyte is only hundreds or thousands of times larger than a spermatozoid, while billions of sperm cells are produced per each oocyte. Its production is regulated only by hormones and does not lead to changes of the phosphorous balance in the brain.

One way or another, it is clear that what we are dealing with here are partial adjustments to an organism's living system. However, as should be already obvious from our previous discussion, it may be possible to radically reformulate the problem and approach it in a *much broader and more general* way if we consider it from the point of view of tektology. This approach will aim to *resolve all systematic contradictions.* We also know of a method that is holistic and not merely partial: it consists in *counterdifferentiation.* The question that remains is how to apply this method.

If while exploring this question we consider only an isolated organism, then we will immediately encounter insurmountable difficulties. First of all, conjugation gives positive results only up to a certain stage of divergence. When it moves past this stage, the integration becomes too disharmonious and is accompanied by too large an expenditure of activity. Advancing any further leads to an inevitable crash and complete destruction. In the human body the extent of cell differentiation is incomparably greater than that of the cells capable of integration in the organisms of different species, even when they are of a relatively high level of development (take the example of infusorium Paramoecium). Any biologist understands that the conjugation of a nerve cell with a striated muscle tissue, for instance, would be an utter absurdity. Every such counterdifferentiation would inevitably and radically disturb other accompanying complex correlations, and with them the foundation of the organism's resilience. A task of this type is resolvable only inasmuch as it is possible to preserve the necessary additional connections after conjugation.

Second, even direct and technically simple conjugation of heterogeneous tissues is impossible without their destruction, since all their functions are steadily bound with their position in the organism, which is, in turn, fixed by the skeletal system (bones, cartilage, and connective tissue).

If this is true, where should we look for a solution? We should go along the same path that nature, our great teacher of tektology, travels searching for and successfully discovering the answer. When nature has to solve this type of problem, it expands its circle of data: it does not confine itself by working with a single organism, but takes two or even more. The copulation and conjugation of single-cell organisms and the merging of sexual cells in higher organisms are some of the methods of fighting against the negative aspects of systematic divergence. The decline of an individual's vitality is overcome through the joint efforts of several organisms. Even so-called protoplasmic immortality may be accomplished in this way.

Until recently, two forms of conjugation between humans have been known to us. The first is sexual—just as in many other species. The second type is the conjugation of experience by means of speech, gestures, and art, as well as other forms of expression and perception, which have developed through the functioning of the nervous and muscular systems. Such conjugation is not only "psychological"—as the instances when it is prolonged clearly demonstrate (for example, between spouses). Thanks to the dependence of all organs and tissues on the activity of the nervous system, the physical resemblance between spouses acquired after fifteen to twenty years of shared life on average is no less, if not greater, than that commonly found between brothers and sisters.

Medicine has already added a third form of conjugation to these two. At the moment it is still *one-sided* and rather *limited*; however, it is already a form of *direct physiological* conjugation. It consists of organ and tissue transplantations: skin grafts for burn victims, blood transfusions, injections of blood serums, and so on. Animal experiments by Alexis Carrel, Prjbram,[2] and others with transplanting sometimes whole and very complex organs—for instance, a kidney or an eye from one specimen to another—open vast perspectives in this direction.

Practically, such transplantations are examples of the already-familiar type of solution to the problem of "specific resistances." Sometimes resistances of an organism become insufficient within its particular parts or functions. It is then necessary to add these resistances from without. Transfusions of another person's blood may be administered to prevent death from blood loss; an organism can be injected with the serum extracted from an "immunized" animal that would paralyze diphtheria microbes and their poisons, and so on. Formulating the task of conjugation in this fashion is deeply *one-sided* and *limited*. Such an approach envisions blood transfusion only from one person to another, never its exchange and mutual blending.

Counterdifferentiation has an altogether different character. It can be viewed as a solution to the common problem of "indeterminably changeable resistances." The struggle against old age belongs to this type of problem. A solution that readily suggests itself is to attempt something similar to the rejuvenation of live cells through conjugation. However, these cells, with their colloidal semiliquid structure, may easily exchange some of their living tissue or even merge with each other completely. In people and in other higher organisms—with their skeleton, skin, bones, and cartilage, and so on—such easy blending of cells is impossible. But what is possible here? Contemporary scientific technology can enable us to practice direct conjugation of liquid tissues such as blood and lymph from different organisms. These are the tissues that compose an organism's inner conjugational environment and support its chemical unity through uninterrupted exchange with other tissues. Technically, the procedure will consist of a slightly complicated version of a normal blood transfusion. Subjects A and B will exchange blood, and neither will experience any quantitative blood loss.

Most multicellular organisms—especially the higher ones—are covered with a protective skeletal layer: for example, cornea and fibrous "skin" in humans. As a consequence, grafting and transplanting living tissues is possible only by wounding the integrity of the protective layer. This results in a partial disorganization of a living system, dangerous to its survival. It is therefore only natural that conjugational methods were used on humans (the most interesting biological test subject for us) only when the wound was already present (for instance, grafting of skin after severe burns), or when inflicting a wound presented a smaller risk for an already considerably disorganized system (an incision or an injection to perform a blood transfusion during an acute anemia or to administer serums to treat infectious diseases). The consequences of such necessary damage may be quite serious, and transplantation or transfusion themselves are even more dangerous if unsuccessful. In the past, a blood transfusion often resulted in the patient's death. For this reason, the idea of reverting to transplantation and transfusion in cases other than extreme and specific pathologies has not occurred to anyone before. And since experimentation on animals was tailored to treating humans, no experiments with mutual transfusion were conducted in that area either.

However, from the tektological point of view, science was not at all obligated to limit itself to partial tasks and one-sided methods. Here, as everywhere else, specialization narrowed and constrained scientific work. Medics and physiologists did not consider the possibilities that followed from the general biological theory of copulation and conjugation. The question of improving well-being through direct physiological exchanges of living matter was not even posed. The miracles of scientific development of recent years make it hard to believe that what was lacking was either courage or intelligence. What was really missing was a corresponding *trend* of thinking. However, now that we have arrived at the general formula for conjugation, its logic *compels* us to pose this question. A decisive answer to it will be found through precise experiments, which will undoubtedly be conducted in the future. It is no accident that systematic experiments with transplantation of living tissue are already underway in a number of laboratories, and that prominent specialists openly promote and search for partial methods of resisting old age, that is, for methods of holistically increasing vitality—something that in nature is achieved precisely through conjugation.

Owing to the extraordinary importance of this question, we will consider its practical aspects in the future.

Many brilliant experiments with transplanting organs and tissues are laying the groundwork for a considerably broader application of the conjugation method. Still, because of technical difficulties it is unlikely that this method will be fully developed any time soon. Contemporary technology permits a *comparatively* easy and comfortable conjugation of liquid bodily tissue—of blood and lymph. On the other hand, methods and techniques for such procedures may already be considered ready and established.

Blood transfusion was almost entirely abandoned in the beginning of the century, but has been recently experiencing a resurgence, especially in the aftermath of the world war. Today it is used not only in cases of blood loss, but also in cases of severe blood infections. Thanks to the renewal of this practice, the tools and surgical techniques for blood transfusion have been perfected so that this procedure poses no *major* practical difficulties. Reliable methods of preventing the coagulation of transfused blood have been discovered. The conditions for blood incompatibility and simple methods of eliminating it have also been found. We now have a classification of blood according to blood poisons, and so forth. In a word, it is now possible to prevent almost all the risks of this procedure.

Since none of the patients lose any blood during the blood exchange, a transfusion of a very considerable volume is possible. Naturally, a complete transfusion is unthinkable, as well as undesirable. Half of the total blood volume of each donor is the highest amount of blood that may be exchanged. However, even this would make the procedure very long. An exchange of one-third of the donor's blood would require considerably less time.

Several repetitions of the procedure are permitted, in case there is a need to increase its effects. If one of the original "conjugating" donors is replaced by another person, the resulting effects may be more complex.

What can such procedure offer? Naturally, it would have been naive to suppose—as the ancient alchemists did—that young blood may simply and mechanically rejuvenate an old organism by supplying it with an excess of "vital force," while old blood could age a young one. However, it would be no less of a mistake to think of blood as a simple, nutritional liquid. Blood is a living tissue that is very complex and of enormous significance for the organism's entire organization. It is home to leukocytes, which fight against microbes; its serum produces antitoxins, the "antidotes" against microbial and other poisons; and finally, hormones—the internal secretions of a number of specialized glands, which regulate many aspects of organism's life—circulate within it. As the inner environment of an organism, the environment for all its organs and tissues, blood bears their structural imprint as their living supplement. Therefore, as precise tests demonstrate, its content is *individual* and is never the same in any two organisms. It cannot but influence all organs and tissues and be influenced by them in turn. During blood transfusion from one organism to another, we inevitably transfer "immunities"—abilities to resists various infections, along with leukocytes of varying "combatant abilities," and hormones with their regulating tendencies, and so on. The fact that none of this has been seriously studied until now may be explained by scientists' attention having been directed elsewhere. Serum therapy as a whole is immutable evidence in favor of our position.

The most likely conclusion is the following: the conjugation of liquid tissues must have not a partial but a *comprehensive* influence on an organism's vital functions. We have all grounds to believe that young blood with its materials taken from young tissue may help an aging organism's fight on the frontlines where it is already experiencing defeat—that is, precisely where it is "ageing." The exact extent to which this procedure may be beneficial can be established only experimentally.

However, don't we have reasons to think that old blood will "age" a young organism? This is highly unlikely. The strength of youth is in its tremendous capacity to assimilate and to process all sorts of material. As is well known, it can easily cope even with a significant loss of blood by restoring it quickly. One can expect that it will also cope with weakened and impaired blood—except perhaps in the case of blood poisoning. Besides, older or otherwise inferior blood must nevertheless contain elements for development that better and younger blood lacks. However, we have no reason to limit such conjugation to combining old and young or strong and weak: expansion of life here depends on the ability *to transgress the limitations of individuality* by establishing a living accord between two previously separate individualities.

Some important specifics suggest themselves. For instance, let's suppose that we have two organisms, which, owing to the individual conditions of their conception and development, have accumulated two different types of toxins and cannot eliminate them fully from their tissues. In this case, a reciprocal blood transfusion must produce a deep cleansing and reinvigoration of the organism and liberate it from harmful, internal poisons.

Further, let's consider the transmission of immunity against various diseases. Since the volume of blood that could be transferred in a reciprocal transfusion may be quite large—in fact, it may constitute a significant part of the entire blood volume of each of the participants—the transmission of immunity may be similarly vast. Besides, we can expect the transmission not only of the immunities gained after recovering from an illness or vaccination by toxins but also of those we previously did not know how to pass down—the immunities that depend on age (adult immunities from children's diseases and vice versa), inherited immunities, and so forth.

Perhaps the main achievement will be the positive increase in the sum of developmental elements. It is true that we still do not know exactly the extent to which blood and lymph serve as carriers of organic properties embodied in the rest of the organs and tissues. However, from an organizational point of view, it is unthinkable that, given their close communication, liquid tissues would not reflect the structure and composition of other organs and tissues.

We have a direct indication of this: if *inheritance of acquired characteristics* exists—and it appears that to a certain extent modern science has to admit its existence—then what medium other than blood or lymph could carry toward the new cells the necessary reproduction factors of the changes that other parts of the body have experienced?

Needless to say, this path contains many difficulties and even dangers. We know from other types of conjugation that combining several individual complexes is not always beneficial. Not to mention the possibility of transmitting diseases, and so on. However, the sole conclusion that we could draw from this is that we need to conduct systematic research and stage our experiments very carefully, starting with experimentation on animals. It should be mentioned that such experiments with animals have technically already been carried out, although they pursued entirely different aims. An experiment in cross-blood circulation was set up to research the influence of inner poisons and the by-products of overexhaustion on the organism. The carotid arteries of two dogs were artificially conjoined in such a way that blood from one of them flowed into the brain of another, and vice versa. However, in one case, such experiments were undertaken with a goal quite similar to ours: the experiments of A. Kahn, published in America in 1916. He injected a bacterial infection into the abdomens of several dogs and then set up a cross-blood transfusion between pairs of infected and healthy dogs for a duration of an hour or longer. In doing so he discovered that infected dogs subjected to this treatment recovered faster than the ones that were not. The results were all the more impressive, since the procedure itself—which involved incisions, damage to large blood vessels, and nervous shock—could not have been beneficial to the dogs' health. We can conclude that resistance to infection increases if two organisms are fighting it simultaneously: the role of conjunction is obvious here.

We saw that the conjunction method is applicable to such diverse complexes as simple drops of water and living cells, psychological images and social organizations, and even to such abstract and ideological systems as languages and dialects. Knowing this, we can expect with a probability close to certainty that it will be applicable to the organizational forms situated *between* these aforementioned types. Between a simple cell and social organization is a multicellular colonial system—a complex organism. And since, as we know, the extremes are capable of deep, real conjugation, which expands the limits of their vitality, it would have been a strange exception if the same would not have been possible for an intermediate element.

The sole reason why this research, which could open an immense field of work and perspectives of unheard-of victories, is not already fully underway is the *individualism* of contemporary scientific thinking, for which the idea of deep physiological exchange of life between two individuals must seem not only strange but directly repulsive. Of course, development will overcome this obstacle.

After almost twenty years of trying to attract the interest of competent specialists to this question, I decided to undertake similar experiments myself, with the help of few sympathetic doctors and with the rather meager means available to us. Over the course of two and a half years, we managed to arrange almost a dozen blood transfusions between old and young people. Although these experiments did not follow the conjunction method fully, they offered some concrete results. Approximately one-seventh to a quarter of blood volume was exchanged. My impression from the experiments—I dare not speak of anything other than "impressions," for owing to the meagerness of our means and equipment our data are hardly sufficient—is that our theoretical foresight was confirmed. Out of eleven participants in the first experiments (four seniors, seven young people—some of whom were subjected to the procedure more than once), approximately ten reported an increased sense of vitality and energy. The most consistent influence was on the nervous system—we observed a marked boost in productivity and improvement in overall well-being. It is hardly possible to attribute these symptoms to suggestion. Even if senior patients might have been positively impressed by the thought of being injected with young blood, young patients receiving old blood should have manifested the opposite psychological effect. As expected, nerve cells proved to be particularly sensitive to the changes of inner environment. However, we also established other objective changes especially among the senior patients, such as rapid improvement in those suffering from atherosclerosis and gout, partial return of gray hairs to their original color (although this effect was temporary and would disappear after several months), and considerable increase in lung capacity as well as muscular force (the last two symptoms were observed in one of the younger participants). In general, even in the most cautious assessment of these results, we must acknowledge that *we have a wealth of material to explore here*. A wide sphere for experimentation opens up before us: the combinations are infinite. And if it turns out that repeated conjugations of this type may accrue positive results, then it will be impossible to predict just how many future successes these experiments promise.

Translated by Anastasiya Osipova

Notes

1. Zenovia A. Sochor explains that "the 'Law of the Least' (*zakon naimen'shikh*) establishes the conditions for the maintenance or the destruction of the system; that is, the stability of the whole is defined by the least stable of its parts." Zenovia A. Sochor, *Revolution and Culture: The Bogdanov–Lenin Controversy* (Ithaca, NY: Cornell University Press, 1988), 47.—Ed.

2. G. Prjbram. See, for example, G. Prjbram, "Obzor mneniy avtorov o znachenii analogii mezhdu kristallami i organizmom" [Review of the opinions of authors on the importance of analogy between crystals and the organism], in *Chto takoye zhizn'* [What is life], from the series "Novyye idei v biologii" [New ideas in biology] (Moscow: "Education," 1913).—Ed.

13 Immortality Day

Alexander Bogdanov

1

One thousand years have passed since the day the genius chemist Fride invented a formula for physiological immunity. Injecting the formula into the bloodstream renewed the body's tissues and sustained its eternal blossoming youth.

The dreams of medieval alchemists, philosophers, poets, and kings had come true.

Cities in their previous forms ceased to exist. Thanks to the ease and universal accessibility of air travel, people were no longer limited by distance and settled all over the Earth in luxurious villas surrounded by greenery and flowers.

Each villa was equipped with a spectrotelephone that connected its apartments with theaters, press agencies, and civic organizations. On a glass screen in the leisure of their own homes all could enjoy the songs of artists, theater performances, the speeches of orators, and conversations with friends.

Where there were once cities, enormous skyscrapers now towered, housing community centers, schools, museums, and other civic establishments.

The Earth was transformed into a single massive fruit garden. Trained forest rangers oversaw the artificial breeding of wild animals in designated parks.

There was no shortage of water. Water was obtained by running electricity through a compound of oxygen and hydrogen. Refreshing fountains poured cascades of water into shady parks. Earth was adorned with symmetrical ponds that shone like silver in the sun and contained all types of fish.

Artificial suns made of radium had already melted the polar ice caps, and at night electric moons cast a gentle glow over the Earth.

Only one danger threatened Earth: overpopulation. For people were no longer dying. The people's legislative committee approved a law prohibiting women from bearing more than thirty children during their endless lives on Earth. Children born over this quota were relocated to other planets in hermetically sealed spaceships when they reached their five-hundredth birthdays, the age of maturity. Humanity's unlimited life permitted very distant journeys. In this way, humanity came to colonize not only Earth, but all neighboring planets in the solar system.

2

Having woken on a luxurious bed made of platinum wires and aluminum, Fride took a quick shower, did his routine gymnastic exercises, put on his clothes woven from a light thermofabric that gave off heat in the winter and kept the body cool in the summer, and ate a breakfast of nutritional chemical bars and an extract of processed wood fiber that tasted of Bessarabian wine. All of that took about an hour. To avoid wasting time, he connected his bathroom via microphone to a newspaper agency broadcasting world news.

A tranquil and happy feeling of strength and health spread throughout his entire body, which seemed to be made of only bone and muscle.

Fride remembered that midnight would mark one thousand years since the discovery of human immortality. A thousand years! Almost in spite of himself, he began to take stock of his life.

The adjacent room held a collection of Fride's written works, totaling about four thousand volumes. His diary, discontinued after eight hundred fifty years of life, was also there. It was written in a simplified syllabic method (not entirely unlike ancient stenography) and occupied sixty enormous folios. Farther behind his study was an art studio, next to it a sculpture workshop, and farther still, a hall in the Varienocturne style that had replaced the previous décor in the decadent style. It was there that Fride wrote poetry. Finally, there was a symphony hall with string and keyboard instruments that he played by means of various mechanical devices allowing him to achieve an unusual fullness and brilliance of sound. Situated above the house was a chemistry lab.

Fride's genius was versatile and reminiscent of the virtuosity of one of his maternal ancestors—Bacon, who was not only a great scientist, but also a playwright whose works had long been misattributed to Shakespeare. Over the course of a millennium Fride had proven himself in all spheres of the arts and sciences.

From chemistry, where, so he thought, he exhausted all the powers of his intellect, Fride moved on to sculpture. In the course of eighty years he became an equally accomplished sculptor, bringing into the world many wonderful things. From sculpture he turned to literature: in a hundred years he composed two hundred dramatic plays and up to fifteen thousand poems and sonnets. Then painting attracted him. As a painter he was mediocre. Still, he mastered the technique perfectly, and after fifty years of practice, all the critics assured him of a glorious future. As a painter of promise he worked for another fifty years before moving on to music: he composed several operas that met with some success. In this fashion, at different times, Fride moved from astronomy to the mechanics of history, and then, finally, to philosophy. After that he no longer knew what to do. His brilliant mind had absorbed everything that contemporary culture had to offer, and he returned once again to chemistry.

Through his chemistry experiments he resolved the final problem society had struggled with since the time of Helmholtz: the question of spontaneous conception of organisms and the animation of inert matter. There were no other problems left.

Fride worked in the mornings. From his bedroom he usually headed straight to the lab.

Warming up his beakers on the electric stove, he hastily recited in his head formulas that were so familiar that there was no need to write them down. During this routine, a strange feeling came upon him, one that had recently become more frequent.

His experiments no longer interested or absorbed him. It had been a long time since he felt the joyful rush of enthusiasm that used to kindle his soul, to inspire and fill him with supreme happiness. His thoughts were inadvertently following familiar beaten paths—hundreds of combinations came and went in redundant and tiresome patterns. He stood, sensing the heavy and anxious emptiness in his soul, thinking:

Physically, man became a likeness of God. He can rule over worlds and space. But could human thought, which the people of the Christian era said was limitless, really have its borders? Could the brain, which includes only a certain number of neurons, be capable of producing only a finite number of ideas, images, and feelings—but no more?

If this is so, then ...

A terror of the future overcame Fride.

Upon hearing the familiar melody of the automatic clock announcing the end of his working time, he breathed a deep sigh of relief—a feeling he never used to associate with his studies.

3

At two o'clock Fride was in the collective dining hall he visited daily, solely to meet his numerous offspring and descendants, many of whom he had never met.

He had around fifty children, two thousand grandchildren, and several dozens of thousands of great- and great-great-grandchildren. His descendants, now scattered around many countries and even worlds, could have comprised the population of a major city in ancient times.

Fride did not feel any familial affection toward his children and grandchildren, as was common for the people of the past. His family was too numerous for each of its members to hold a special place in his heart. He loved them all with an abstract and noble love, one that was reminiscent of a love for humanity in general.

In the dining hall he was greeted with due ceremony and was introduced to a still very young man of two hundred fifty: his grandson Margo, a distinguished astronomer.

Margo had just returned from a twenty-five-year-long absence. He had been on an expedition to Mars and now spoke freely about his travels. The Martian population—the megalantropes—had quickly mastered all of the cultural achievements of Earth. They wanted to visit their teachers from Earth; however, their immense height precluded them from fulfilling their wish. Presently they were setting to work on the construction of large air ships.

Fride was distractedly listening to Margo's tales of Martian flora and fauna, of its canals and the cyclopic constructions built by its dwellers. And all of this, described by Margo with such passion, did not touch him in the least. Three hundred years ago, he had been among the first to fly to Mars and had spent almost seven years there. Later, he made two or three additional brief excursions to the planet. By now each nook and cranny of Mars was as familiar to him as those of Earth.

However, so as not to offend his grandson by his lack of attention, he asked:

"Please tell me, my young companion, while on Mars, did you meet my old friend Levionach? And if so, how is he?"

"I certainly did meet him, our venerable patriarch," Margo answered eagerly. "Levionach is busy constructing a tremendous tower as tall as the Elbrus."

"I knew it, I knew it," murmured Fride with a mysterious smile. "I predicted that upon reaching a certain age, all Martians would be consumed with a passion for tall buildings. And with that, my dear young companion, I must bid you farewell. I have an important task I must hurry to. I wish you all the luck in the world."

4

Margarita Anche, a blossoming woman of seven hundred and fifty, and Fride's current wife, was the president of an amateur philosophical society. Fride's relationship with her was already becoming a burden.

While still several miles away from her villa, Fride announced his approach by means of phonogram. Fride and Anche lived separately so as not to infringe upon each other's independence.

Anche greeted her husband in the alcove of mysteries and miracles—a wondrous pavilion where everything was illuminated with a soft ultrachromolite hue, the eighth color in the spectrum of light. It was unknown to ancient peoples with their underdeveloped sight, just as green was unknown to primitive people.

A beautiful silk tunic—cut above the knee to allow her free movement—gracefully and lightly enveloped her slender frame. Her loose black hair fell in waves along her back. An aroma of a subtle and sensuous perfume followed her.

"I am very glad to see you, dear Fride," she said, kissing her husband on his pronounced, distinctive forehead, which looked as if it were sculpted out of marble. "I need you for a very important piece of business."

"I guessed as much, from our previous telephonoscope conversation," responded Fride. "I must confess I was somewhat surprised by your mysterious look. So, what's the matter? Why such urgency?"

"I wanted it that way, my dear," said Anche with a playful smile. "It may be folly, but sometimes I am visited by desires that I have difficulty chasing away. By the way, where are we going to celebrate the Holiday of Immortality tonight? Also, you might recall, today is the eighty-third anniversary of our marriage."

"Oh dear," thought Fride, and answered reluctantly:

"I don't know! I haven't thought about that yet."

"But, certainly, we are going to celebrate together?" asked Anche, with some anxiety trembling in her voice.

"But of course," said Fride. An unpleasant feeling was spreading through him, and for that reason he hastened to change the topic:

"What is this important business of yours?"

"I'll tell you right away, my dear. I wanted to prepare a surprise for the new millennium. An idea, which I will acquaint you with, has been occupying me for several decades, and only now has acquired a final definition."

"Hmm, something from the area of irrational pragmatism?" joked Fride.

"Oh, no!" Anche retorted with a graceful smile.

"In that case, something that has to do with politics?" Fride went on: "You women are always ahead of men in these respects."

Anche laughed.

"You are a wonderful oracle, dear. Yes, I am working on organizing a cell to undertake a civil revolution on Earth and I need your help. You must become our ally and help disseminate my ideas. Given your connections and influence, that won't be difficult."

"All depends on the character of your plans," countered Fride, after a short pause. "I cannot promise you anything in advance."

Anche crossed her eyebrows slightly and continued:

"My idea is to abolish the last remaining legislative chains that bind the people of Earth. Let each given man individually enact what in ancient times was called the state. Let him or her be autonomous. No one is to restrict them. Central power is to have control only over the organization of common wealth."

"But aren't things essentially this way already?" contradicted Fride. "Tell me, how and where is a citizen's will infringed upon?"

Anche flared up and continued passionately:

"And what about the law that limits women to having only thirty children? Is this not a restriction? Is it not a barbarous violence toward women? It is true that you men do not feel the burden of this law?"

"But isn't this law born out of economic necessity?"

"Then we have to leave its resolution not to a fluke of nature, but to the wise intervention of reason. Why should I reject my thirty-fifth son, the fortieth, and so on, and keep the thirtieth on Earth, when my fortieth son may be a genius, and the thirtieth—a pathetic mediocrity! Let only the strong and distinguished ones remain on Earth, and let the weak ones leave it. Earth must be an assembly of geniuses."

Fride retorted coldly:

"These are improbable fantasies, and they are not even new. They were expressed one hundred and fifty years ago by a biologist called Madlen. We cannot break rules that are wise. By the way, I must tell you that ancient women did not think the way you do. They had what is called maternal compassion: they loved the weak and deformed children more than the strong and beautiful ones. No, I will not be your ally. More than that, as a member of the government and a representative of the Council of the Hundred, I will veto your actions."

"But you, being a genius, should not be afraid of revolts!"

"Yes. But as a genius I foresee all of the terror that will befall Earth if the question of relocation were decided by citizens' free will. This would trigger such a struggle for power on Earth that it would destroy mankind. Although, mankind will unavoidably perish anyways, but for other reasons; it will seal itself off in a hermetic cycle of monotony," concluded Fride, as if he was talking only to himself. "But why should we bring the fated moment nearer?"

Anche was silent. She had not at all anticipated a rejection.

Coldly turning her classical profile to Fride, she said woundedly:

"Do as you will! I can't help noticing that recently something is amiss in our relationship. I do not know; perhaps it has become a burden to you."

"Perhaps," Fride responded dryly, "one must get accustomed to the thought that love does not last forever on Earth. You are the eighteenth woman in my life whom I have married and the ninety-second whom I have loved."

"But of course!" said Anche, angrily biting her lip, pink stains marring her golden complexion. "But for some reason you husbands demand that your wives remain faithful to you to the end, and always claim it your prerogative to cheat on her first."

Fride shrugged: "That's the rule of strength, which you've just been advocating."

Anche was trembling with anger, but masterfully took hold of herself and responded with a proud dignity:

"So we are to part. Well then. I wish you all the best in your future life."

"I sincerely wish you the same!" responded Fride, trying to ignore the bitterness of her words.

His sole feeling was that of a heavy languor. Thirty-one times he had endured these words from a woman, accompanied by the same gestures, the same expressions, and the same tone.

"How old all of this is getting! And how trite!" he thought, while getting into an elegant, toy-like airplane.

5

Fride spent the evening on a flying platform five thousand meters above Earth, with a large group of youth gathered to celebrate Margo's return. They were seated around a round revolving table, the top of which would glide on rails of air, carrying back flowers, fruit, and stimulating and exciting drinks that were wondrously aromatic and pleasant to the taste.

Down below, Earth was illuminated with beautiful bright lights, the lights of cars moving down the network of smooth highways—all sportsmen who from time to time indulged in this type of outmoded transportation. Electric moons, with their phosphorescent light, were pouring a soft blue onto the gardens, villas, canals, and lakes. Seen from a distance, with the play of light, its reflections and half-shadows, Earth seemed enveloped by a translucent silver mesh.

The youth, especially young Margo, who had not seen Earth for twenty-five years, admired the beautiful sight that opened before them.

Margo turned a mechanical knob, and the chair on which he was seated rose up on its legs so that everyone could see him as he spoke.

"Friends! I suggest that we drink a toast in honor of the universe!"

"Excellent!" The gathered guests joined in happily. "A toast and a hymn!"

During the celebrations people often sang national hymns composed by the patriarchs of great families. This is why Margo followed his first suggestion with a second:

"Friends! Since we are honored today by the presence of our esteemed patriarch Fride at this table, I suggest that we sing his hymn 'The Immortal One.'"

All eyes were now on Fride. He sat absorbed in his thoughts, and upon hearing his name, nodded in assent.

Accompanied by a majestic symphonion, clear male and female voices joined in the hymn, composed in sonorous and bold major tones. The hymn consisted of eight-line stanzas, each concluding with these words:

Blessed is the one soul of the universe,
Spread around grains of sand and stars,
Blessed is omnipotence, since it is
The source of eternal life.
Blessed is immortality, which made people like gods!

The sound of this magnificent chorus soared above and seemed to be simultaneously a prayer and an exalted breath of the sky itself, bringing its mysterious blue depth closer to Earth.

Only Fride sat there, indifferent to all that was happening around him. When the singing was over, everyone regarded him again. One of his more or less close grandsons, the chemist Lynch, took it upon himself to break the silence:

"Venerable patriarch! What is the matter with you? You are not joining us in the singing of your hymn."

Fride lifted his head. For an instant he thought that he shouldn't mar the young crowd's happiness with his doubts; however, this thought was immediately replaced by another: sooner or later they all will inevitably experience the same thing as him.

And Fride said:

"This hymn is the greatest error my mind has committed. Omnipotence and immortality deserve curses, not praise. Yes, let them be damned!"

Everyone turned to the patriarch in amazement. He paused, looking at his audience with an expression of deep suffering and torment:

"Eternal life is an unbearable torture. Everything in this life is repeated; such is the cruel law of nature. Entire worlds are created out of chaotic matter, ignite, fade away, collide with others, get pulverized into dust, and then are formed anew. And so it goes on like this without end. Our thoughts, feelings, desires, actions, all get repeated, even the very idea that 'everything repeats itself' returns to my mind for the thousandth time. This is intolerable!"

Fride held his head in his hands. He felt he was going mad.

They all stood astonished by his words.

A moment later Fride spoke again, loudly and sternly, as if challenging somebody to a battle:

"What a great tragedy human life is—to receive power from God just to transform into an automaton that repeats itself with the precision of a mechanical clock! To know in advance what the Martian Levionach will do or what your beloved woman will say! An eternally living body joined to an eternally dead spirit, cold and indifferent, like an extinguished sun!"

No one knew how to respond. Only the chemist Lynch, having come to his senses after the initial shock of Fride's speech, addressed him:

"Dear teacher! It seems to me that there is a way out of this situation. What if we were to resurrect the cells of the brain and recreate ourselves, to achieve reincarnation!"

"This is not a solution," scowled Fride bitterly. "If such resurrection is possible, it would only mean that the present, currently existing 'I' with all of my thoughts, feelings, and desires, would disappear without a trace. Someone else, unknown and alien to me, would go on thinking and feeling in my stead. In antiquity people composed fables about a man's soul, after death, entering another being and forgetting about his previous life. How would my renewed and resurrected state be different from such primitive beliefs about death and reincarnation? In no way at all. Should humanity have used its genius to gain immortality simply to return to the problem of death?"

Fride abruptly fell silent, rolled his chair toward the end of the platform and, as he waved goodbye, added:

"Forgive me, my friends, for leaving you. I regret that I ruined your good time with my speech."

Already getting ready to fly back to Earth, Fride shouted from his airplane:

"One way or another, only death can put an end to the torments of the spirit!"

These perplexing last words shook everyone and cast on their spirits a vague premonition of some impending tragedy. Margo, Lynch, and the rest all rolled their chairs to the edge of the platform and, for a long time, anxiously followed the movement of Fride's airplane, its glowing blue lights gliding through the vast expanse of the night.

6

Fride decided to commit suicide—however, he faced the difficulty of choosing an exact method for dying. Contemporary medicine was capable of reviving corpses and restoring individual body parts. All of the ancient means of killing oneself—cyanide, morphine, carbon monoxide, strychnine—were of no use.

He could have blown himself up or flown into space to become a satellite of some planet. However, Fride chose self-immolation, and moreover, self-immolation in its ancient barbarian form—being burned at the stake, although the technology of his time allowed for near-instantaneous combustion of large masses of material with the use of radium.

"To burn at the stake! At the very least, it will be beautiful."

He wrote his will:

"After one thousand years of my existence I have come to the conclusion that life on Earth is a cycle of repetitions, especially intolerable for a man of genius, whose entire being yearns for innovation. This is one of nature's antinomies. I resolve it with suicide."

He built a pyre in the alcove of mysteries. He bound himself with chains to an iron pole, around which he had piled up kindling.

Mentally, he surveyed all that he was leaving behind on Earth.

Not one desire, not a single attachment was he able to seize on! A terrible loneliness pursued him, a kind of loneliness the ancients could never have imagined. Back then, in the old times, people were lonely because of their inability to discover in others what their spirit yearned for. Now loneliness came for the spirit that no longer searched for anything, in fact could not search for anything; it had itself become dead.

Fride was departing Earth with no regrets.

One last time he remembered the myth of Prometheus and thought:

"Divine Prometheus stole fire and led people to immortality. Let this fire grant the immortal people what wise Nature had intended for them: death and the renewal of spirit in eternally living matter."

At midnight the explosion of fireworks marked the arrival of the second millennium of human immortality. Fride pressed an electronic button, which lit the fuse, and the pyre went up in flames.

Terrible pain, of which he had some vague childhood recollection, disfigured his face. He frantically struggled to pull himself free, and an inhuman scream resounded in the alcove.

But the iron chains held him firmly. Tongues of fire twisted around his body, hissing:

"Everything repeats itself!"

Translated by Anastasiya Osipova

Bibliography

Bogdanov, Alexander. "Goals and Norms of Life." In *O proletarskoy kul'ture: 1904–1924* [On proletarian culture: 1904–1924], 37–70. Moscow-Leningrad: Izdatel'skoe tovapishchestvo "Kniga," 1924.

Bogdanov, Alexander. "Immortal Fride: A. Bogdanov's Fantastic Narrative." *Probujdenue-SPb* [Awakening—St. Petersburg], no. 16 (1912): 497–505.

Note: The text was first published under the title "Immortality Day" in 1914 in *Volatile Anthologies* (*Letuchie Al'manakhi*), no. 14. After that it was republished again only in 1991 in *Ural Pathfinder* (*Ural'sky sledopyt*) no. 7, with illustrations by N. Moos.

Bogdanov, Alexander. "Tektology of the Struggle against Old Age." In *Tektologiya: Vseobschchaya organizatsionnaya nauka* [Tektology: Universal organizational science], 242–250. Moscow: International Alexander Bogdanov Institute and "Finansi," 2003.

Note: Original publications include the following:
Vseobschaya organizatsionnaya nauka (Tektologiya) [The universal science of organization (Tektology)]. Vol. 1. St. Petersburg: Semenov, 1913.

Vseobschaya organizatsionnaya nauka (Tektologiya) [The universal science of organization (Tektology)]. Vol. 2. Moscow: Self-published, 1917.

Tektologiya: vseobschaya organizatsionnaya nauka [Tektology: The universal science of organization], 3 vols. (vols. 1–2 in their 2nd ed., vol. 3 in 1st ed.). Berlin, Petrograd, and Moscow: Z. I. Grzhebin, 1922; 3rd ed., Leningrad and Moscow, 1925–29. Reprint of the 3rd ed. in 2 vols.: Tom 1, Tom 2, Moscow: Ekonomika, 1989.

Chizhevsky, Alexander. *Kosmicheskiy pul's zhizni: Zemlya v obyatiyakh Solntsa. Geliotapaksia* [Cosmic pulse of life: The Earth in the Sun's embrace], 300–320; 478–491. Moscow: Mysl, 1995.

Fedorov, Nikolai. "Astronomy and Architecture." *Vesi*, no. 2 (February 1904): 20–24.

Muravyev, Valerian. "A Universal Productive Mathematics." In *Vselenskoe Delo* [The deed of the universe], no. 22 (1934): 116–140.

Svyatogor, Alexander. "Biocosmist Poetics." In *Kreatoriy Biokosmistov* [Creatorium of the Biocosmists], 3–11. Moscow, 1921.

Svyatogor, Alexander. "Our Affirmations." *Biocosmist,* no. 1 (March 1922): 3–6.

Svyatogor, Alexander. "The Doctrine of the Fathers and Anarcho-Biocosmism." *Biocosmist* no. 3–4 (May–June 1922): 3–21.

Note: *Biocosmist* was the magazine of the Russian and Moscow Anarchists-Biocosmists.

Tsiolkovsky, Konstantin. *Budushchee zemli i Chelovechestva* [The future of Earth and mankind]. Kaluga, 1928.

Tsiolkovsky, Konstantin. "Panpsychism, or Everything Feels." In *Monizm Vselennoy* [Monism of the universe], 277–298. Kaluga, 1925.

Tsiolkovsky, Konstantin. "Theorems of Life." In *Monizm Vselennoy* [Monism of the universe], 299–304. Kaluga, 1925.

Note: Despite producing approximately 150 manuscripts on cosmic philosophy, Tsiolkovsky published only two such works during his lifetime, *Monizm Vselennoy* (1925, 1931) and *Prichina Kosmosa* (The cause of the cosmos, 1928). Both editions of *Monizm Vselennoy* were self-published in the city of Kaluga, each in editions of two thousand. Neither included "Theorems of Life." This piece was written as the addendum and clarification to the original book, and was typewritten (rather than printed) in 1928–30 with the author's handwritten remarks. It is now stored in the Russian Science Academy archives (Foundation no. 555, Inventory 1, Case no. 430).

Author Biographies

Nikolai Fedorovich Fedorov (1829–1903) was an Orthodox Christian philosopher, Russian Cosmist, and librarian. He was born as the illegitimate son of Rurikid Prince Pavel Ivanovich Gagarin and a woman of lower-rank nobility. After studying cameralism at the prestigious Richelieu Lyceum in Odessa, Fedorov taught history and geography at several provincial schools in the Middle East between 1854 and 1868. He then moved to Moscow, working as an assistant at the Chertkov Library before becoming an official in the reading and catalog room of the library at the Rumyantsev Museum. There he began hosting philosophical talks attended by the Moscow intelligentsia, including Leo Tolstoy, Vladimir Solovyov, Afanasy Fet, and Valery Bryusov. After his retirement, Fedorov worked at the library of the Moscow Archive of the Ministry of Foreign Affairs. A fervent Christian, Fedorov despised money and lived in small, unfurnished rooms, eating poorly and scarcely sleeping. During his lifetime, he rarely published, and did so only anonymously or under a pseudonym. His writings were inspired by the works of theologian Sergei Bulgakov and philosopher Nikolai Berdyaev. *The Philosophy of the Common Task*, Fedorov's major, two-volume work, was published posthumously in 1906 by his close friend, the judge Nikolai Peterson, and philosopher Vladimir Kojevnikov. In the 1920s and '30s, Fedorov's philosophy gave rise to a small group of followers including Maxim Gorky, Andrei Platonov, and Boris Pasternak. Fedorov's contributions to Russian philosophy gained renewed attention in the 1970s and '80s.

Konstantin Eduardovich Tsiolkovsky (1857–1935) was a rocket scientist, pioneer of astronautics, major proponent of Russian Cosmism, and founder of the Soviet space program. Deaf from the age of ten, Tsiolkovsky was a reclusive and largely self-taught scientist. At the age of sixteen, he was sent to Moscow, where he spent most of his time studying in libraries. Tsiolkovsky met Nikolai Fedorov at the Chertkov Library, where the latter worked as an assistant librarian. Driven by Fedorov's "philosophy of the Common Task," Tsiolkovsky aimed his scientific research at the colonization of space, the achievement of immortality, and free space travel for all. He moved to Kaluga in 1982, where he was to remain for the rest of his life. Teaching arithmetic, geometry, and physics at the local school, Tsiolkovsky otherwise led an ascetic life dedicated to scientific experimentation. He was a member of the Academy of Science, from which he received his first grant in 1899 for conducting experiments in aerodynamics. As early as the 1880s and '90s, Tsiolkovsky was designing airships, multistage rockets with liquid propellants, space stations, and spacecraft. To popularize his inventions, Tsiolkovsky wrote fantasy novels such as *On the Moon* (1893), *Dreams on Earth and Heaven* (1895), and *Outside the Earth* (1928). In *The Will of the Universe: The Unknown Intelligence* (1928), he proposed a panpsychist understanding of the cosmos, while affirming mankind's future colonization of the galaxy. Tsiolkovsky was awarded the Order of the Red Labor Banners in 1932 on the occasion of his seventy-fifth birthday. He died in Kaluga, where the State Museum of the History of Cosmonautics opened in 1967 and was named after him.

Alexander Leonidovich Chizhevsky (1897–1964) was a Soviet scientist, biophysicist, poet, and painter, and founder of heliobiology. His father was a highly educated military general from an eminent noble family. Chizhevsky was raised by his grandmother, who taught him foreign languages and drawing, which he briefly pursued by taking courses with one of Degas's students at the Academy of Fine Arts in Paris. Chizhevsky spent his childhood traveling in Italy and France, before his family moved to Kaluga in 1913. Having learned about ancient Greek and Egyptian civilizations during his trips throughout Europe, Chizhevsky cultivated an early fascination for the Sun and taught himself the principles of astrology. At the age of seventeen, he visited Tsiolkovsky at his home in Kaluga. This first encounter marked the beginning of a long-term friendship and collaboration between the two scientists. After studying at the Commercial and Archeological Institutes of Moscow, Chizhevsky defended his doctorate thesis "On the Periodicity of the World-Historical Process" within the university's departments of history and philology. In this preliminary research, later published under the title *Physical Factors of the Historical Process* (1927), Chizhevsky proved the effect of solar activity on global-scale phenomena such as natural catastrophes, epidemics, socioeconomic crises, and political upheavals. In 1921, he began teaching at the Moscow Archeological Institute. Since 1918, he had been investigating air-ionization therapy at his home in Kaluga, later leading experiments on animals while working at Vladimir Durov's Zoo-Psychology Laboratory from 1924 to 1931. Chizhevsky participated actively in Moscow's intellectual circles, frequented by Gorsky, Lunacharsky, Mayakovsky, and many others. His Biocosmic theories gained recognition as his texts were translated and read by an international community of scientists. In 1939, Chizhevsky was invited to preside over the First International Congress of Biophysics in New York City. Two years later, however, his explanation of revolutions was found to contradict Communist ideology, and he was sentenced to eight years of forced labor in a camp in the Southern Urals. During his detention and his later rehabilitation in Kazakhstan, he was nonetheless allowed to continue his research on air-ionization therapy. Upon his return to Moscow, Chizhevsky worked at an air-ionization laboratory until his death in 1964.

Alexander Aleksandrovich Bogdanov (born Malinovsky, 1873–1928) was a Soviet philosopher, revolutionary activist, writer, physician, and economist. He studied medicine in Kharkov, as well as mathematics, physics, chemistry, and biology in the Natural Science Department of Moscow University. In 1894, he was arrested by the Okhrana at a student protest, and exiled to Tula where he lived with Vladimir Bazarov's father. With Bazarov, he published a new three-volume translation of Marx's *Capital*, while independently writing articles on political economy and natural philosophy under various pseudonyms. He finally adopted his wife's father's name, "Bogdanov," under which he published the first socialist utopian novel, *Red Star*, in 1908. One of the leaders of the Bolshevik party, Bogdanov was fiercely rivaled by Lenin, who published *Materialism and Empirio-Criticism* in 1909, countering Bogdanov's own treatise on empiriomonism. Lenin accused Bogdanov of philosophical idealism, defeating him at a conference in Paris organized by the magazine *Proletary* in 1909. After his expulsion from the party, Bogdanov joined his brother-in-law

Anatoly Lunacharsky and Maxim Gorky in Capri to form the political organization Vpered. They opened political party schools on the island of Capri in 1909 and in Bologna in 1911, training factory workers for the development of proletarian culture. After the 1917 Revolution, Bogdanov served as the director of the Socialist (later Communist) Academy of Science and taught economics at the University of Moscow. In 1918, he cofounded the Proletarian Cultural and Education Organization (Proletkult) and acted as its main theoretician. In December 1920, the Proletkult was denounced as a "petit bourgeois" organization by the magazine *Pravda*, leading to Bogdanov's withdrawal and the movement's ultimate dissolution. From 1913 to 1922, Bogdanov worked on his three-volume philosophical work, *Tektology: Universal Organization Science*, widely considered a forerunner of systems analysis and cybernetic theory. Bogdanov founded the world's first Institute of Hematology and Blood Transfusion in 1926, where he practiced "rejuvenation" by means of blood transfusions with his younger students. By October 1927, the Institute had successfully carried out 213 transfusions with 158 patients, and transfusion centers opened in all republics of the Soviet Union. Bogdanov died the next year while donating his blood to save a student who was suffering from blood disease. His brain was transferred to Moscow's Brain Institute for research and preservation.

Valerian Nikolaevich Muravyev (1885–1932) was a Russian philosopher, politician, diplomat, publisher, and Cosmist. He was born to a family of old Russian nobility. His father was a distinguished lawyer, who worked as the minister of justice from 1894 to 1905 and later as an ambassador in Rome. Muravyev grew up in England and graduated in 1905 from Saint Petersburg's elite Imperial Alexander Lyceum. He then studied law and economics at the École des Sciences Politiques et Sociales in Paris. From 1907, he worked as a secretary of diplomatic missions in Paris, The Hague, and Belgrade. In Paris, Muravyev entered masonic and occult circles, learning from Eastern religions and the teachings of the Ephesians. During World War I, Muravyev was the director of the Balkan Department in Russia's Ministry of Foreign Affairs. After the February Revolution, he became the head of the Political Committee at the Provisional Government's Ministry of Foreign Affairs. From 1912, Muravyev began publishing articles in support of the liberal Constitutional Democratic Party, cofounded by the Bolsheviks' major critic, Pyotr Struve. Muravyev first opposed the October

Revolution and spoke against the peace treaties of Brest-Litovsk. In 1918, he contributed to Pyotr Struve's famous anthology of critical essays, *De Profundis*, which was censored upon its publication. However critical of the Bolsheviks, Muravyev also rejected parliamentary democracy and believed in the Third International's ability to create a powerful world order. At that time, Muravyev was also involved in philosophical circles such as Nikolai Berdyaev's Free Academy of Spiritual Culture (Vol'naya Akademiya Duchovnoy Kul'tury). He befriended Trotsky, who recommended him to be appointed as the head of the Information and Economic Law Department of the People's Commissariat for Foreign Affairs in the early 1920s. However, in February 1920, Muravyev was arrested for his former involvement with the anti-Bolshevik organization National Center, and sentenced to death by the Supreme Revolutionary Tribunal. With Trotsky's intervention, Muravyev was released two years later, in 1922. He then worked as a translator in the People's Commissariat of Foreign Affairs and was an employee at the Library of the National Economy Council and at the Workers' and Peasants' Inspectorate (WPI), finally obtaining the position of scientific secretary of the Central Institute of Labor (CIT) under the direction of the proletarian poet Aleksei Gastev. He published reviews and translations of foreign publications on occupational science and work organization in CIT's magazine. His most important philosophical work, *Mastery of Time as the Primary Task of Work Organization*, published in 1924, was largely inspired by Fedorov's ideas. In 1929, Muravyev was arrested for "anti-Soviet agitation" and sentenced to three years in labor camp, probably because of to his ties to Trotsky, who was then in exile. According to different sources, Muravyev died either in a labor camp in the Solovetsy Islands around 1930–1931 or from typhoid in 1932 while in exile in Narym, Siberia.

Alexander Fedorovich Agienko (known as **Svyatogor**) (1889–1937) was an anarchist-futurist poet and founder of the Biocosmist movement. His father was a priest living in the Kharkov Governorate. As early as 1909, Svyatogor expressed his futurist ideas in the notorious publication *Vekhi* (Milestones), a collection of seven essays whose contributors were selected by Pyotr Struve. Under the influence of Fedorov's philosophical texts, Svyatogor began to investigate questions of immortality and resurrection of the deceased around 1913. He founded the Verticalists group in 1914.

In Ukraine, Svyatogor promulgated his tenets of "volcanism," an antecedent to Biocosmism that proclaimed the abolition of death and domination over the universe, under such slogans as "Revaluation of all values!" and "Down with Kant!" After the February Revolution, Svyatogor moved to Moscow, where he befriended the anarchist actor Mamont Victorovich Dal'skii. He spent his time expropriating "bourgeois apartments" until the Bolsheviks appointed him commander of the Black Guards, who were to take part in the events of October 1917 in both Petrograd and Moscow. He joined the group of anarchist-futurists who published the Moscow newspaper *Anarchy* from spring 1918, before briefly returning to Ukraine where he fought against the Austrian and German occupiers. Back in Moscow, Svyatogor wrote for the Bolshevik press and worked for the People's Commissariat. Additionally, he was involved with the Pan-Russian Section of the Anarchists-Universalists, led by Abba Gordin. In December 1920, Svyatogor cofounded the anarchist group of Biocosmists with the poet Alexander Borisovich Yaroslavsky. Profoundly influenced by Fedorov's and Tsiolkovsky's writings, the Biocosmists proclaimed the overcoming of limitations of time and space under the slogan "Immortalism and Interplanetarism." Wishing to dissociate themselves from the "epigones of ancient anarchism" to form a new "dictatorship of the proletariat," the Biocosmists-Immortalists broke off from the Anarchists-Universalists with the publication of their manifesto in December 1921. To organize the activities of the new group, Svyatogor founded the club Creatorium of Biocosmists, later renamed "Creatorium of the Russian and Moscow Anarchists-Biocosmists." He edited the bimonthly journal *Biocosmist* in Moscow, while Yaroslavsky edited the journal *Immortality* in Petrograd. Groups of Biocosmists-Immortalists were forming in Kharkov, Pskov, Kiev, Omsk, and Irkutsk, counting the poets E. Grozin, V. Anist, Pavel Ivanicki, Nikolay Degtjarev, B. Gejgo-Uran, and Pyotr Lidin among their members. In 1922, they had organized forty-five poetry readings and debates in Petrograd. In 1923, the Petrograd "northern group" of Biocosmists, led by Yaroslavsky, split from the Creatorium. They led evening lectures on regeneration, eugenics, rejuvenation, and anabiosis, until the journal *Immortality* was shut down by the authorities on charges of pornography. Moving away from the organization, Svyatogor transposed the Biocosmist program into the Free Labor Church, organized by Reverend Ioannikiy Smirnov.

He broke off from it in 1923, joined the Central Council of the League of Godless Militants, and began to publish antireligious articles and tracts for the magazine *Antireligioznik*. His last article, published in 1936, was entitled "Missionaries—Agents of Imperialism." On June 25, 1937, Svyatogor was arrested as a member of an "anti-Soviet mischief group." On November 4, 1937, he was sentenced to eight years detention in a labor camp, disappearing from history's tracks.

Index

Note: page numbers in italics indicate tables or figures.

Russian Cosmism
Edited by Boris Groys
Published by e-flux and The MIT Press

e-flux

www.e-flux.com

journal@e-flux.com

www.ingramcontent.com/pod-product-compliance
Lightning Source LLC
LaVergne TN
LVHW091124080826
845145LV00008B/2030

* 9 7 8 0 2 6 2 5 5 2 8 8 2 *